BLACK ELK'S RELIGION

Black Elk at Manderson, South Dakota, 1947. Photograph by Joseph Epes Brown.
Courtesy National Anthropological Archives, Smithsonian Institution.

Black Elk's Religion

The Sun Dance and Lakota Catholicism

Clyde Holler

SYRACUSE UNIVERSITY PRESS

First Edition 1995
95 96 97 98 99 00   6 5 4 3 2 1

The paper used in this publication meets the minimum requirements of American
National Standard for Information Sciences—Permanence of Paper for Printed Library Materials, ANSI Z39.48-1984. ∞™

Library of Congress Cataloging-in-Publication Data

Holler, Clyde.
    Black Elk's religion : the Sun Dance and Lakota Catholicism /
Clyde Holler. — 1st ed.
        p. cm.
    Includes bibliographical references and index.
    ISBN 0-8156-2676-2 (cloth : alk. paper). — ISBN 0-8156-0364-9
(paper : alk. paper)
    1. Sun dance. 2. Oglala Indians—Religion. 3. Oglala Indians—
Rites and ceremonies. 4. Oglala philosophy. 5. Black Elk,
1863–1950. 6. Catholic Church—Missions—Great Plains—History.
I. Title.
E99.O3H65   1995
299′.785—dc20   95-20991

Manufactured in the United States of America

Another sunlight might make another world.

— Wallace Stevens

CLYDE HOLLER holds a Ph.D. in the philosophy of religion from Boston University. He has previously published articles on native American religion and on Kierkegaard.

Contents

Acknowledgments

This book could not have come into being without the love and encouragement of my family—my father and mother, my sister, my Aunt Lynn, my cousins, and my departed relatives, especially Grandfather Holler and Uncle Al.

The original discussion group for this project was comprised of Alan R. Sandstrom, Todd Nichols, and Pamela Effrein Sandstrom.

The following people read various versions of the manuscript and provided helpful criticisms: Alan R. Sandstrom, Paul B. Steinmetz, S.J., Todd Nichols, Christopher Vecsey, Sunny Salibian, Catherine L. Albanese, and Stephen J. Stein. Paul Steinmetz deserves special thanks for corresponding with me frequently during the late stages of the project. Pamela Effrein Sandstrom provided bibliographic support.

Martin and Karen Brokenleg provided hospitality when I was in South Dakota. Thomas E. Mails shared information. Cynthia Ann Powers shared her impressions of the 1983 Sun Dance at Three Mile Camp.

During the early stages of the project, I often worked late and ate at Manual's. Special thanks to everyone at this unique establishment.

It remains to thank my editor, Cynthia Maude-Gembler, for her efficiency and support.

Preface

Perspective is one of the component parts of reality. Far from being a disturbance of its fabric, it is its organizing element. . . . Every life is a point of view directed upon the universe. Strictly speaking, what one life sees, no other can. . . . Reality happens to be, like a landscape, possessed of an infinite number of perspectives, all equally veracious and authentic. The sole false perspective is that which claims to be the only one there is.

—Alfred North Whitehead, *The Modern Theme*

As no two people see the same view along the Way, all trips from here to there are imaginary; all truth is a tale I am telling myself.

—Brion Gysin, *The Process*

These quotations, from the novelist and the philosopher, are meant to make a serious point. This is not "the truth" about Black Elk and the Sun Dance. It is instead the organized musings of a scholar on a religious tradition that is not his own. To some extent, it is akin to a book about Roman Catholics written by a Baptist, or a book about American culture written by a Frenchman, perhaps more so. There are advantages and disadvantages to the scholar's perspective, just as there are advantages and disadvantages to any outsider's perspective. The outsider sees some things that insiders do not see, either because they take them for granted or because they are prevented by their involvement from seeing their situation truly and objectively. On the other hand, outsiders inevitably overlook things that insiders take for granted, misunderstand others, import false assumptions, and produce an interpretation with which insiders are dissatisfied.[1] This is particularly true with religion, and since religion is hardly separate from politics in native North America, native American religion produces even more than the usual passion. Since the very existence of a book on the Sun Dance written by an outsider is somewhat controversial, I think it is best to explain my perspective as clearly as possible.

Perhaps I can begin to do this by explaining how I came to the study of native American religion, something I'm frequently asked both by scholars and by others. Nothing in my formal education prepared me for this study, which I came to when I was already fairly well along in a career as a scholar specializing in Kierkegaard and nineteenth-century continental thought.[2] But in 1981 while teaching philosophy at Indiana University–Purdue University at Fort Wayne, I was asked to develop a course in Religion and Culture with the idea of increasing our meager enrollments. After the usual lengthy negotiations—and over the strenuous objections of the English de-

1. N. Ross Reat introduced the terms "insider" and "outsider" to religious studies in 1983 get at some of the differences between the believer's and the unbeliever's perspectives on a religious tradition. Although Reat's discussion is enlightening, my usage of these terms is based loosely on the terms "emic" and "etic" as they are used in anthropology by cultural materialists to distinguish between the point of view of the native informant (emic) and the point of view of the outside scientific observer (etic). For the usage of the term in cultural materialism, see Marvin Harris (1968, 568–604; 1980, 32–45).

2. I enjoyed two years at Shimer College, an experimental liberal arts college where the "great books" curriculum focused on what we have now discovered are the thoughts of dead, white males. As a philosophy major at the University of Chicago, I was trained in the analysis of concepts in the context of English linguistic philosophy. As a lay Episcopalian, continuing my education at the Episcopal Theological School allowed me to deepen my knowledge of the Christian tradition, acquire the tools of biblical research in the liberal tradition, and specialize in nineteenth-century Protestant theology. As a graduate student in the philosophy of religion at Boston University, a long-standing engagement with the thought of Kierkegaard led to my dissertation on tragedy in his pseudonymous literature. In short, little in this curriculum focused on America, much less on native America.

partment, which feared it would hurt enrollment in courses such as "Nineteenth Century Irish Poets"—the course was approved and I was left to decide how to teach it. After consulting with scholars from other institutions, I decided to accept the suggestion of Stephen J. Stein at Indiana University, who reported that he spent half of the semester on *Black Elk Speaks* and half on *The Autobiography of Malcolm X.* That sounded interesting, and I have always been partial to teaching primary texts, so I thought I would give it a try. This was my first formal contact with native American religion.

During the segment on *Black Elk Speaks,* one of my students raised his hand and said, "Look, just how faithful is this thing to what Black Elk really said?" Since I had learned from harsh experience not to fake it, I promised to find out. Alan R. Sandstrom, the coordinator of our anthropology program, steered me to David Brumble's bibliography of Indian autobiography, which hinted both that it was not completely faithful and that there was not much work done on the subject. After reviewing the existing literature, it struck me that here was a wonderful research opportunity, for it represented a gap in the research on a very important book. That summer, I went to the Neihardt Archives in Columbia, Missouri, to examine the original transcripts of Neihardt's interviews with Black Elk. From my perspective, they revealed significant differences in the religious positions of Neihardt and Black Elk, which led to an article in which I tried to disentangle Black Elk from his tragic portrait in Neihardt's novel (1984a).

Since I had no previous preparation in American religion, I had to work extremely hard on that article, doing much background work on Lakota culture, history, and anthropology to develop the competence to discuss the subject intelligently. I discovered that, although there was a great deal of anthropological work on the Sioux, only one other philosopher, George W. Linden, had published on Black Elk. After my dissertation on Kierkegaard, I found it intellectually exciting to be working in a field in which so little philosophical work had been done. As I got further into the subject, I began to think of native American religion as my cross-cultural specialty within the field of philosophy of religion. At that time, scholars in religious studies were doing much thinking about what was implied in teaching religion in a state institution, and as that was my setting, developing a cross-cultural approach made sense. Since I found I could not fully exploit the data embedded in the anthropological literature without understanding the methods and theories that engendered it, I audited Sandstrom's course on the anthropology of religion and began to conceive religious studies as the humanistic discipline most in dialogue with social science.

The point of view of this investigation is thus that of a philosopher of religion working within the religious studies paradigm. Since religious studies is a relatively new discipline and the idea of a dispassionate study of religion may seem contradictory, even to other scholars, it seems worthwhile to outline my understanding of religious studies. Religious studies is generally understood to be distinct from both philosophy and theology. Theology presupposes the point of view and commitments of a particular religion or religious community; philosophy attempts to understand the issues of life and thought without recourse to religious authority. As the search for truth, it stands in a relationship of advocacy to its subject just as theology stands in a relationship of advocacy to religion.[3] Religious studies, however, attempts to understand religion from a more disinterested point of view. Although the same subjects may be taught by religionists as by theologians—Christian Scriptures, for instance— the point of view of religious studies does not presuppose or require faith. Although the same courses may also be taught by religionists and philosophers—Philosophy of Religion, for instance—philosophers are traditionally inclined to attack religious belief from a philosophical point of view, while religionists tend to approach religion more sympathetically. Religious studies can also be understood as the study of religion appropriate in state-supported institutions of higher education, where advocacy of any particular religion is properly proscribed. To some extent, it is also the heir of the old "world religions" courses, which were taught—often in the English depart-

3. Owen C. Thomas, my mentor in theology at the Episcopal Theological School, held that philosophy and theology were the same kind of enterprises, theology being a species of the genus philosophy. In his view, philosophy is the attempt to organize and interpret the data of human experience in accord with certain key categories or organizing principles that are chosen by a decision that is analogous to the decision of faith. Theology is the attempt to organize and explain human experience in accord with the key categories of the Christian faith. See Thomas 1973, 4.

ment—as a necessary component of a private liberal arts education. Religious studies is an inherently interdisciplinary field, having been founded by scholars who had their formal training in other humanistic disciplines, such as literature, history, and philosophy. To a lesser extent, religious studies has also attracted scholars who have been trained in the social sciences, and it can be said that the field maintains an active dialogue with the social sciences, as is evidenced by the fact that the *Journal of the American Academy of Religion* publishes in social science format. The religious studies paradigm thus supports a variety of perspectives, methods, and research strategies. Perhaps it is best described as the attempt to understand religion with the traditional tools and techniques of the humanities, in dialogue with the social sciences.

Passionate believers, as well as passionate unbelievers, tend to find the objective study of religion pointless and misguided. Since the believer is primarily in a relationship of faith to his or her religion, critical scrutiny is at best irrelevant and at worst sacrilegious. For an equally passionate unbeliever, the objective study of religion is either a total waste of time or a mendacious attempt to sneak faith through the back door of the academy. In response to both, I would argue that the dispassionate study of religion produces insights that are not available from any other perspective. To recur to the quotations above, a little perspectivism is not necessarily a dangerous thing. To paraphrase Whitehead, the only false perspective is the one that claims to be the truth.

With that in mind, I simply do not agree with the notion that "only native Americans should study native Americans." One reason I am not overly sympathetic to this opinion is that no one has ever shared it with me without also sharing his or her negative opinion of my own culture, education, and religious upbringing. In other words, if it only works one way—it is special pleading. Since this exclusionist ideology often proceeds from a well-meaning desire to control interpretations of the past to serve the real and pressing needs of the present, it is not simply advocated from prejudice. As a philosopher of religion, however, I have no comparable political agenda. This means minimally that I do not care who wins the next tribal election nor do I advocate any particular solution to the urgent practical problems faced by native Americans today.

The epigram from Gysin's character goes a bit further than Whitehead in saying that there is no truth, or that the only truth is the story I am telling myself. Since many scholars today are inclined to make the leap from Whitehead to Gysin, I should perhaps make it clear that I am not willing to join them in the jump. Especially given the recent outbreak of the "French flu" in both literary and social scientific circles, I must say that in confessing that I have a perspective, I am not necessarily proclaiming that I am a solipsist. I do not believe that nothing is true, that all truth is fictional, or that we scholars might as well give up and go home, except that this is the way some of us make our living. For one thing, a properly nuanced hermeneutical philosophy does not necessarily intend this kind of vulgar relativism. For another, I am disinclined as a philosopher to participate wholeheartedly in ad hoc discussions of the most refractory epistemological problems in the context of disciplines that lack the necessary conceptual vocabulary to fruitfully discuss the history of philosophy since Kant.

Lest anyone misunderstand my perspectivism, I hope that my exposition justifies the conclusion that I am curiously devoted to the old-fashioned understanding of scholarly objectivity, particularly as it relates to the sifting of historical evidence. That is to say, I believe both that there are factual statements in this book and that they can and will be corrected in the light of the evidence. I also believe that my conceptual understanding can and will be clarified and corrected by criticism. No matter how convincingly post-Kantian hermeneutical reflection demonstrates that "all I can ever have is my understanding of Black Elk," it has not thereby demonstrated that I cannot improve my understanding or that any and all understandings are equally valid.

From this antediluvian point of view, I must say that it seems to me ironic that some of my anthropological colleagues have surrendered the scientific fort without having put up much of a fight. Since so many of them now agree with Gysin—or say they do—it seems important to make another point about my perspective. Just as I do not understand myself as a "wannabe," a person who "wants to be" an Indian, I do not want to be an anthropologist, either. Since this is an unavoidably interdisciplinary study, I have trespassed in many areas in which I have no formal training, including literary criticism, American history, government relations, and anthropology. Since I have trespassed most often on the anthropologists' turf, I want to make it clear that I am not trying to "do anthropology," however that field is currently conceived. What I am doing is philosophy of religion within the religious studies paradigm. For this reason, I expect that the academic specialists who will be most satisfied with my work are others working within the emerging discipline of cross-cultural philosophy of religion and particularly those religionists interested in the Lakota. Despite this, I have tried to write for the general reader, as well as for other scholars who may wonder what a cross-cultural perspective would mean to their work.

From the outset, the spirit of my work on the Lakota has simply been to demonstrate that humanistically trained scholars have something to contribute to the understanding of this material, which has usually been handled by anthropologists. As I went forward, however, I discovered that the data cast a different light on some of the basic elements of the philosophy of religion, such as the concept of syncretism and the theory of religious truth. I also found that my perspective as a humanist was different from that of the social scientists I was reading. In looking at the change and adaptation that characterizes contemporary native American culture, where they tended to see a process of dissolution and degeneration, I saw something more like creative change and evolution. I also discovered that many of the anthropologists I spoke to assumed that contemporary native American groups were too acculturated to reward further study, while I found quite the opposite to be the case. In an article on Black Elk's appropriation of the Christian tradition, I argued that the kind of creative change and evolution characterized by Black Elk's adaptation of the Sun Dance to modern times was the sign of a living—not a dying—tradition (1984b).

As I proceeded, I also found that the study of native American religion stretched the methods and techniques that are generally employed in the humanities. Humanists are trained primarily to work with texts, which may be one reason for the relative dearth of work on native American religion by humanists. The study of a religion whose theology is expressed in ritual and storytelling rather than in sacred literature requires something different in method and approach. When I began work on the Sun Dance, my idea was to try to study the contemporary ritual with a humanistic equivalent of the anthropological "participant/observer" method, and I traveled to South Dakota to observe a dance as it took place. I can only say that I found it to be an incredible—and deeply moving—experience that brought the religion I had been studying fully to life.

The most basic result of my work on the Lakota has been a perspectival shift in my philosophical thinking, something the anthropologists call "acquiring a cross-cultural perspective." That is to say, I now consider cross-cultural data when I philosophize. Among other things, the classic questions in the philosophy of religion such as "What is religion?" acquire a different aspect when the data implicitly includes, say, the religion of the contemporary Aztec Indians in highland Mexico or that of the Tsembaga Maring in New Guinea. I must also report that, from this perspective, much of what is said in philosophy and philosophy of religion—even from a philosophical perspective informed by contact with the world religions—seems simply ethnocentric and inadequate. We humanists have mostly ignored the religion of technologically primitive cultures, perhaps because of an uncritical tendency to equate primitive technology with primitive thought. But the "other" that we find in the world religions is not so decisively other as the other we find in native North America or in other technologically primitive cultures. For this reason, native North America is a fascinating study that casts new light on religious change and adaptation. The fellow in the English department who was always asking, "Who is the Indian Shakespeare?" is not going to understand this, but my encounter with native North America has been the greatest intellectual challenge and adventure of my adult life. I recommend a similar encounter highly to those of my colleagues in the humanities who may have ears to hear, for this is an endeavor that greatly repays serious thought.

Introduction

The idea of this book is to investigate Black Elk and the Lakota Sun Dance with an eye to their mutual interaction and influence. Although I say something about my perspective in the preface, I emphasize that my point of view is that of a philosopher of religion working within the religious studies paradigm, which I take to be the scholarly discipline that applies the traditional tools and techniques of the humanities to the study of religious phenomena.

Black Elk and the Sun Dance are intrinsically interesting and important studies. Black Elk is the greatest religious thinker yet produced by native North America, and the Sun Dance is the central religious ritual of his Lakota tradition. By juxtaposing them, I hope not only to illuminate the Sun Dance, but also to further illuminate Black Elk's religious thought. Both Black Elk and the Sun Dance were affected by rapid and forced cultural change. Since, the Sun Dance comes into scholarly view in 1866, roughly the same year Black Elk was born, the history of the Sun Dance in reservation times parallels Black Elk's intellectual development, from the waning years of native autonomy to the forced confrontation with Christianity and Christian culture on the reservation. Taken together, it is the story of how a living religion changes and develops in response to changing economic and cultural circumstances as well as the story of how a great religious thinker responds to the same challenges personally and intellectually.

When I began work on this project some years ago, I intended to simply write about the Sun Dance, relying on the foundational work that I published on Black Elk in 1984 for my understanding of his life and religious thought. The recent proliferation of critical work on Black Elk, partly in response to my earlier work, has made this impossible. This is especially true since there is in this literature a wide diversity of conclusions about Black Elk and his religion. In response to this critical proliferation, by which I am delighted, chapter 1 examines the positions of the major contributors to the discussion. This chapter also provides my preliminary response to this new critical work; my final thoughts on Black Elk and his life work are presented in the conclusion.

The contemporary Sun Dance is the central ritual of traditional Lakota religion. Before the reservation period, when Lakota cultural autonomy had not yet been seriously threatened and Christian missionary influences were as yet unknown, it was the central religious ritual of the Lakota. The difference between these positions is profound and the entire exposition is in a sense a commentary on this difference. Since discussions of the Sun Dance typically start—and end—with a description of an ideal Sun Dance, synthesized from both contemporary and historical sources, this difference has often been overlooked. Such accounts have usually been based quite uncritically on Walker's famous monograph, *The Sun Dance and Other Ceremonies of the Oglala Division of the Teton Dakota* (1917).[1] The motive for drawing this picture from Walker has most often been to assess the degree of difference—and thus degeneration—in the contemporary dance.[2] At the very minimum, this approach ignores the difference between an ideal account, collected by interview, and an actual dance as observed in performance. At the maximum, it becomes the vehicle for invidious comparisons in which a negative value judgment on religious change and adaptation is hidden from view. For this and other reasons, I have resisted the temptation to begin with a synthetic account of the Sun Dance. Since the point of this study is to

1. Walker's account has usually been accepted as an irreducible baseline for the Lakota dance, despite the fact that it is based on information acquired relatively late in the reservation period while the Sun Dance was already under ban. As we will see below, although Walker's material is indeed valuable, it must be approached from a critical perspective that is duly alert to his romanticism and his anachronistic attempt to reconstruct the "precontact" form of the Sun Dance.

2. For an example of this procedure, see William K. Powers's accounts of the dance (1975, 95–100, 139–43; Nurge 1970, 287).

delineate as clearly as possible the history and development of the dance, the best procedure is to proceed inductively, by critical examination of Sun Dance accounts as they appear in chronological sequence. To begin with a summary and synthesis would prejudge the results of the analysis itself, as well as obscure a point that I am particularly at pains to make, which is that no two Sun Dances are the same.

Since I have taken care to begin this study with historical materials that in effect introduce the basic ideas of the Sun Dance and Lakota religion, I do not think that the lack of an introductory synthesis will confuse the matter unduly. If the reader wants an introduction to the Lakota Sun Dance, my account of Fool's Crow's dance at Three Mile Creek in 1983 should suffice.[3] Besides providing an account of this dance, I have included a diagram of the ritual arrangements. For readers who desire more, the best introductory account for those unfamiliar with the dance is probably the fictional account in Ella C. Deloria's novel, *Waterlily*. Her account is particularly vivid and can be recommended—though with some caution—to readers who want to acquire a good, general idea of both the dance and its social context.[4]

With that in mind, a few brief remarks should suffice to introduce the ritual elements and terminology of the dance. Among the Lakota, the Sun Dance is an annual, communal festival, taking place during the summer. It is celebrated outdoors, in a ritual space defined by a tree, which is cut and replanted for the purpose, forming the center of a circle. All the ritual action of the dance itself takes

3. See pages 169 to 178.
4. Deloria draws her account primarily from the Sword manuscript collected by J. R. Walker, which is discussed in the third chapter. The strength of her account is her imaginative reconstruction of the social context of the classic dance. However, either because she never had the opportunity to observe the dance or because she is striving for dramatic effect, there are several anomalies in her account. For one thing, she describes the giving of flesh offerings by females as an innovation. For another, she overemphasizes the painfulness of Lowanda's sacrifice, since it is unlikely that a warrior, even a young one, would faint while giving flesh offerings. Deloria also thinks that those who danced suspended were upright—an impossibility given the piercing in the small of the back or shoulders or both—and describes the female spectators as screaming, which is unlikely.

place within or around this circle, the spectators watching from the periphery, generally under a shade, an awning made of evergreen boughs. The ritual space thus created is large, typically from forty to a hundred feet in diameter, depending on the number of pledgers and spectators anticipated. The circle is oriented with reference to the cardinal points, which have sacred connotations for the Lakota, thus defining the ritual space as a model of the traditional cosmos. An opening in the shade at the east admits the rising sun and provides an entry for the dancers. Additional structures are a resting area for participants in the *catku* (the place of honor directly across from the opening to the circle), a preparations tipi outside the circle, and sweat lodges for the purification ritual known as *inipi,* which are also outside the circle. In the classic dance, the scouting of the tree, the cutting of the tree, and a charge on the dance grounds were important features of the dance that also took place outside the circle.

The ritual, which is multitextured and multilayered, with many ritual actions taking place concurrently, is under the general direction of a holy man, who is today known as the intercessor. The intercessor is assisted by numerous other holy men and officials. The dance requires singers, who accompany the Sun Dance songs with a drum. An altar is always present, and the primary symbolic touchstones are the buffalo, represented by his skull, and the sun, represented by the sacred color red. The symbolism and imagery of war, once a central part of Lakota culture, pervades the classic dance and survives in minor ways in the contemporary dance.

The essence of the dance is sacrifice, all dancers having made a vow to *Wakan Tanka* to suffer. The basic pledge is to dance in the hot sun, without food and water, for the duration of the dance, typically forty-eight hours (day and night) in the classical period and four days (sunrise to afternoon) in the contemporary era. The more extreme forms of the sacrifice entail piercing, the cutting of the flesh to allow the insertion of skewers, which are subsequently torn loose to complete the sacrifice. Although there are various forms of piercing, the most basic is the attachment of the skewers to a rope tied to the tree. The pledger then strains against the rope until the skewers are torn free, releasing the pledger from his vow and signifying his bravery and willingness to suffer. Although the nature and extent of the sacrifice in former times is disputed, in the contemporary dance the wounds, though extremely painful, are not life-threatening. Women may dance and give flesh offerings but were not pierced until recently, usually in dances associated with the American Indian Movement (AIM). The dancers and spectators may also give flesh offerings, small pieces of flesh typically cut from the upper arms.

The Sun Dance is a highly variable phenomenon. There is, of course, no written text to govern performances. Each holy man performs the ritual in accord with his vision, meaning that dances performed by different holy men vary. But successive dances held by the same holy man also vary in response to changing pledges, conditions, situations, and needs. Formerly the traditions and rituals of the dance varied from band to band, a diversity that is mirrored to a certain extent today by differences in the dances held by different groups on different reservations. In short, no two Sun Dances are the same. Rather, the Sun Dance is a canvas on which the intercessor paints, in dialogue with the tradition and the needs of his people.

I have endeavored to examine critically all good accounts of the dance, with special attention to early accounts. The criteria for inclusion was essentially that an account either be a credible first-person, eyewitness account of an actual dance or a description of the dance collected from a qualified informant. Although a high degree of variability exists in the literature with respect to terminology in both amateur and professional accounts, I have attempted to avoid confusion as much as possible by consistently using the terms introduced above in my exposition. In the citations, the author's actual usage has been retained for accuracy, which should not be confusing as long as the essential ritual elements described above are borne in mind. A glossary has been provided to assist the reader in identifying common terms and their usual variants. For instance, the Sun Dance circle is variously described as "the sacred hoop," "the mystery circle," the "mystery hoop," and so forth. In general, I have employed the terms in use in the Fools Crow tradition as represented in the works of Thomas E. Mails and Paul B. Steinmetz, on the theory that this is the most authoritative and best attested contemporary tradition.

The issue of terminology raises considerable difficulties for the beginner in the study of Lakota religion, both because of variations in the technical vocabulary and because of differences in Lakota orthography. The best general account of these problems is in W. K. Powers's *Oglala Religion* (1975, 3–24); what the reader absolutely must know is summarized below.

There are three basic divisions in the group that is popularly known as the Sioux. The Santee speak a dialect known as Dakota and occupied the easternmost territory. In historical times, they were concentrated in Minnesota and were thus the first to be encountered by the early explorers, military men, and settlers. The Yankton speak a dialect known as Nakota, and they occupied a point midway between the Santee and the Teton in prereservation times. The Teton speak a dialect known as Lakota and occupied the westernmost point, comprising parts of South Dakota, Nebraska, Montana, and Wyoming. Although this study is primarily concerned with the Teton (the Lakota), the Santee and Yankton divisions are mentioned in passing, particularly early in the exposition.

One of the terminological problems is that in identifying themselves in their native tongue, native speakers tend to say "I am Lakota/Nakota/Dakota." When speaking English, they say instead "I am Sioux." The problem with this is that "Sioux" is apparently a French term that means "snake" or "cutthroat," and its use is disliked by many of the people to whom it is applied, even if they must occasionally use it themselves. Another problem is that "Dakota" was widely used, especially in the older anthropological literature, as a technical term for "Sioux." Even in this literature the term had an equivocal reference—to the Santee (Dakota speakers) and also to Santees, Tetons, and Yanktons considered collectively (the Sioux). Recognition of this problem led to constructions such as "Teton Dakota," an oxymoron. Another problem is that there is no native equivalent to the term "Indian" or "native American," when used in speaking of any person of aboriginal American origin. Again, the term "Indian" is disapproved both by many of the people who use it and many to whom it is applied.

I have not attempted to emend these terms in the citations. In the first place, it would be highly anachronistic to do so. In the second place, the reader will have to come to terms with terminology in going further with the subject, and it is something that causes little practical difficulty after some exposure. For similar reasons, in discussing historical texts, I will occasionally use "Dakota" and will, as appropriate, use the terms that are currently subject to various degrees of disapprobation—"Sioux" and "Indian." I hope that it becomes clear that I mean no disrespect in doing so. In certain contexts, these terms are simply unavoidable, as their continued use among native speakers evidences. For instance, they continue to be used by the Lakota-owned newspaper, *Indian Country Today* (formerly the *Lakota Times*). Since "Dakota" has fallen out of use as a synonym for "Sioux," there is no other useful way to refer to the Teton, Yankton, and Santee taken as a totality. Similarly, "Indian" cannot always be conveniently replaced by "native American"—especially in the sense of "pan-Indian phenomena."

The reader needs also to be aware that each of the three main divisions had subdivisions. The customs and rituals of these subdivisions were not at all uniform, but exhibited considerable variability. To a certain extent, they remain as markers of identity on the reservation today, as evidenced by a T-shirt I saw in Pine Ridge that said "It's hard to be humble when you're Oglala!" To a large extent, however, these divisions have been replaced as political units by the various reservation communities, such as Pine Ridge and Rosebud. Nonetheless, the reader will encounter some of the historical divisions: Santee (Mdewakanton, Wahpeton, Sisseton, Wahpekute); Yankton (Yankton, Yanktonais); and Teton (Oglala, Brulé/Sicangu, Hunkpapa, Mnikowoju, Sihsapa/Black Foot, Oohenunoa/Two Kettle, and Itazipco/Sans Arcs). These terms also exhibit considerable orthographic variation, which should not create a problem if they are sounded.

I have encountered some thorny problems with respect to tenses. Descriptions of Sun Dances typically include two kinds of statements—statements about what the author observed and statements about what the author was told by informants. In reporting ritual actions they observed, our authors naturally tend to use the past tense. However, in reporting information obtained from informants, anthropologists and others typically use an idiom that might be termed "the prescriptive present," which reflects in part the native idiom. In other words, a statement such as "The pipe is then offered to the four directions, while the holy man sings the prayers appropriate to this great occasion" generally means that this action was not observed by the author. If the author had observed this action, he or she would have written, "The pipe was offered . . . while the holy man sang. . . . " In other words, the former statement, obtained from an informant, is a statement about what is customarily or properly done. It is correctly understood as prescriptive, meaning "The pipe *should* then be offered and the holy man *should* sing. . . . " These statements simply cannot be recast in the past tense for the exposition, because to do so blurs the distinction between what the observer has witnessed and what the informant has reported. In many accounts, including those of professional observers, these un-conscious verbal markers are our only clue to what was observed as opposed to what was reported by informants. Unfortunately this can be more gracefully handled in the original exposition, which typ-ically devotes several sequential paragraphs to each kind of informa-tion. To achieve concision in a summary, it is often tempting to report both kinds of statements in a single paragraph, creating the impression that one is "changing tenses."

A related problem comes with the use of the historical present. A native speaker of English, who is holding an open book, naturally replies to a question about it in the present tense: "It says here that the dance lasts two days." It makes no sense at all to me to convert these statements into the past tense. On the other hand, there can be a confusion between "Densmore" (the text) and Densmore, the au-thor of that text. Native speakers of English will continue to use the historical present in certain statements about Densmore the text ("Densmore says the dance lasts two days."), but they tend in some contexts to report actions of the same author in the past tense ("Densmore assumed that all dances lasted two days."). These prob-lems conspire to produce some fluidity in tenses in the exposition. Since I know that this sort of thing makes certain people crazy, I have tried to keep it to a minimum simply out of respect for their feelings.

The division of the subject requires some comment. Accounts of the classic dance primarily fall into two categories, eyewitness ac-counts and accounts compiled with the aid of qualified informants. Although eyewitness accounts generally contain varying degrees of information gained by informants, the distinction is clear-cut in the case of the accounts produced during the ban. These accounts were necessarily based solely on informant information, for no public dances were available for observation. For this reason, I have devoted separate chapters to these accounts. The distinction is useful not only because these accounts are chronologically distinct, but also because the point of view in the eyewitness accounts is primarily that of an outside observer, while the point of view in the retrospective accounts is to a relatively greater degree that of the native informant. Remember, however, that almost all Sun Dance accounts—classic and contemporary—have been written by outsiders. Except George Bushotter's Lakota account of the classic dance, which was written under the direction of an anthropologist, all accounts of the classic dance are the product either of outside observers or of outsiders working with informants. In evaluating these sources, due allowance must thus be made for problems of translation and the normal problems of cross-cultural explanation and understanding. Even in the contemporary period, the number of Sun Dance accounts written directly by insiders is not great.[5]

In sifting all the sources on the dance, due allowance must also be made for the fact that the accounts are of different types, written by people from various walks of life—explorers, military men, missionaries, "ordinary people," and anthropologists. The diversity of these sources—and their points of view—means that the information in these texts cannot simply be abstracted from their context. Rather, due attention must be given to the point of view and prejudices of its author. For the more important accounts, such as J. R. Walker's, sufficient attention must be given to the author's point of view to ensure that the dance itself—rather than the author—is the true object of our attention. Even the social scientific accounts, such as Frances Densmore's, are not without assumptions, and they too present the dance through the lens of a point of view or scientific paradigm.[6] If we wish to see actual Sun Dances rather than an ideal

5. Amoitte's and McGaa's accounts are among the few examples. Lame Deer and Crow Dog's biographies, which were both coauthored by Richard Erdoes, might also be included.

6. The best advice for humanists who are trying to grasp the social scientific theories and paradigms behind the older anthropological literature is probably to consult Marvin Harris's *The Rise of Anthropological Theory: A History of Theories of Culture*. Although Harris's point of view is clear, he is also remarkably clearheaded.

Sun Dance that never was, we must be prepared to come to grips with an unusual diversity of points of view.

The division of the subject is to a certain extent suggested directly by its history, for the ban imposed a hiatus on the public performance of the dance. The most natural division of the subject would thus seem to be strictly chronological: the dance from contact to the ban, the ban, the accounts collected by interview during the ban, and the dance after the ban. I experimented with this arrangement, but I found that it placed too great a demand on the attention of the reader, since the two chapters on the classic dance were separated by the chapter on the ban, a very different subject. For this reason, I have presented my account of the ban after the chapter on accounts of the Sun Dance obtained during the ban. Although this creates a certain anachronism, because the actual real-life context of these accounts (the form critic's *Sitz im Leben*) is the ban, I believe it is justified on heuristic grounds. The order of the exposition is thus (1) third-party observer accounts of the classic dance, (2) retrospective accounts of the classic dance obtained through interviews during the ban, (3) the ban and the state of the dance during the ban, and (4) the revival of the dance in contemporary times.

An astute observer might object to the discussion of Black Elk in the chapter dealing with the revival of the dance on the grounds that his account is an informant account produced during the ban (or more properly, during the de facto ban).[7] But its placement at the beginning of the chapter dealing with the revival of the dance is justified because Black Elk's influence on the revival of traditional religion was very great.

I am very ambivalent about my choice of the word "classic" to denote the dance from contact to the ban. Despite its unavoidable connotations as a term of value, it is meant primarily in a chronological rather than a normative sense. The word "early" would not be appropriate, because the Lakota dance first comes into view in 1866,

---

7. As will become clear in the first chapter, I regard it as a very serious mistake to characterize Black Elk as an informant. In my view, he was a creative and consciously innovative religious thinker, and—as will become clear in the fifth chapter—his account of the Sun Dance is in no sense an unvarnished account of the Sun Dances of the past. The fourth chapter discusses the ban and the de facto ban on piercing that lasted at least until the early 1950s.

which is not very early, either in Lakota culture or in American history. What is needed is a simple synonym for "the dance taking place after contact, from the time it is first described in the literature until it was banned in 1883." Since no such word comes to mind, "classic" will have to do. Its value connotation could possibly be justified on the grounds that this period's dance has obtained a normative status in the literature. However, because I deprecate making invidious comparisons between the contemporary dance and the dance described by Walker, I think it is best to simply say that I do not use the term to imply a value judgment. It will become clear that the "classic" dance was not in any way pristine, but was itself essentially a product of the reservation period.

A little reflection should be sufficient to realize that, since all accounts of the dance are ipso facto a product of contact, the dance in its precontact form—in Walker's mind this apparently meant with horses but without firearms—is simply not available for inspection. That is to say, it is not possible to establish the form of this dance through historical inquiry. It is possible to reconstruct it speculatively, as Walker tried to do, by accepting the assurances of his informants that "it was ever thus," but because innovations in religion are rarely described as such by those who introduce them, this procedure stands on extremely shaky methodological ground.

Similar cautions should be issued about the term "traditional," which is a value-laden term that is simply unavoidable in the discussion of the contemporary dance. Since it is frequently applied to things that are clearly innovations, it cannot be taken at face value. Rather, its usage signals that an appeal is being made to the authority of the tradition; to call something traditional in a religious context is to say that it is both legitimate and authoritative. "Traditionalist," as it is used on the reservation today, properly describes an element that is at once a political and religious party, that element or those elements who identify themselves as traditionalists. When used in reference to life-style, it implies respect for the former aspects of life and social relations that can be preserved in the present—such as, the avoidance of direct address between husband and mother-in-law. In this sense, it could properly be used of a Christian Lakota who does not profess "traditional religion" but who does live—or attempts to live—in a traditional way. When used in a religious con-

text, it implies continued allegiance to the native religious system—
although not necessarily to the exclusion of Christianity. As a potent
political force to be reckoned with on the reservation today, the traditionalists represent one of the two main factions in contemporary
reservation politics. In some sense, politics on the reservation today
is still the heir to the "progressive-traditionalist" conflicts that we encounter during the early reservation period, the progressives allied
with the agent and the traditionalists resisting the same. Today's traditionalists tend to live in the country, tend to resent the government
employees who live in Pine Ridge and Rosebud, and tend to look to
traditional religious leaders for leadership. For this reason, the
reader must realize that "the traditionalists" are both a political and
religious force on the reservation today—as even a casual reading of
Indian Country Today will reveal.

Since tribal religion becomes traditional religion only when it is
challenged from outside by another religious system, it is anachronistic to use the term "traditional religion" to describe the religion
of the Lakotas during the period of religious autonomy. Traditional
religion, as one choice among others, is wholly a creation of the reservation period. Part of the function of the label, particularly in po-
lemical contexts, is to obscure the fact that "traditional religion" is
not the same as the earlier tribal religion, thus ensuring that the
adaptive function of religion remains latent by implying that "it was
ever thus." However, even though it is technically anachronistic to
use "traditional religion" to refer to Lakota religion before the reservation period, its usage is ensconced, and is simply unavoidable in
some contexts.

It will become clear that part of my conception of critical scholarship is to reject romanticism in the sense of the projection of contemporary values upon historical events. This policy has led me to
some positions that may not be "politically correct." For one thing, I
think it is anachronistic to simply demonize the missionaries, agents,
and government anthropologists for not leaving the Indians alone—
something that would surely have resulted in their extermination.
Similarly, I do not think it is very astute to demonize Neihardt for
writing a novel instead of an ethnographic monograph. Regardless
of what we today believe is right or wrong—and without submitting
to mindless relativism—it simply is not good history to ignore the

fact that people who are "politically incorrect" by today's (relatively) enlightened standards may have had the right on their side in their own time, and even if not, they were real people facing real choices and challenges, not cardboard cutouts of demons. This is not to deny that greed, ethnocentrism, and self-interest rule the hearts of men. It is simply to say that to see the past clearly, even the demons have to be perceived as agents with a portion of the right on their side.

Good history, however, also requires that we realize that traditional religion did not "fade away" during the ban, but was brutally and vigorously repressed as a policy issued from the highest authority. It is distressing to note how many times this obvious fact is glossed over or ignored in discussions of the "decline" of traditional religion. It is extremely important to see the ban clearly and not blink it, both for a proper understanding of Black Elk as well as for a proper understanding of the Sun Dance and Lakota religion today. As I will argue, the repression that was intended to promote religious change retarded it by denying to traditional religion the opportunity to openly confront Christianity and changing cultural and economic conditions. In the end, traditional religion would probably have adapted sooner if it had not been repressed, something that was apparently impossible in the context of the times.

For those who have never attended the Sun Dance or another traditional Lakota ritual, it might be said that Lakota ritual is incredibly dense. Many more ritual actions take place in a small portion of a traditional ritual than occur in an entire Christian worship service. At the Sun Dance, many ritual actions take place simultaneously, something else unfamiliar in a Christian context. In fact, the Christian model of "worship" is probably not adequate to the understanding of Lakota ritual, since the purpose of traditional ritual is to invoke and harness supernatural power, not necessarily to worship in the Christian sense. In addition, Lakota ritual is very fluid, since each holy man has the responsibility and the freedom to interpret traditional religion according to his vision—that is, in response to the situation he is addressing and the spiritual resources available to address it.

BLACK ELK'S RELIGION

1

※

The Search for the
Historical Black Elk

The influence of the Lakota holy man, Black Elk, has traveled far
beyond his tribe and seems far from having waned. Although his
influence on contemporary Lakota religion has been profound, his
influence on American religion as a whole has also been profound,
and it seems best to regard him as an authentically American religious genius, the greatest religious thinker yet produced by native
North America. His enormous influence can ultimately be traced to
his collaboration with the American poet John G. Neihardt, which
resulted in *Black Elk Speaks,* a recognized classic in American religion. Without this collaboration, it is unlikely that Black Elk would
be known today outside his tribe. But recent critical work has demonstrated that *Black Elk Speaks* can no longer be regarded uncritically
as an authoritative source on Black Elk's religion and thought.
Rather, the full range of primary source material and critical secondary work needs to be considered to obtain an authentic understanding of the life and thought of this complex and captivating
figure.

The primary materials for this work are both textual and contextual. The primary textual materials now include four books—*Black
Elk Speaks, When the Tree Flowered, The Sacred Pipe,* and *The Sixth
Grandfather*—as well as a number of archival materials. Besides these
texts, there is also a flourishing oral tradition surrounding Black Elk,
who is regularly cited in support of diverse religious and political
positions. There is also a contextual aspect to the analysis, since any

1

serious consideration of Black Elk's life and thought must take into account the cross-cultural context of the collaborations that produced these texts, the old Lakota culture that nurtured the young Black Elk, and the political, economic, and religious situation on the reservation during Black Elk's mature years. In recent years, the publication of the first truly critical work on Black Elk has produced a secondary literature of real value in forming an estimate of Black Elk's work. The days are now past when an uncritical conflation of Neihardt and Black Elk will pass for serious scholarship, and it is now incumbent on scholars to engage the full range of source material in forming an estimate of Black Elk's life and thought.

Before surveying that source material, it may be helpful to draw attention to two scholarly precedents that are to a certain extent analogous to the problem presented by Black Elk. In certain respects, the problem of Black Elk parallels the problem of Socrates. Socrates is well known, and his influence has been enormous, but we possess no work that is directly from his hand. Nor is this accidental, for his teaching seems to have been entirely situational and oral. It is not that no works by Socrates survive, but that he wrote none. His reputation is based instead on his portrait by Plato, who was deeply influenced by Socrates, both as a man and as a philosopher. However, since Plato presents Socrates as a character in his dialogues, which express his own philosophy, it is by no means clear where Plato begins and Socrates leaves off. To some extent, the situation with Black Elk is similar, for Black Elk's teaching was wholly oral, while his reputation is largely based on his literary portrait by Neihardt, who retained his own philosophical and religious identity despite being deeply influenced by Black Elk.

It could be said that the situation is analogous in another way as well. With respect to Socrates, the non-Platonic evidence is disappointing, consisting of a number of amusing but historically dubious anecdotes from subsequent works, a portrait of Socrates as a buffoon by the comic poet Aristophanes, and a defense of Socrates as a hard-working pragmatist by the military man, Xenophon. In other words, none of the non-Platonic material offers anything like the soaring conception of Socrates presented by Plato. Something of the same thing could be said about Neihardt's Black Elk, since nothing in the literature matches his soaring portrait in *Black Elk Speaks*. The secondary literature on Black Elk also provides us with a startling diversity of interpretations that to some extent recall the diverse portraits of Socrates—genius, pragmatist, buffoon—with Lakota holy man John (Fire) Lame Deer providing the portrait of Black Elk as a buffoon by characterizing him as "a catechism teacher" and "cigar-store Indian" (Mathiessen, xxxvii).

Since Black Elk is essentially a religious thinker, another analogy is useful in understanding the problem—the quest for the historical Jesus. The Christian Gospels, which were written in Greek, reflect the oral teaching of the Jewish religious leader, Jesus, who spoke Aramaic. The Gospels were not written immediately after the death of Jesus. Instead, his teaching passed into the oral tradition and was modified continually to meet changing circumstances until it was finally fixed in literary form by the authors of the Gospels. By this time, Jesus was himself the object of the faith of the Christian community as the Christ. Hence, what the Gospels most directly reflect is not the historical teaching of Jesus, but the state of the Jesus tradition and the situation and teaching of the Christian church at the time of their composition.

This is precisely the case with the oral tradition surrounding Black Elk today. Black Elk is regularly invoked—on the reservation and off—in support of political and religious positions in response to issues that he could not have anticipated. His teachings are continually modified and applied to new situations, as religious practitioners routinely invoke his authority in support of their own. It is important to note that it is a decisive misunderstanding of this process—an anthropologist might call it ethnocentric—to regard this continual modification and "reading back" as dishonest. It is instead the normal functioning of an oral tradition to appropriate the teachings of a great religious master in this way, preserving them by applying them to new situations and circumstances. Nonetheless, for this very reason, the testimony of this oral tradition must be used with extreme caution in historical reconstruction.

Another point of bringing up the analogy with the quest for the historical Jesus is that the search for the Jesus of history is not disinterested, since Jesus as the Christ is the object of passionate religious devotion, and the results of historical inquiry into his life and teaching potentially affect competing political and religious interests.

Scholars do not agree on Jesus in part because of the equivocal nature of the evidence. But they also disagree because of his vast importance to Christians and to competing interests in the Christian community. These interests reflect competition among the world religions, competition among Christian denominations, competition within denominations, and among factions in local congregations. Because all competing factions in the Christian community appeal to the Jesus tradition as the ultimate authority, historical inquiry cannot be disinterested—there is something "riding on the results" of the inquiry. The situation with respect to Black Elk is similar, for he has been claimed not only by traditionalists and Catholics, but also by antitraditionalists and anti-Catholics—as well as by admirers of John Neihardt, people who "want to be" Indians, religionists, and anthropologists. It may seem inappropriate to include religionists and anthropologists in this list, but it is well to remember that scholars are human beings with values, passions, interests, and jealousies. For us, too, something is riding on the outcome. Michael F. Steltenkamp provides a list of the special interests competing for the interpretation of Black Elk, which appears to be fairly exhaustive except for the omission of his own.

> Environmental activists, Indian militants, anthropologists, historians, religionists, students of Americana, and others have gleaned from Black Elk passages that bolster or refute whatever conventional Native theme they choose because, it appears, his representation has become *the* conventional stereotype par excellence. (1993, xv)

Turning from these analogies to the problem of the historical Black Elk, the first logical starting point for inquiry is the texts themselves. The interviews that Black Elk gave Neihardt in 1931 resulted in the work on which Black Elk's reputation rests. During these interviews, Black Elk spoke in Lakota and his son, Ben Black Elk, translated. The proceedings were recorded in shorthand by Neihardt's daughter, Enid, who provided Neihardt with a typescript, roughly arranged in the chronological order Neihardt was to use in *Black Elk Speaks*. This typescript, which is available in the Neihardt Archives at the University of Missouri, is the first text to result from this meeting (1931). The second text is *Black Elk Speaks* itself, which was published in 1932. The third text is a retranscription of Enid's original shorthand notes (1980), which was undertaken as part of Raymond J. DeMallie's reconstruction of the original interviews. This version of the transcript is in the original order of the interviews as appearing in Enid's stenographic notebooks, and includes some material omitted from the 1931 transcript. In conjunction with this project, Enid Neihardt's diary and her stenographic notes for some of Neihardt's correspondence relating to the book were also transcribed, which is particularly valuable because most of Neihardt's correspondence was removed from the archives by his biographer, and is not available to other scholars. The fourth text to emerge from the 1931 interviews is *The Sixth Grandfather*, DeMallie's redaction of the transcripts and reconstruction of the interviews (1984). Since DeMallie produced this text through comparison and combination of the 1931 and 1980 transcripts, it can be regarded for most purposes as the closest possible approximation of what transpired when Black Elk first interviewed Neihardt and other elders.[1]

Neihardt interviewed Black Elk again in 1944, using the material he obtained in a book titled *When the Tree Flowered*, which focuses on Lakota tribal history and mythology. The original transcript of these interviews was produced by Hilda Neihardt in the field on a typewriter, and DeMallie includes this material in *The Sixth Grandfather* as well. In 1948, Black Elk spoke for the record a final time to anthropologist Joseph Epes Brown. The result was *The Sacred Pipe*, which focuses on traditional Lakota religion and ritual, explained and interpreted in terms commensurate with Christianity.

Of these texts, *Black Elk Speaks* and *The Sacred Pipe* have attracted the most attention. For many years, they were read quite uncritically—both as sources for Black Elk's thought and as sources for anthropological reconstruction of the aboriginal Lakota past. With respect to *Black Elk Speaks*, it was assumed that Neihardt's creative role as an author was minimal and that the essential message and thrust of the book was Black Elk's. With respect to *The Sacred Pipe*, it

---

1. Specialists may wish to consult the original transcripts, for in assembling his text, DeMallie has given priority to the 1980 transcript, which has required heavy emendation owing to the time-critical nature of shorthand transcription. The accompanying archival versions of Enid's diary and Neihardt's letters also help give the transcripts context.

was widely assumed—despite its obvious Christian orientation—that the text describes pristine Lakota rituals, untouched by the influence of Christianity and contemporary life. In other words, the reader of these works is encouraged to conceive of Black Elk as an unreconstructed traditionalist, as a passive informant on the past, completely unaffected by modern reservation life. Neihardt's gripping portrait also created the impression that Black Elk was a broken man after the events at Wounded Knee in 1890, consumed with despair and nostalgia for bygone days.

So it was something of a shock to readers of these works when Paul B. Steinmetz reported that research by fellow Jesuit Michael F. Steltenkamp revealed that Black Elk accepted Catholicism in 1904 and began work as a catechist shortly afterward (Steinmetz 1980, 158–59). Black Elk had been an active Christian leader for twenty-seven years when he was first interviewed by Neihardt in 1931. Both *Black Elk Speaks* and *The Sacred Pipe*, however, completely ignore Black Elk's modernity, treating him simply as an informant on the past—on the glory days of the Lakota—rather than as an active creator of the Lakota religious present. The resulting image of Black Elk as an old man living in an uncorrupted past—as an informant—rather than as an active creator of the Lakota present has been completely shattered by subsequent research.

The first stirring of a scholarly reevaluation of Black Elk can be found in literary research by Sally McCluskey (1972) and Michael Castro, which focused on Neihardt's appropriation of Black Elk.[2] Subsequent critical work has moved in two directions. Research by Castro (1983), Holler (1984a), DeMallie (1984), and Rice (1991) has focused on further disentangling Black Elk from Neihardt and *Black Elk Speaks*. At the same time, research by Holler (1984b), DeMallie (1984), Steinmetz (1990), Rice (1991), and Steltenkamp (1993) has focused on forming a proper estimate of Black Elk's relation to Christianity. The keynote of this critical research has been to go beyond the fictional Black Elk—who mirrors the stereotype of the end

---

2. Castro reported on his research to the Modern Language Association in 1979 in a paper titled "Poetic License in Neihardt's *Black Elk Speaks*." This paper was summarized in Brumble (1981) and Castro generously provided me a copy when I began research on the subject in 1982.

of the trail—to the life and thought of Black Elk himself. The essential result of this inquiry into the relationship between Ncihardt and Black Elk has been that *Black Elk Speaks* and *When the Tree Flowered* have been superseded as primary sources for Black Elk's life and thought by the publication of *The Sixth Grandfather,* DeMallie's reconstruction of the Black Elk interviews. As a corollary, much of the secondary literature on Black Elk—a vast amount—has been superseded as well.

The purpose of this book is neither to recapitulate the earlier stages of this discussion nor to reiterate the complex textual and contextual argument presented in my essay "Lakota Religion and Tragedy" (1984a). However, to summarize the results of this first line of inquiry, it can now be regarded as certain that Black Elk never spoke the "death of the dream" speech that ends *Black Elk Speaks,* that Neihardt considerably simplified the vision and omitted its warlike implications, and that the book's essential religious and social perspective—its message—is Neihardt's and not Black Elk's. In a positive sense, this means that Black Elk did not believe that the dream had died; he was emphatically not simply an old man living in despair. As my earlier work demonstrates, Black Elk's evaluation of the viability of the traditional Lakota religion and lifeways was diametrically opposed to Neihardt's. In the face of this critical research, interpretations of Black Elk that depend on the attribution of the "death of the dream" speech to Black Elk—and they are legion—can no longer stand, even if their purpose is to elicit sympathy for the Lakota.

Neihardt's book itself stands as a work of art and as a secondary source on Black Elk, reflecting Neihardt's impressions and understanding of the great holy man. It is integral to the mission of the artist to interpret. Critical understanding of Black Elk has been hampered by admirers of Neihardt who have adapted an unnecessarily defensive posture toward criticism. Neihardt was a literary artist; *Black Elk Speaks* is a work of art. As McCluskey's research shows, Neihardt understood this much better than some of his admirers. If *Black Elk Speaks* did not interpret, if it did not reflect Neihardt's understanding of Black Elk, it would not be a work of art. Defenders of Neihardt who insist on his faithfulness to Black Elk's message simply reveal the shortcomings of their understanding of literature. Since the artist is not a tape recorder, it is ironic that defenders of Neihardt's faithfulness to Black Elk's message unintentionally depreciate his art and deny him his true vocation as an artist.[3] Neihardt's memory is better served by a critical appreciation of his work as an artist than by the misguided attempt to deny that *Black Elk Speaks* is art.[4]

DeMallie wrote in 1984 that "today Black Elk's Catholicism represents the biggest gap in our understanding of him as a whole human being" (Deloria 1984, 124). Since part of the mission of the present work is to contribute to the understanding of Black Elk's religion, it is important to survey the results of the second line of inquiry into Black Elk's life and thought, which seeks to clarify his relation to Christianity. DeMallie's sketch of Black Elk's life, which accompanies his redaction of the Black Elk interviews, is a good place to start.

DeMallie notes that Black Elk's first significant contact with Christianity came when he was required to become an Episcopalian to travel to Europe with Buffalo Bill's Wild West in 1887 (1984, 10). Black Elk apparently traveled with Buffalo Bill in part to learn more about the white man and his religion, and letters that he wrote from

---

3. It could be said that a similar lack of appreciation for literary art has hindered the understanding of both the Platonic dialogues and the Gospels—for the oral teachings of Socrates, Jesus, and Black Elk were necessarily interpreted when they were taken up into literature.

4. It is ironic that Raymond J. DeMallie must be included among the ranks of the misguided defenders of Neihardt's faithfulness to Black Elk's message: "Neihardt was an extraordinarily faithful spokesman for Black Elk; what he wrote was an interpretation of Black Elk's life, but not one that was embellished in any way" (1984, 51). In another place, DeMallie states, "Neihardt was an extraordinarily faithful spokesman for Black Elk. Although his psychic empathy for Black Elk might have led him to take great liberties with the material, he did not do so. Comparison of *Black Elk Speaks* to Enid's stenographic record of the interviews only underscores the fidelity of Neihardt's literary interpretation" (Deloria 1984, 120). These are odd statements from the author of *The Sixth Grandfather,* a work whose raison d'être is to reveal the differences between Black Elk and Neihardt. Since DeMallie also says that the fact that Black Elk never spoke the death of the dream speech "points up the inappropriateness of using *Black Elk Speaks* in any comparative study as representative of traditional Lakota culture and religion" (1984, 77–80), it is perhaps best to consider his remarks on Neihardt's faithfulness simply a courteous nod to Neihardt's admirers and literary executors.

Europe and shortly after his return seem to indicate a significant degree of engagement with Christianity: "So thus all along, of the white man's many customs, only his faith, the white man's beliefs about God's will, and how they act according to it, I wanted to understand" (9–10). His return to Pine Ridge in 1889, however, immediately preceded the first stirring of the Sioux Ghost Dance, and Black Elk's involvement with the Ghost Dance was profound. Nonetheless, DeMallie interprets the Ghost Dance as a cruel disappointment to the Lakota, and "to none more than Black Elk" (11), suggesting in another place that he easily abandoned the Ghost Dance and its teachings (87). As I argue in "Lakota Religion and Tragedy," this seems less than clear, given Black Elk's continued use of the Ghost Dance image of the "happy promised land" (1984a, 39). In any case, according to DeMallie, a result of the massacre at Wounded Knee was a general turning away from the white man's ways and religion: "Like so many other Lakotas who had been adapting well to civilization before the ghost dance, Black Elk seems to have turned his back on the white men's ways after the Wounded Knee massacre" (12).[5] Although he notes that Black Elk's first wife, Katie War Bonnet, must have been a Catholic as her children were baptized in 1893, 1895, and 1899 (13), DeMallie suggests that Black Elk was mainly absorbed in his *yuwipi* practice at this time, something that brought him into conflict with the Jesuits. DeMallie notes that Black Elk's acceptance of Catholicism in 1904 was the culmination of a "slow process that stretched over two decades," but he associates it strongly with his decision not to use the "soldier weed" that was given in his vision to wipe out the whites, saying that Black Elk "refused to take the responsibility for such wholesale destruction" (14). Although he also notes that Black Elk's wife died in 1903 and that baptism was the prerequisite for participation in the "social and material benefits of church life" (15), he seems most inclined at this point in his discussion to interpret Black Elk's acceptance of Catholicism in terms of the renunciation of violence and, consequently, freedom from the responsibilities of his vision: "Black Elk's conver-

5. Oddly, DeMallie says the exact opposite later in his discussion: "To judge from Black Elk's own life experiences, after the ghost dance he and his people felt that their religion was lost to them forever, and they turned to Christianity" (1984, 92).

sion was unquestionably genuine. By accepting Catholicism he at last put himself beyond the onerous obligations of his vision, and he never practiced the Lakota religious ceremonies again" (14).[6] Similarly, DeMallie interprets the collaboration with Neihardt as a conscious and deliberate shifting of responsibility: "But the vision, and his failure to live up to it, must have been a heavy burden. This burden he could at long last transfer to another man" (28).

At the same time, on DeMallie's reading, Neihardt's visit was something of a "reconversion experience" and turning point in Black Elk's life. Up to this point, he seems to DeMallie to have been a model of a successful, assimilated Catholic. According to DeMallie, Neihardt reawakened the traditionalist who had been slumbering in Black Elk and from this point forward his involvement in traditional religion seems to accelerate: "It was as if something long bound up inside the old man had broken free at last, an impulse to save that entire system of knowledge that his vision represented and that for more than twenty-five years he had denied" (28).

These two notions, that Black Elk was motivated by a desire to shirk his vision-given responsibility and that something "broke free" in Black Elk when he met Neihardt, merit further discussion. It is true that Black Elk seems to have accepted the Christian critique of the warrior society. At the same time, it is true that in a traditional sense, sharing his power vision with Neihardt constituted a giving away of his power to Neihardt. But there is little evidence, however, that Black Elk sought to evade his responsibility for his people in a larger sense. As Julian Rice points out, Black Elk worked tirelessly to fulfill the traditional role of the holy man as an advocate of his people long after the Neihardt interviews (1991, 12). With respect to DeMallie's theory that Neihardt's visit prompted a relapse into traditionalism, it must be said that this idea can neither be proven or disproven. The truth is that there is very little evidence for what Black Elk was thinking in the years between 1904 and 1931 aside from what is presented in *Black Elk Speaks*. It seems to me to be more plausible to assume that Black Elk never ceased to be engaged with traditional religion, perhaps remaining deeply in dialogue with traditional leaders who were not as committed to Catholicism as he was.

6. As we will see, this last point is a matter of interpretation and some dispute.

In view of the content of the Neihardt interviews, this seems to make more sense than the assumption that Black Elk denied traditional religion for twenty-five years and was seized with a sudden impulse to preserve it on Neihardt's arrival.

After his retirement from active church work, Black Elk served as the "medicine man" in the Duhamel Sioux Indian Pageant, a tourist attraction held each summer along the highway from Rapid City to Mount Rushmore. In this pageant, Black Elk demonstrated the offering of the pipe, the Sun Dance, and the other rituals that he was to systematize in *The Sacred Pipe* (DeMallie 1984, 71). DeMallie suggests that his primary motive for participation in the pageant was to disprove the Jesuits' assertion that the old religion was devil worship (66). According to DeMallie, Black Elk could affirm the truth of the two religions in a way that the Jesuits could not: "The two systems were not compartmentalized; rather, they were stages in his life" (66). In his old age, though, he "turned his attention increasingly to Lakota tradition," a process that apparently "began with Neihardt's first visit in 1930" (71). Reginald and Gladys Laubin, who met Black Elk at the pageant in 1936 and returned to visit him every subsequent year, reported that he seemed mainly interested in the old days and that he never mentioned Catholicism, and a visitor to Black Elk's home in his final two years of life was told by his son that Black Elk wondered whether his life as a Catholic had been a mistake (71–72). Similarly, Hilda Neihardt states that according to Lucy Looks Twice, Black Elk's daughter, Black Elk said on his deathbed that "the only thing I really believe is the pipe religion" (119).

Whether it is correct or not, DeMallie's notion of an increasing commitment to traditional religion in Black Elk's later years raises the question of how deeply his Christianity influenced the material that he gave to Neihardt. DeMallie identifies as evidence of this influence phrases from the Bible, universalism and an emphasis on salvation, and pacificism, declaring that it is not possible to determine whether Black Elk reinterpreted *Wakan Tanka* as the Christian Godhead (89–92). At this point—as opposed to his earlier discussion—DeMallie seems most inclined to interpret Black Elk's conversion as a matter of convenience, as a pragmatic response to a difficult situation. He points out that Black Elk's conversion "must not be misunderstood as indicating a loss of faith in traditional religion," saying that it was "a pragmatic decision, not an emotional conversion" (92). Although this is inconsistent with his earlier remarks on Black Elk's renunciation of the soldier weed and desire to avoid the responsibility of his vision, DeMallie in the end seems to interpret Black Elk's Catholicism as a practical necessity, as Black Elk himself implied when he said to Neihardt that he became a Catholic because "my children had to live in this world" (47).

Michael F. Steltenkamp's *Black Elk: Holy Man of the Oglala* (1993) comprises an impassioned plea for the reevaluation of Black Elk's life, work, and religion. Steltenkamp's portrait turns DeMallie's on its head by interpreting Black Elk as a fervent Catholic progressive, whose traditionalism was opportunistic and perhaps insincere. Steltenkamp's book is the final product of a project that he conceived shortly after his arrival on the Pine Ridge Reservation in the early 1970s. According to his account, he was surprised to find that Black Elk's books were relatively unknown among the Lakota. Black Elk's considerable reputation in the reservation circles in which Steltenkamp moved was based instead on his work as a Catholic catechist. His first idea for a book was to write the story of Ben Black Elk, Black Elk's well-known son, but the death of Ben in 1973 foiled this ambition, and he turned instead to writing Black Elk's life story as it was told by his sole surviving child, Lucy Looks Twice.

In stark contrast to DeMallie, Steltenkamp presents Black Elk essentially as a progressive Catholic convert who never looked back. He regards most—if not all—prior interpretations of Black Elk as unduly romantic, accusing all other classes of commentators of special pleading (xv). Considerable passion is in his position, and his distaste for commentators that do not agree with him is so great that he simply dismisses Julian Rice's work as misleading "armchair ethnology" and speculation (179, n. 8). This is an unfortunate attitude, since Rice directly engages Steltenkamp's argument as it was presented in his dissertation, and much might have been learned if Steltenkamp had replied directly to Rice. Despite his lack of adequate engagement with the work of other scholars and with source material that does not support his case, Steltenkamp correctly opposes the image of Black Elk that has grown out of uncritical readings of *Black Elk Speaks,* that of an old man living in despair, consumed with nostalgia for bygone days. He convincingly argues that Black Elk was instead a vigorous advocate for his people for many years, in no sense a prisoner of the past. Steltenkamp's stress on Black Elk as an agent, as an active creator of his people's present, is the major constructive contribution of the book.

In evaluating Steltenkamp's position, it is important to understand the point of view and testimony of his mentor, Lucy Looks Twice, which stands at the center of his argument and constitutes the book's major contribution to the primary information available on Black Elk. Lucy was the oldest of three children born to Black Elk and his second wife, Anna Brings White. (Ben was born to Black Elk's first wife, Katie War Bonnet.) Looks Twice was born in 1907, three years after Black Elk accepted Catholicism. She seems to have had a wholly Catholic upbringing, with extensive contact with the Jesuits in her early years (73–77). She attended school at the Holy Rosary Mission, and the self-understanding expressed in Steltenkamp's account is that of a Lakota Christian, despite the occasional traditional elements that surface in her recollections. That Lucy's upbringing was relatively untouched by overtly traditional elements reflects both the times—the old religion had been banned and elements of Lakota language and culture were vigorously repressed in the Catholic schools—and, perhaps, the newly Catholic Black Elk's enthusiasm for his work as a catechist. As a young woman, she strongly disapproved of the Neihardt interviews in general and Ben's role as a translator specifically (19, 86). She also seems to be at the center of the later recriminations with the Jesuits who were so scandalized by *Black Elk Speaks* (79–87). She might therefore best be regarded as representing the first generation of Lakotas who were raised in a Catholic environment, although her religious commitments seem to have changed shortly after speaking to Steltenkamp; Hilda Neihardt reports that after her husband, Leo, died in 1974, Looks Twice was disappointed in Christianity. At the suggestion of friends, she read *Black Elk Speaks* for the first time, subsequently becoming a pipe carrier (117–19).

The immediate context of Steltenkamp's interviews with Looks Twice in 1973 was the recent occupation of Wounded Knee by the American Indian Movement (AIM). A central figure in the occupation was the traditionalist holy man, Wallace Black Elk, who is not related to Black Elk, although he claims Black Elk as his "uncle" or spiritual mentor (a distinction his followers do not always observe[7]). Wallace Black Elk's attitude toward Christianity is one of scorn and ridicule, expressed in constant sarcasm and mockery of Christianity in general and Catholicism in particular.[8] Since this Black Elk was very much in the news during the Wounded Knee occupation, Looks Twice's desire to disassociate her father from both the occupation and the anti-Christianity of Wallace Black Elk is understandable: "The past couple of years I've been shocked to hear people say that my father never actually believed in the Catholic religion. I know they're really making a mistake. So please pray that they won't spoil my father's past life and destroy his work for the church" (Steltenkamp 1993, 141). Unfortunately, while Steltenkamp places much emphasis on these remarks, their immediate context (see 140, 179, n. 11) tends to drop out of sight in his conclusions. The unwary reader may be left with the impression that her remarks are directed primarily toward scholarly interpretations of Black Elk as a traditionalist—like Rice's—rather than toward Wallace Black Elk and the occupation of Wounded Knee by AIM. So it is a little disingenuous of Steltenkamp to say, "Lucy's bias, if it could be called that, was simply to tell what she knew about her father's life" (179, n. 12). On the basis of Steltenkamp's account, it would be more accurate to say that her bias was that of a militant Lakota Catholic who disapproved of Neihardt from the beginning and whose response to the contemporary revival of traditional religion was strongly negative. Her distaste for the Wounded Knee occupation (see 189, n. 6) itself

7. Promotional materials for a workshop held with Black Elk at the Cloudmont Ski and Golf Resort in Mentone, Alabama, December 6–8, 1985, describe him as "a 19th generation Lakota Medicine Man, Spiritual Teacher, and grandson of the Oglala Holy Man, Black Elk (*Black Elk Speaks*)."

8. For instance, in recalling his education, Black Elk says: "Those Christian people would preach against everything we did. They'd say, 'Don't go out there and eat those roots and herbs. Those are serpent food, devil's food. We have a hospital, so you come over here and eat those registered pills.' So we were supposed to go over there and eat the right kind of poison. So we'd go over there, and they would have that St. Joseph's aspirin. At the same time, over here Jesus is the healer. So what's wrong with Jesus? Why do I have to eat those pills from St. Joseph? So all this was going through my head. So I had a heck of a time trying to understand" (Wallace Black Elk, 25–26).

represents one pole of opinion about a highly polarizing event that is still quite divisive today (Steinmetz 1990, 168).[9]

It is also well to remember that no one, not even his daughter, can know for sure how Black Elk would have responded either to the Wounded Knee occupation or to the revival of traditional religion on the reservation today. The understanding of a great man proposed by one of his children is certainly of interest, but it cannot simply be regarded as decisive for scholarship without further ado. Steltenkamp, however, encourages us to do precisely that, particularly when he misrepresents Looks Twice's point of view as unbiased. In so doing, Steltenkamp fails to use proper caution in evaluating the oral tradition that surrounds Black Elk on the reservation today.

Steltenkamp's use of Looks Twice's oft-quoted story of Black Elk's conversion in 1904, in which a priest named Father Lindebner forcibly ejects Black Elk from a tipi where he was performing a healing ritual—another pillar of his interpretation of Black Elk—is a clear example of this lack of caution. Looks Twice herself stipulates that Black Elk "never talked about that incident" (34) and her story certainly is of dubious historicity. Steltenkamp himself notes both that other credible sources say that Black Elk simply asked for instruction in Catholicism and received it (183, n. 12) and that the story bears a suspicious resemblance to a diary entry by one of the Jesuits, which indicates that it may well be a "twice told tale" (37–38). It also harmonizes remarkably badly with Black Elk's story about a priest who died soon after interfering physically with one of his healing rituals (DeMallie 1984, 239). Despite these and other contrary indications, and despite DeMallie's contention that Black Elk's acceptance of Catholicism was the culmination of a slow process, it is clearly important to Steltenkamp that Black Elk have a "conversion" and he essentially accepts Looks Twice's account: "Black Elk's own presentation of the drama of Payabya [the locality identified in Looks Twice's story], whether whole or partial in its statement of concrete fact, unambiguously signaled for him the decisive call from Wakan Tanka through a Wanikiye Blackrobe" (41–42). The alert

9. For the opposite pole of opinion on Wounded Knee 1973, Mary Crow Dog's autobiography presents her perspective as a participant.

reader will notice that in a few paragraphs, the essence, if not the details, of Looks Twice's story has been attributed to Black Elk himself, which is clearly unjustifiable based on the evidence Steltenkamp himself presents. The conclusion that he draws from this story is similarly dubious. According to Steltenkamp, after his conversion, Black Elk became a zealous catechist and a consistently progressive Catholic. He "appreciated his earlier tradition" (136), but he retained no meaningful commitment to it. There is thus in Steltenkamp's interpretation no trace of the traditionalist fervor that DeMallie believes Neihardt awakened in Black Elk.

In this context, Looks Twice states that after his conversion, Black Elk put his medicine practice away and never took it up again (34). The reader will recall that DeMallie makes the stronger claim that Black Elk "never practiced the Lakota religious ceremonies again" (1984, 14). Although Steltenkamp does not make this claim himself, it is implied by his characterization of the pagan Black Elk as a *pejuta wicasa*, a *yuwipi* man, rather than as a *wicasa wakan*, a holy man. According to Steltenkamp, "Lucy's narrative rightly characterizes her father as a *pejuta wicasa* before his work as a catechist. . . . Current parlance would accord her father the title of *wicasa wakan* once he became a catechist, a phrase likewise designating the priests with whom he worked" (23; see 181, n. 6). Obviously, if Black Elk was not a *wicasa wakan* before beginning his church work, but became one only after accepting Catholicism, by putting his medicine practice away he would have been renouncing all his traditional spiritual power. If this were the case, it would certainly justify DeMallie's statement that he never practiced Lakota religious ceremonies again.

This issue is clearly of central importance to the understanding of Black Elk's life and religion. In the first place, it seems clear that Black Elk was in fact a *wicasa wakan,* as he is clearly understood to be in the oral tradition, despite Steltenkamp's claim to the contrary. The distinction is that the *wicasa wakan* (holy man) had a higher status than the *pejuta wicasa* (medicine man) in Lakota culture, for he had the right and responsibility to conduct religious rituals, to intercede with the sacred powers on behalf of the people. Although the holy man might well also be a healer, the healers proper were not holy men. Direct evidence that Black Elk was a *wicasa wakan* is his gift to Neihardt of a morning star pendant, which is described by

Neihardt in one of the drafts of his correspondence as "a beautiful old sacred ornament that he had used a long while in the sun dances in which he has officiated as a priest" (DeMallie 1984, 28). At the bare minimum, this statement proves that Black Elk represented himself to Neihardt as a *wicasa wakan,* in this case, as a Sun Dance intercessor. As additional evidence, it is unlikely that a *pejuta wicasa* would have been permitted to enact the Horse Dance, which was subsequently accepted as a part of the tradition, as Fools Crow's remarks make clear: "Another religious dance whose song was a prayer was the Horse Dance. I was one of the riders in the last true and sacred Horse Dance, which was also held that day at Whiteclay in 1931" (Mails 1979, 79). The creation of new rituals was the sole province of the *wicasa wakan.* Furthermore, Black Elk states in his account of his power vision that he "was to be a sacred man when I got back to earth" (DeMallie 1984, 122). At this point in the transcript, "sacred man" is glossed by "wakan shasha" [*wakan wicasa*] and "holy man." In explaining his reasons for wanting to go to Harney Peak to Neihardt, Black Elk also said, "I had been appointed by my vision to be an intercessor of my people with the spirit powers" (DeMallie 1984, 293). It might also be said that Black Elk's entire approach to life and religion was decisively that of a *wicasa wakan.* In view of this and other evidence, it must be said that Steltenkamp's claim that Black Elk became a *wicasa wakan* only on becoming a catechist must be regarded as a spectacular bit of special pleading.

A related problem with Steltenkamp's picture of Black Elk's conversion is that he does not mention the ban on the Sun Dance while speculating on Black Elk's motives. The ban on the Sun Dance and on traditional healing made it extremely difficult for the holy men to make a living. Since the ban on traditional healing was necessarily more difficult to enforce, the holy men were not entirely out of work, but the Sun Dance was probably their main source of income. Since the ban effectively eliminated his income as a *wicasa wakan,* Black Elk was left with his practice as a *yuwipi* man, and he may well have been experiencing economic stress.

Although the ban is certainly not pleasant to contemplate from our present relatively enlightened perspective, its omission from discussions of Black Elk's conversion produces anachronistic and distorted results. Black Elk first performed the Horse Dance in 1881

(DeMallie 1984, 7), a date that roughly coincides with the last great public dances before the ban on the Sun Dance took effect in 1883. Since this was Black Elk's public announcement of his vocation as a holy man, it is unlikely that he officiated at a Sun Dance before this time. This means that to have officiated at the Sun Dance for "many years"—as he apparently told Neihardt that he did—he would have had to have officiated at secret dances during the ban. It can be said that defiance of the ban would have been fully consistent with Black Elk's militant posture during the Ghost Dance disturbances: "My relatives, there is a certain thing that we have done. From that certain sacred thing we have done, we have had visions. . . . So therefore the Wasichu if they want to, they may fight us, and if they fight us, if we are going to we will win; so have in your minds a strong desire and take courage" (DeMallie 1984, 268). Given his attitude in 1890, it seems entirely possible that Black Elk took part in the small, secret dances that kept traditional religion alive during the ban, either before going to Europe or after the Ghost Dance disturbances or both. It is even possible that he maintained some degree of involvement after his baptism in 1904. The record seems to be silent on this issue, probably with good reason. Black Elk presumably would have known better than to elaborate on such points in his remarks to Neihardt. In the first place, the dance was still under ban in 1931; to have mentioned any involvement would have constituted admission of a crime. In the second place, as subsequent events would show, he was going to get in enough trouble with the Jesuits for simply talking about his vision and his early years without elaborating further on his involvement with the Sun Dance, the ritual that the Jesuits most hated and condemned.[10] Black Elk knew the Jesuits and their principles and prejudices intimately, and there is no reason to assume that he was surprised by their response to *Black Elk Speaks*.[11]

10. From the standpoint of traditional Christian theology, the Sun Dance is not merely inhumane and barbaric, but is also a profane mockery of Christ's redemptive work on the cross, which was interpreted as the final sacrifice early in the history of the church.

11. Since the information that Black Elk had officiated at the Sun Dance appears only in Neihardt's correspondence, and not in the introduction to *Black Elk Speaks*, where Neihardt might well have used it, it is even possible that Black Elk explicitly requested Neihardt not to make any mention of his participation in the Sun Dance.

As Steltenkamp would say, there is certainly an element of speculation in these extrapolations from Black Elk's comments to Neihardt about the morning star pendant. It should be clear, however, that the effect of the ban on Black Elk and on men like him was to force them to rely on healing rather than on the Sun Dance to make a living. In this light, his remarks to his daughter about his qualms of conscience—which apparently centered on the trickery or psychological supports necessary to traditional healing—make much more sense (35). In later years, Black Elk said to Looks Twice that he did not believe in *yuwipi* but that "praying with the pipe is more of a main thing" (26). This should perhaps be understood as expressing Black Elk's regret that he was forced into a *yuwipi* practice by economic circumstances. Remember that J. R. Walker arrived on the Pine Ridge in 1896 and soon after began working with the medicine men on the cure of tuberculosis, taxing them with their dishonesty and convicting them of the "trick with the worm" (Walker 1980, 10–11). Since tuberculosis was such a terrible killer on the reservation during these years, these charges may well have had a considerable effect on Black Elk's conscience. If he did take up a medicine practice in part in response to economic stress, his income as a catechist may have helped enable him to quit it, probably with much relief. But note also in this connection that on at least one occasion, at Looks Twice's suggestion, Black Elk submitted himself to the ministrations of a *yuwipi* man, apparently with good results (Steltenkamp 1993, 123–25).

However it was with his medicine practice, Black Elk's remarks to Looks Twice presuppose a distinction between the pipe—the preeminent symbol of traditional Lakota religion—and *yuwipi*. Although Black Elk apparently did abandon his medicine practice, it should not thereby be inferred that he necessarily put away traditional religion as well. On the testimony of Ben Marrowbone, Black Elk defended the pipe to the catechists on at least one occasion (Steltenkamp 1993, 105), and he seems to have quietly maintained his contact with traditional spiritual leaders like Fools Crow (Mails 1979, 45). Although there is no evidence of his subsequent participation in

---

Similarly, practical considerations cannot be dismissed with respect to Black Elk's reported refusal to demonstrate the *yuwipi* to Neihardt (DeMallie 1984, 14, n. 16).

the Sun Dance, Looks Twice notes that in 1928, Black Elk did attend the first public Sun Dance on the Pine Ridge reservation since the early 1880s—the dance was still technically under ban—and invited Elk Head, the Keeper of the Pipe, to his camp after the dance, where Looks Twice met him (107). He also held the *inipi* (sweat lodge) on at least one occasion (60–61) and "split the clouds" with the pipe on at least one occasion (117).

As I have argued in "Lakota Religion and Tragedy" (1984a, 21–28), the entire process of transmitting his sacred knowledge to Neihardt was itself a traditional ritual, which was punctuated with other rituals, from the holding of a feast and the building of a shade to the final ritual on Harney Peak that ended the instruction (De-Mallie 1984, 294–96). In view of these rituals, it cannot be said that Black Elk never again practiced traditional religion, even if the Duhamel performances are judged insincere. A final observation may be relevant to the possibility that Black Elk continued to be involved in some way with the Sun Dance or traditional religion or both during his years as a catechist. As DeMallie points out, while Black Elk pledged not to participate in the rabbit dance at the Catholic Indian Congress in 1929, a number were held as a part of the festivities surrounding Neihardt's instruction only two years later (1984, 38). According to Hilda Neihardt, Black Elk himself was the singer and drummer at one of these dances (87). This would seem to indicate that the Jesuits' condemnation of the rabbit dance made little impression on Black Elk. How much less impression would their condemnation of the Sun Dance—a far more important and sacred rite than this merely social dance—have made on a man such as Black Elk?

In any case, according to Steltenkamp, Black Elk was a *pejuta wicasa* who was converted in 1904, became a catechist, and remained faithful to Catholicism until his death. He was "not a disconsolate elder mourning the loss of a past forever gone" (146). Instead, he exemplifies one of the central cultural traits of the Lakota, a "resilient willingness to let go" of the past (160). His worldview was essentially that of one who has "a spiritual approach to life in which religious thought dictates behavior" (161–62). Steltenkamp further characterizes Black Elk in his conclusions as essentially "a social critic who derived his own strength and inspiration from the Lakota-Catholic religious sphere and who, in turn, used that framework to challenge his people unto renewal" (171).

Just as *Black Elk Speaks* was something of an embarrassment to the old Jesuits, both *The Sixth Grandfather* and *The Sacred Pipe* are something of an embarrassment to Steltenkamp's position, for few readers of these works would credit the idea that they are merely appreciations of a faith Black Elk has left behind. Steltenkamp understandably has little to say about *The Sixth Grandfather,* but he does characterize *The Sacred Pipe* as "simply another attempt to rally his people's religious fervor by whatever means were at his disposal" (164)—not as an attempt to revitalize traditional religion (155, 159) or as a "Lakota counterpoint to Catholic sacraments" (163).

It is worth noting that any consistent attempt to describe Black Elk as a progressive Catholic, a convert who retained no meaningful commitment to traditional religion, could be maintained only in the face of formidable difficulties. It could be argued that Black Elk simply abandoned traditional religion for Catholicism only if the following points could be defended:

1. Black Elk was a sincere Catholic who understood his conversion as an either/or choice between Christianity and traditional religion

2. *Black Elk Speaks* and *The Sacred Pipe* do not fairly represent Black Elk's religion

3. The ritual Black Elk performed on Harney Peak, calling on the Grandfathers to "make the tree flower," did not occur as Neihardt reported it

4. Lucy Looks Twice's understanding of her father is an irrefutable source for his own self-understanding

5. Black Elk's participation in the Duhamel pageant was not in earnest

6. The testimony of Fools Crow and others who regard Black Elk as the greatest of the Teton holy men (Mails 1979, 53) can be ignored

7. The extraordinary influence of Black Elk on the contemporary revival of traditional religion is a decisive misunderstanding

If these propositions—and others that they entail—could be maintained, it would be possible to argue that Black Elk was not a religious traditionalist in a meaningful sense. Although it is perhaps not impossible that this position could be rigorously defended, Stel-tenkamp does not attempt to do so, either because his position is in fact more nuanced or because he recognizes the difficulties. Although something like this seems to be implied by many of his statements, the position sketched above should probably not be at-tributed to Steltenkamp, who seems implicitly to recognize that Black Elk's religion is more complex than this model implies.[12]

In the end, while providing a needed corrective, Steltenkamp overbalances the scale toward Black Elk's Catholicism, falling prey to the very either/or that he cautions against (157). The real Black Elk was not either a traditionalist or a Catholic; he was both at the same time. His conversion was not conversion as understood by the Jesuits who were so scandalized by the publication of *Black Elk Speaks*—the substitution of one religion for another—but, as Steltenkamp him-self implies, the acceptance of Christianity as the further extension of his vision.

Despite his overemphasis on Black Elk's Catholicism, Stel-tenkamp has a great deal right. Certainly interpretations of Black Elk that simply ignore his Christianity are no longer viable. Likewise, as he points out, Black Elk did not live as a paralyzed victim of West-ern subjugation (xv) or a despairing old man, but as a vital presence. Steltenkamp correctly notes that the picture of Black Elk as a pris-oner of the past is a form of stereotyping (145–46) and that the romanticism rampant in many discussions of Black Elk does nothing to remedy the real problems of the Lakota today (148). Steltenkamp is correct in implying that the real Black Elk is infinitely more inter-esting than either Neihardt's portrait or the romantic stereotype

12. Just as it is frustrating that Steltenkamp declines to engage his critics, it is frustrating that he declines to state his thesis, relying instead on oblique suggestions to carry the argument forward. For instance, Steltenkamp replies to DeMallie and Stein-metz on Black Elk's conversion thusly: "As this study progresses, a more curious and complex series of experiences will be shown to unfold within the holy man's life that beg a more expansive interpretation than those proposed thus far" (42). His indif-ference to argument attains something of a zenith in his discussion of Neihardt's influence on *Black Elk Speaks:* "When scholars adopt such contrary positions, it is diffi-cult to determine exactly what this holy man of the earlier works actually thought" (155).

(22). He is also correct in maintaining that Black Elk's approach to life was essentially religious (164) and that Black Elk believed that effective strategies for social change flow from the sacred (170). Finally, Steltenkamp is correct in pointing out that Black Elk lived spiritually and productively through many changes, showing an adaptiveness that helps explain how an entire people has carried on against seemingly overwhelming odds (14–15).

Ultimately, Steltenkamp's vigorous corrective to uncritical interpretations of Black Elk should help occasion a much-needed re-evaluation. As such, his overbalancing of the scale toward Black Elk's Catholicism might best be regarded in the light of the passion that he brings to the subject, both as a Catholic and as a scholar who believes that a great injustice has been done. Steltenkamp's overstatements reflect the considerable frustrations of a scholar who believes that the truth has not been told, who has been laboring for many years to make himself heard over the roar of a popular, romantic stereotype. With this book, Steltenkamp has finally been heard.

In contrast, Julian Rice's *Black Elk's Story: Distinguishing Its Lakota Purpose* (1991) portrays Black Elk essentially as a traditionalist, in part through direct engagement with Steltenkamp's dissertation. As befits an English professor, much of Rice's interpretation focuses on discussion of Neihardt and his literary shaping of the Black Elk material. In constructing his portrait of Black Elk—which is also a portrait of Neihardt, for Rice believes that they are different in ways that illuminate their traditions—Rice relies primarily on *The Sixth Grandfather,* contrasted with *Black Elk Speaks* and *The Song of the Messiah,* the final book in Neihardt's epic poem, *The Cycle of the West.* Rice points out that from the point of view of recent criticism, *The Sixth Grandfather* is a better text than *Black Elk Speaks.*

> The text of *The Sixth Grandfather* is a better text than *Black Elk Speaks* because it has not been oversimplified. It retains a greater range of mood and experience spoken by a more authentic voice. . . . Future students of the Black Elk material will find [it] to have the ironies, reversals, and shifts of voice found in most of the Western literature now considered worthy of extended thought and

comment. *Black Elk Speaks*, on the other hand, may perhaps be relegated to the ranks of nineteenth century curios, reflecting white misconceptions of Indians. (13–14)

The Sacred Pipe is not nearly as congenial a text for Rice, who characterizes it as "overtly Catholic" (xi) and containing an "excessive Christian commentary" (6). Although this is hardly an apt characterization, since the point of the book is to relate the two traditions, it does indicate decisively where Rice's sympathies lie.

Rice interprets the 1931 material as an indication that Black Elk was a "Lakota elder still immersed in the traditional religion" despite almost thirty years of Christianity (x). (It is mildly ironic that this was Neihardt's own estimate of Black Elk's Catholicism, given the gulf that separates them in Rice's interpretation.)[13] He characterizes Neihardt as a Christian poet in the typological tradition, who believed that native Americans had to be crucified for their own redemption by God's chosen instrument, the Aryan race (xi). According to Rice, Neihardt was therefore a racist (17), although not of the most virulent type (34–35). The groundwork of Rice's interpretation of Black Elk is a contrast between Lakota and Christian culture, which he believes have broadly different values and emphases. While Lakota culture is "directed toward physical and spiritual continuance on the earth" (xi), Christian culture is directed toward an otherworldly "spiritual evolution beyond time" (xi). This basic contrast is elaborated in Rice's other works, particularly in *Deer Women and Elk Men: The Lakota Stories of Ella Deloria* (1992), which relies on a series of comparisons of the stories with Shakespeare's tragedies to make essentially the same point.

With this somewhat superficial view of Christianity, it is perhaps not surprising that Rice believes that Black Elk's Christianity was "more social than spiritual" (xi). He is very much inclined to think that Black Elk became a Christian for reasons of expediency: "Black Elk may well have chosen baptism at the age of thirty-seven for a warrior's reasons, to protect the people from persecution, and to help them adjust to reservation life" (xi). Steltenkamp would agree

13. Steltenkamp quotes Neihardt in an interview with F. W. Thomsen as replying to the question of whether Black Elk's Christianity colored his thinking by saying: "It might have, here and there in spots, but fundamentally no" (1993, 187, n. 5).

wholeheartedly with the latter half of that statement, but he would certainly never accede to the notion that Black Elk's Christianity was insincere. Rice suggests that Black Elk sought "channels in Church practice through which to continue Lakota tradition," preserving traditional values until they could be openly revived (2). As might be expected, Rice estimates the years with Duhamel very differently from Steltenkamp, saying that he "spent nearly the next decade teaching non-Indians the value and validity of Lakota culture at an annual pageant in the Black Hills" (3). Despite his Catholicism, Black Elk thus "spent his last years working actively to preserve the Lakota religion using every available vehicle" (4). He closes his biographical sketch by noting DeMallie's statements that the Laubins, annual visitors to the Duhamel pageant, never heard Black Elk mention Catholicism and that Charles Hanson, a visitor to Black Elk in 1948, reported that Ben Black Elk suggested that Black Elk regretted his Catholicism (4).

On Black Elk's conversion, Rice characterizes DeMallie's position as being that it was expedience, Steltenkamp's as being that it was a "fortunate fall," and my own as denying that a "conversion in any meaningful sense ever occurred" (5). Although DeMallie seems to be of two minds on this issue, he does finally seem to come down on the side of expediency, and it could be said that Rice's characterization of Steltenkamp's position is ironically apt. As for my position, as I say above, Lucy Looks Twice's story of Black Elk's conversion seems to be dubious, and it seems unlikely that Black Elk had a "St. Paul on the road to Damascus" experience, much less one occasioned by physical intimidation. However, Rice's statement that "for Holler, Black Elk became a Catholic to find metaphors that would infuse the Lakota religion with life and assure its continuance" (6) reflects his view more than mine. Although I do not believe that a conversion in the sense of a substitution of Christianity for traditional religion occurred with Black Elk, it seems to me that he did accept Christianity as a valid expression of the sacred. Although *The Sacred Pipe* could certainly be read as supporting Rice's contention, its firm grasp of Christian concepts alone indicates that his engagement with Christianity was deeper and more profound than Rice implies. Also, Black Elk clearly accepted some elements of the Christian critique of traditional religion and modified the Sun Dance accordingly, indicating that he was on a more serious mission than a hunt for metaphors.

In any case, Rice states the alternatives.

> Thus far we can see three Black Elks from the biographical record and from the text edited by Brown: 1) a Black Elk who was a sincere Catholic but who returned to Lakota religion after the Neihardt interviews [DeMallie]; 2) a consistently active and committed Catholic who never turned back [Steltenkamp]; and 3) an ingenious, syncretic Lakota-Christian [Holler]. (8)

In response, Rice points out that these images might well be equally valid, since people and writers go through stages and develop over time. As DeMallie implies, Black Elk might well have been a more fervent Catholic in the years he was working as a catechist, turning again to traditional religion in his later life. But Rice is inclined against such a developmental sequence based on statements in the Neihardt interviews in which "Black Elk is sharply critical of missionary influence and clearly angry about their wrongfully imposed suppression" (9). In the end, Rice suggests that Black Elk may not have been able to be fully consistent, and that he in fact contradicted himself—perhaps purposefully. For Rice, what is most important is that Black Elk never changed in his essential self-understanding as a Lakota holy man whose primary responsibility was to protect the people: "The purpose of his speech, as defender and spokesman for the people, never changed" (10). He emphasizes that because Black Elk's self-understanding was formed by traditional culture, the cross-cultural aspects of understanding Black Elk must always be borne in mind. Rice believes that the idea that Black Elk "made a complete transition to twentieth century Catholic consciousness"—a position he attributes to Steltenkamp—"is improbable" (10). Ultimately, Rice suggests that it is impossible to tell when Black Elk is being sincere and when he is being deceptive. Like the Brulé leader Spotted Tail, he knew the value of faking out the whites with "an image of intelligence and charm" (11). Furthermore, "as in warfare, he could be deceptive" (12). In making this point, Rice refers to Black Elk's telling of the story of Sharp Nose (DeMallie 1984, 371–76), who lied about the sacred to protect his people, suggesting that Black Elk may have been doing the same (148). For Rice, what really matters is Black Elk's endurance, his persistence in standing up for his people, and his heroic "refusal to vanish" (13).

Ironically, much of this is what is important to Steltenkamp about Black Elk, and it is unfortunate that he simply dismisses Rice without attempting a rebuttal. It could be said that Rice seems to have the clear meaning of Black Elk's texts more on his side, but Steltenkamp might have found some resources for reply. For one thing, there seems to be no testimony from any of Black Elk's associates that his Christianity was insincere—including Fools Crow, who could hardly be accused of having a Christian bias.[14] The old Jesuits, except those who spoke Lakota, probably had no way of knowing whether the content of Black Elk's Lakota teaching was orthodox.[15] There is no evidence, however, that it was insincere. Steltenkamp might have said that—warrior or not—the assumption that there was this much deception in Black Elk's character is just as unlikely as the assumption that he made a complete transition to twentieth-century Catholic consciousness. He might also have pointed out that the evidence seems instead to indicate that Black Elk readily accepted Christianity as a valid extension of the insights expressed in his power vision, and as a practical bridge to the white world and a better life for his people. Steltenkamp might have turned up the heat by accusing Rice of romanticism in his constant use of the warrior image, demanding to know how this romanticism would benefit the contemporary Lakota. Perhaps the opportunity for such a rebuttal is not yet lost, as Steltenkamp—who seems a little inclined to this sort of polemic—might yet get in the spirit.

Rice could clearly be accused of a certain kind of romanticism. His procedure is essentially that of the Boasians, such as Ella C. Deloria, who conceived of cultural description, in DeMallie's words, as

14. Although Paul B. Steinmetz believes that Fools Crow regarded Christianity as superior (1990, 186), his biographer, also a Christian minister, saw the matter differently: "Before I met him, he and his wife, Kate, had been attending mass fairly regularly at a Pine Ridge parish. But he remained a staunch traditionalist, and in his later years the frequency of attendance decreased. Whenever we were staying together in a town or city, Dallas Chief Eagle attended mass, but Fools Crow did not go with him. There was never a question as to which came first with Fools Crow, and I suspect that the parish priests knew this too" (Mails 1991, 12).

15. Christopher Vecsey notes that almost all the German Jesuits, including Eugene Buechel, Placidus Sialm, Emil Perrig, Louis J. Goll, and Florentine Digmann, spoke Lakota (n.d., 6).

"an idealized and generalized synthesis of the past, a testament to the old and valued customs of the Sioux" (Deloria 1988, 237). Rice's discussions presuppose an ideal Lakota world that poses a sharp contrast to the strife and disharmony present in the Christian world. It might be doubted whether the Lakota culture presupposed by Rice's interpretation ever existed or could have existed. Certainly it bears little resemblance to either the ethnographic record or to the realities of reservation life during Black Elk's time. Although Rice casts much light on Black Elk's self-understanding as a holy man and on the old Lakota mental world, the contrast between Lakota ideality and Christian reality is arranged to Christianity's disadvantage, particularly because many Lakotas profess allegiance to both traditions. The greatest shortcoming of Rice's conception is thus that it fails to take seriously Black Elk's engagement with Christianity in the context of the reservation life as it was lived in his day.

Paul B. Steinmetz's conception of Black Elk is embedded in a comprehensive model of Lakota religious identity that takes into account not only traditional Lakota religion and Christianity, but also the Native American Church and a Lakota fundamentalist group, The Body of Christ Church. As a Jesuit who worked on the Pine Ridge Reservation from 1961 to 1981, Steinmetz possessed an enviable platform for fieldwork among the Lakota, perhaps unequaled by anyone since agency physician J. R. Walker. Like Walker, Steinmetz devoted many years of his life to actively helping the people, and was able to develop intimate relationships with both traditional holy men and ordinary people without the necessity to rely on paid informants or brief, intensive periods of fieldwork. The results of Steinmetz's reflections on this experience are presented in his dissertation, which was prepared under the direction of Åke Hultkrantz (a European authority on the American Indian) and subsequently published as *Pipe, Bible, and Peyote among the Oglala Lakota* (1980). Steinmetz's book, which was significantly revised in 1990, thus combines his perspective as a Catholic priest among the Lakota with academic reflection informed by engagement with the European history of religions perspective, American anthropological theory, and the work of other scholars.

But Steinmetz is more than an informed observer of the contemporary reservation religious scene. In 1965, he began to incorporate the elements and symbols of traditional Lakota religion into his

Catholic rituals. According to Steinmetz, his involvement began in 1961 with the decoration of the church under his direction in Oglala, South Dakota, with traditional Lakota symbols, which led to changing the patronage of the church from St. Elizabeth to Our Lady of the Sioux. In 1965, Steinmetz prayed with the pipe for the first time at a funeral, separating the pipe to symbolize death and rejoining it later to symbolize the resurrection and eternal life. According to Steinmetz, the Lakota consulted the *yuwipi* man of the community, John Iron Rope, who gave his approval to this use of the pipe (36). In the intervening years, Steinmetz gained the support of many of the reservation's eminent holy men, including Pete Catches, Sr., who directed his vision quest, and Frank Fools Crow, who indicated his support by inviting Steinmetz to participate in the tribal council's Sun Dance of 1971. Although Steinmetz notes that his use of the pipe in Catholic worship and his participation in this and other rituals was opposed both by militants and other Lakotas who believe the two traditions should remain separate, he seems to have enjoyed the support of many of the traditional holy men.

Steinmetz is thus at once a qualified observer of the Lakota religious present as well as an influential creator of that same present, a fact that must be borne in mind in evaluating his model of Lakota religious identity, for he is at once analyst and advocate. The axis of his model of Christian-traditionalist interaction is a distinction between related positions, which Steinmetz calls "Lakota Ecumenist I" and "Lakota Ecumenist II."

> Ecumenist I designates those Lakota Christians who separately practice their traditional and Christian religions but see common religious forms between the two traditions. Ecumenist II designates those Lakota Christians who see the Christian religion as a fulfillment of the Lakota religion through the symbolic identifications they made. (6)

Almost all contemporary Lakota profess some degree of Christian belief, for almost all are members of one of the Christian denominations. Many also profess some degree of belief in traditional Lakota religion simultaneously. There are Lakotas who reject Christianity entirely (especially those in the American Indian Movement) and Lakota Christians who reject traditional religion entirely (especially those Lakota fundamentalists in The Body of Christ Church), but most Lakotas possess both Christian and traditionalist loyalties. Insofar as they compartmentalize these beliefs, or practice these religions separately, they belong in the Ecumenist I category, along with Lakotas who oppose Steinmetz's praying with the pipe. Although he admits that "beyond doubt, the Ecumenist I group contains the majority of the Lakota people" (193), Steinmetz claims for the Ecumenist II group "the medicine men and more serious thinkers" (6).

Steinmetz's model is clearly and explicitly Christian, presupposing both the superiority of Christianity to traditional religion and the superiority of the Ecumenist II position to that of the Ecumenist I. As Bruce David Forbes pointed out in his review of the first edition, "apparently the only way that Steinmetz can conceive of an integration of religious traditions is to have Christianity fulfill the others. . . . His treatment still implies a hierarchy of religions with Christianity at the pinnacle" (87). Steinmetz's position, however, is nuanced by his appreciation of the Lakota tradition and his belief that traditional religion—as interpreted in the light of Christianity—is valid. The model for this understanding is the relationship between Judaism and Christianity as it is understood in Christian theology. According to this model, a special relationship exists between Christianity and Judaism such that Judaism is a preparation for Christianity, which is its perfection and completion. Judaism, so understood, is a preparation for the Christ.[16] Steinmetz explicitly appropriates this model in his discussion, saying that Black Elk makes "Lakota religious tradition an 'Old Testament' foreshadowing of Christ and reaching its fulfillment in Him" (187–88). In another place, Steinmetz attributes to George Plenty Wolf the insight that "traditional Lakota religion is a preparation for Christ in a way similar to the Old Testament for the Jews" (189).

Although it is understandable that Steinmetz uses this model, which is readily available in his tradition, there are anomalies in its application to the Lakota. For one thing, the early Christians were

---

16. Unlike others who do not believe in the Christ, Jews are generally not missionized, for the "old covenant" God made with them is held still valid, although it has been superseded for all other people by the "new covenant" of Christianity. This is an evident point of difference with respect to the Lakota.

Jews whose religious consciousness changed, not because of missionary influence from outside the Jewish community, but because of their relationship to Jesus as the Christ. More important, the early Christians did not continue to practice Judaism—for instance, by sacrificing in the temple in Jerusalem. Instead, they ultimately left Judaism to follow the Christ, interpreting the death of Jesus on the cross as the final sacrifice. The logical outcome of the use of this model for Lakota-Christian interaction would not be Christian tolerance of traditional belief—and continued practice of traditional religion by Lakota Christians—but the demand that the Christian Lakotas leave behind their pagan past, precisely as it was enunciated by the Episcopal Missionary Bishop Henry Hobart Hare: "So of all Christian peoples, and so too now of those Dakotas who had embraced Christianity. . . . When urged to join in heathen dances and customs as of old, their reply was: 'No, we cannot, we have taken an oath to give up all these things and follow Christ'" (Howe, 89).

In any case, it is clear that for Steinmetz, the Lakota tradition is valid only insofar as it is compatible with Christianity and accepts its fulfillment and perfection in it. For this reason, the Ecumenist I position is inferior to the Ecumenist II position, since the latter explicitly acknowledges the superiority of Christianity. Steinmetz characterizes the Ecumenist I position as consisting of "those Lakota Christians who have both Lakota and Christian identities, or a split identity" (191). It is thus in some sense an "imperfect stage" (192) of the Ecumenist II position, and it is inherently unstable, although it can achieve some stability if the "recognition of common religious forms is sufficiently deep" (192). Since most Lakotas occupy this position, it can be inferred that they need the healing insight provided by the Ecumenist II's understanding of Christianity as the fulfillment of traditional Lakota religion. As Forbes pointed out in his review of the first edition, this is no longer phenomenology, but advocacy (86). In his revised edition, Steinmetz admits that this is so, but comments, "I feel that I am discovering the Ecumenist II viewpoint in their religious imagination and not projecting my own onto it" (177).

However that may be, it should be clear from this discussion that Steinmetz's ministry among the Lakota was both pastoral and prophetic, to use terms in vogue in American religious circles in the

1960s. The pastoral dimension of the Ecumenist II model is that it is
directed toward healing the sense of conflicted loyalties and split
personalities that Steinmetz perceives in the dual religious participation of most Lakotas. In his funeral homily for Ben Black Elk, Steinmetz says that Ben once revealed to him that he felt deeply
conflicted and troubled about his divided loyalties to both traditional
religion and Christianity. According to Steinmetz, these doubts were
largely resolved by the insight that "the Sacred Pipe and Christ really
are one, that they fulfill each other" (203). Steinmetz calls this "the
vision of Benjamin Black Elk" and it is the deeper meaning behind
the picture on the dust jacket of Ben kneeling before the altar with
the pipe.[17] The Ecumenist II has resolved this conflict, which was,
after all, created by the earlier teachings of the Christian denominations. On the other hand, the prophetic side of Steinmetz's ministry
lies in his going beyond the understanding of most of the people,
calling upon them to join him in a place they do not yet stand.

The foregoing discussion of Steinmetz's Ecumenist I and II categories is a necessary propaedeutic to discussion of his understanding
of Black Elk, for Steinmetz believes Black Elk occupies the Ecumenist II position. For Steinmetz, Black Elk's messiah vision "drama-
tizes the starting point for the Ecumenist II position," because in it
Black Elk discovers "the presence of the unknown Christ in his
Lakota tradition" (182). In his first edition, Steinmetz credited Black
Elk only with a deep, unconscious integration of the two traditions
based on his reading of the vision (1980, 159). As I pointed out in
"Black Elk's Relationship to Christianity," if this were so, he could
not rightly be claimed as a representative of the Ecumenist II position (Holler 1984b, 41). Partly in response to my remarks, Steinmetz
has modified his position considerably, acknowledging a more active
and creative role for Black Elk and attempting to locate him more
securely within the Ecumenist II paradigm. Although he retains the
remark that "Black Elk's life as a Catholic catechist did require him

17. Although amusing, it is insensitive of William K. Powers to caption this in his
essay on dual participation as a "promotional photo" (1987, 104), although it conveys
his response to Steinmetz's ministry even more clearly than his essay, which condemns
the use of the pipe in the Eucharist as a cynical priestly ploy that is not even worthy of
the name of syncretism (1987, 99).

to suppress traditional Lakota religion much of the time into his un-
conscious, which surfaced in the Neihardt and Brown interviews,"
he adds the comment that "Black Elk did consciously integrate the
two religious traditions in a remarkable way" (185).

It is important to understand precisely what this implies. Steinmetz's earlier understanding of Black Elk was akin to Steltenkamp's
in making Black Elk almost wholly Catholic, tending to explain away
Black Elk Speaks and *The Sacred Pipe* as aberrations, repressed relics
that accidentally surfaced. His reconsidered Black Elk is still more
Catholic than traditional, for he accepts Lucy Looks Twice's story of
Black Elk's conversion as historical, glossing Looks Twice's admission
that the story is not Black Elk's with brackets: "'My father never
talked [i.e. normally] about that incident'" (184). In response to my
observation that Black Elk's "conversion" was not what is normally
considered a conversion—the substitution of one religion for another (1984b, 47)—Steinmetz replies that "Black Elk had made a
total commitment to Christ." As evidence, he cites the fact that according to Father Sialm, Black Elk came to him during a retreat for
catechists with the statement, "We catechists resolve never to commit
a mortal sin" (188). Steinmetz nuances this remark by saying that to
"equate conversion with the substitution of one religion for another
is an inaccurate notion which does no justice to the deep psychological relationship a person has with his or her past" (189). Instead,
"conversion to Christianity does not mean giving up a religious tradition but rather giving it a Christian meaning" (188). That is to say
that Black Elk is the precise archetype of the Ecumenist II.

> Black Elk reads back into his Lakota tradition the insights he ac-
> quired as a Catholic catechist. This is exactly what the early Chris-
> tian converts from Judaism did with the Old Testament, making it a
> foreshadowing of Christ which reaches its fulfillment in Him. And
> so, Black Elk does the same, making Lakota religious tradition an
> "Old Testament" foreshadowing of Christ and reaching its fulfill-
> ment in Him. (187–88)

In response, I would say that there is no doubt that Black Elk made a
real commitment to Christianity. To say that he made a "total" commitment to it seems again to imply substitution. (I confess I cannot appreciate the decisiveness of the resolution on mortal sin in this context.)

The essential question about Black Elk's relationship to the Ecumenist II category is not whether his Christianity was sincere, but whether he understood Christianity to be superior to traditional religion, in the sense of a correction, clarification, and fulfillment of what was there only dimly grasped. I believe that the key here is an aspect of Ben Black Elk's statement that Steinmetz appears to have overlooked. Ben Black Elk says that traditional religion and Christianity "fulfill each other," and I believe that this is what Black Elk himself might have said in response to Steinmetz's claim that Christianity fulfills traditional religion. It seems to me that the clear sense of Black Elk's remarks in the introduction to *The Sacred Pipe* is that he sees the two traditions as equally valid (Holler 1984b, 42–43). Black Elk does not merely "appreciate his former tradition" as Steltenkamp would have it, or see it as an "Old Testament foreshadowing," as Steinmetz would have it; he regards it as a living tradition that should not simply be discarded for Christianity. In other words, I could accept Steinmetz's description of Black Elk's conversion as "giving the Lakota tradition a Christian meaning" if it were mutually balanced with the observation that Black Elk also gave Christianity a traditional Lakota meaning—and perhaps a Ghost Dancer's as well.[18]

But Steinmetz clearly sees that the situation of Black Elk is complex, and he is more realistic than Steltenkamp in allowing for the constraints on free speech entailed in his position as a catechist: "Black Elk seems to be telling [his people] privately to practice a Lakota Christian religion, since Lakota religion has acquired a Christian value. However, as a Catholic catechist he was unable to preach this publicly" (188). In the end, Steinmetz suggests that while the Ecumenist II was Black Elk's true position, he alternated between the two positions situationally, owing to these concerns: "I believe

---

18. In his prepublication critique of my manuscript, Steinmetz replies to these points thusly: "Total commitment does not imply substitution, but is compatible with the incorporation of one religious tradition into another. I agree that Black Elk did give Christianity a traditional Lakota meaning. The Ecumenist II position does not make mutual influence impossible. In the days of Black Elk when there was a strong emphasis on avoiding sin, Black Elk's statement that the catechists would never commit a mortal sin is a strong statement of total commitment. It was Black Elk's whole point in saying it."

that Black Elk fluctuated between the two positions, being in the Ecumenist I position when talking to the priests and being in the Ecumenist II one in talking to Fools Crow and others privately. This fluctuation explains why different people see Black Elk in such different light" (188).

It may be that Steinmetz cannot dispense with the subordination in his model and conceive traditional religion and Christianity on a truly mutual basis because of similar constraints. Could he do so, I believe he would be closer to the heart of Black Elk's message. However, another aspect of Steinmetz's model that requires comment. In a later chapter I argue that Black Elk clearly accepted some aspects of the Christian critique of traditional religion, modifying the Sun Dance in the light of them. This mutual influence, however, which is suggestive of the Ecumenist II position, operates on the level of interpretation and meaning, not on the level of ritual. Black Elk was not permitted the opportunity to ritualize as a Christian priest, so this is a moot point. However, in *The Sacred Pipe*, Black Elk does not do as Steinmetz does and take Christian symbolism into Lakota rituals. On the ritual level he is best understood in the light of the Ecumenist I position—as are most of the contemporary holy men. In *The Sacred Pipe*, Black Elk seems to be saying most clearly that Lakotas should pray with the pipe and go to the center of the sacred hoop—that is, practice traditional religion and dance the Sun Dance—not that they should incorporate the pipe into Christian rituals or incorporate the cross into the Sun Dance. In other words, although we do not know what Black Elk would have thought about Steinmetz praying with the pipe—this sort of thing would have been impossible with the Jesuits of his day—his practice seems to have been to keep the two traditions separate on the level of ritual. It could be argued that this is simply a function of his times, but it is also the practice of most of the Lakota holy men today.

One final point may be decisive in evaluating Black Elk's relationship to Steinmetz's Ecumenist I and II categories. These categories presuppose a distinction between traditional religion and Christianity that Black Elk may not have felt as strongly as it has been felt by outside observers. If his vision and his relationship with sacred power was truly paramount in his religious understanding, Black Elk may have seen one thing—the sacred—where others see two things—traditional religion and Christianity. As I will argue in my conclusion, if Black Elk regarded these two traditions as two expressions of the same sacred reality, much of the tension that commentators have perceived in his dual participation is dissipated. Such a position would properly be characterized in Steinmetz's terms as Ecumenist I—two expressions of the same thing—rather than Ecumenist II—Christianity fulfills traditional religion.

In the end, Steinmetz appropriates Black Elk for his own position, to lend authority to it. This should perhaps not be judged too harshly, for essentially every other Lakota holy man has done the very same thing, which is another testament to Black Elk's wisdom and enduring influence.

The foregoing sketch of the second major thrust of recent critical research, the inquiry into Black Elk's relationship to Christianity, has left us with a diversity of opinion. Although he is not completely consistent, one of DeMallie's suggestions is that Black Elk was a zealous Catholic whose interest in traditional religion was reawakened by Neihardt, whereupon he became increasingly traditionalist in orientation, verging on a repudiation of Catholicism in his final years. His other suggestion is that Black Elk's conversion was essentially expediency. Steltenkamp presents us with a picture of Black Elk that is almost a reverse of DeMallie's first suggestion. For Steltenkamp, Black Elk was a committed and zealous Catholic whose continued engagement with traditional religion was more apparent than real. Rice presents us with an image of Black Elk as a warrior and a thoroughgoing traditionalist. Steinmetz presents us with a Black Elk who is still in a sense a traditionalist, but who clearly affirms the superiority of Christianity to traditional religion, as its correction, perfection, and fulfillment.

My position will become clearer after the analysis of the Sun Dance and Black Elk's reinterpretation of it that follow. I can say in a preliminary way that I cannot accept DeMallie's picture of Black Elk's religion as being characterized by stages, so that he is by turns a traditionalist, a Catholic, and a born-again traditionalist. Nor can I accept Steltenkamp's portrait of Black Elk as a consistently progressive Catholic who retains no meaningful commitment to traditional religion. This position is not even accepted by his fellow Jesuit,

Steinmetz, who points out that the understanding of conversion as substitution does no justice to the deep psychological links the convert has with the past.

On the other hand, Rice clearly errs in estimating Black Elk's Christianity as superficial and insincere. A careful reading of *The Sacred Pipe* reveals that Black Elk has mastered the Christian tradition as it was presented to him and is fluent in his application of its insights to the task of explaining and updating traditional religion. As Steltenkamp's book shows, he also raised a daughter who was, at least for many years, a militant Lakota Catholic. Finally, as for Steinmetz's portrait of Black Elk as the archetype of the Ecumenist II, one who views Christianity as fulfilling traditional religion, I must say that I very much doubt that Black Elk accepted the implied superiority of Christianity to traditional religion. As will become clearer in my conclusion, I believe that although there is some truth in all these positions, they each in their own way fall prey to the temptation to perceive an opposition between Black Elk's traditionalism and his Christianity, creating an "either/or" that is foreign to Black Elk's way of thinking and experiencing religion.

Finally, despite its diversity and lack of critical consensus, this recent work represents a major advance over precritical interpretations in appreciating Black Elk as an active and creative presence. Each of these four commentators sees Black Elk clearly as an agent, who was actively engaged with his people's present, rather than as a passive victim of acculturation or a nostalgic informant on his people's past. In my view, this movement is real progress, and making it matters infinitely more than the precise position one arrives at after having made it. It amounts to a perspectival shift or paradigmatic change in our view of native American religious leaders of Black Elk's generation, reversing as it does the central thrust of several generations of work that took place in the shadow of the Boasian paradigm of salvage anthropology and the parallel assumptions of the acculturation model of cultural change. From our new vantage point, it is clear that salvaging the vestiges of the past was never the primary concern of "informants," such as Black Elk, who were decisively oriented to the problems of their people in the present, not to reveling in the glories of a romanticized past. The assumption

that the American Indian would soon be vanquished by assimilation—and the obsession with the past that came with it—is itself far
from vanished. The image of "the end of the trail" retains its grip
both on Hollywood and the popular imagination, as well as on some
scholars. But it is a giant step in the right direction to see Black Elk
as the creative religious thinker that he really was, rather than as a
pitiful old man consumed with a longing for a past that never was.

2

The Classic Sun Dance Observed
1866–1882

The Lakota Sun Dance comes into clear view relatively late in terms of the culture that produced it. The first good description of a Teton dance is of a dance in 1866—the year of Black Elk's birth as given by his daughter, Lucy Looks Twice![1] Sun Dances, however, are known to have taken place from the beginnings of white contact with the Sioux. George E. Hyde even found evidence of the Teton Sun Dance as an annual summer festival held on the Missouri River after the buffalo hunt partly for getting up large war parties against the "Omahas, Arikaras, or Mandans" while the Teton were still in Minnesota (1937, 32–33).[2] Since Hyde places these expeditions between 1700 and 1750, they indicate that from a relatively early time the Teton Sun Dance was an annual communal affair, associated with the buffalo hunt, that functioned as an impetus to war.

The earliest accounts of the Sun Dance focus on the Santee, for they were the first to be encountered by the explorers, military men,

1. Neihardt reported that Black Elk was born in December 1863 and DeMallie accepts this date (1984, 3). However, Looks Twice argues that December was when Black Elk was baptized, saying that he was born in June 1866. The year 1866 is also given in the Holy Rosary Mission Archives. See Steltenkamp (1993, 131, 136).

2. Hyde is considered reliable, but he was not in the habit of documenting his assertions. In his preface to Hyde's *Spotted Tail's Folk,* Harry H. Anderson stated that Hyde could, if pressed, usually "supply the basis for key statements of fact" (Hyde 1961, vii) and Olson accepts most of his work in his *Red Cloud and the Sioux Problem* (vii–viii). However, I have been unable to trace his assertion about these early Sun Dances on the Missouri to their source.

and missionaries who provided the earliest information on the Sioux. These early sources are worth exploring, even if they focus on Santee rather than Teton religion and even if what they report is sometimes based on hearsay or untrained observation. Among other things, these early sources make it clear that the Santee did not practice the Sun Dance in the same way or to the same extent as did their Teton allies. From the moment it comes into view, the Santee dance has a more individualistic focus, taking place at various times during the year, while the Teton dance has a communal focus, taking place as an annual festival. Although it is reasonable to suppose that each evolved from a common form, it is important to bear in mind that the Teton dance, which comes into our view later, did not evolve from the Santee dance described in the earlier accounts discussed below. Rather, both probably had their distinctive forms for some time before contact. For this reason, it is best to conceptualize Santee and Teton religion as undergoing a parallel and mutually interactive development throughout the historical period.[3]

One of the earliest accounts of the Sun Dance was written by the French cartographer, Joseph Nicollet, who led expeditions in 1838 and 1839 to map the area between the Missouri and Mississippi rivers. During his expeditions, Nicollet visited the quarry at Pipestone, Minnesota, encountered many of the famous traders and hunters, and met missionaries Stephen R. Riggs, Thomas S. Williamson, and Father Pierre-Jean DeSmet. In the process, he gathered valuable ethnographic information, although it is likely that his primary informants on Sioux religion were these same missionaries. Although he did not witness a Sun Dance, Nicollet notes in his entry for July 23, 1839, that his party came upon a camp where a Sun Dance had been held in what is now Barnes County, North Dakota (Bray, 179). According to Nicollet, the dance was held by the Indians whose camp they had just left, who were Yanktons, Yanktonais, and Sissitons (177). Nicollet was aware that the different divisions of the

---

3. Since the distinction between Santee and Teton is not important to all our sources, it is possible that some of the material collected by these early authors represents Teton, rather than Santee, practice. There is also the possibility that some Santee informants spoke of Teton customs without having made the distinction clear to the interviewer.

Sioux had different Sun Dance customs, emphasizing that while "the Mandan, Minitarri, Arikara, and all the Sioux of the Missouri [the Teton] practice [the Sun Dance] with cruel tortures, [it] is carried out here more gently by the Sioux of the prairies" (179). It is not clear who Nicollet's informant on the Sun Dance was, or if the account he provides is related to the site he observed. According to Nicollet, however, the dance takes place inside a circle of buffalo skins with an awning of buffalo skins stretched above, which are attached to a post in the center of the circle. At the top of the post is attached a crossbar. The pledgers are young men who have made a vow to be successful in the hunt or in war and who "are willing to submit to certain tortures so that the spirits will grant them the fulfillment of their vows" (179). They dance with their eyes open to the sun all day and night for as long as possible without eating or drinking, "indeed until one approaches death" (179). As they dance, they blow the whistle associated with war, while the old ones sing. When they faint, they are revived with herbs.

Gideon H. Pond's "Dakota Superstitions" includes an account of the Sun Dance by a Congregational missionary, Stephen R. Riggs, giving the details of a Sun Dance he witnessed "more than a quarter of a century" ago. It is not clear when Riggs wrote these words, but Pond's letter of transmittal is dated December 14, 1866. Subtracting twenty-five years from this date yields 1841. Since Riggs arrived at Fort Snelling in June 1837, the dance he describes most likely took place between 1837 and 1841. It is not clear when Riggs wrote his account of the dance—whether immediately afterward or many years afterward—and the imprecision in dating makes it impossible to determine whether Riggs's account should take precedence over Nicollet's as the earliest description of a Sioux Sun Dance. However, it is apparently the earliest eyewitness account of a Sioux Sun Dance in the literature.

Riggs begins by mentioning that the Dakota appeal to the sun as a witness and pray to it as *Hunkayapi* (a relative). It communicates with men in dreams and visions, especially to notify them that they are to dance the *wiwanyag-wacipi*, the Sun Dance, "with the promise of success in hunting or war" (Pond 1867, 234). According to Riggs, "Generally the object of dancing to the sun is to secure victory over enemies. In this respect it is a *waihdusna* or self-immolation to the sun; it is an offering up of one's strength and manhood to secure the aid of the sun in the day of battle" (234). It can also be a thank offering for recovery from illness. A man may pledge to dance the Sun Dance if he recovers from an illness, or, on the warpath, in return for victory in battle. These statements could apply equally well to both the Santee and the Teton Sun Dance.

Riggs then gives the details of a Sun Dance he observed, noting that he was present for only a few hours about the middle of the day. The location is not specified, but because Riggs mentions the name of the chief dancer, Makpiya Sna, and states that he later committed suicide, it may be supposed that the location was not far removed from the area of Riggs's missionary activity. This was a small Sun Dance that may be taken as typical of the Santee dances of the time. A few tents had been fastened together and stretched over poles to the north, to form a semicircle. Three dancers stood in the "focus of the radii" with their faces turned to the sun. Their faces and upper bodies were painted and they wore feathers in their hair. Each wore a red or blue blanket around the waist, which "hung down like a woman's skirt" (234). Each dancer had a whistle made of a swan's wing bone. There were men with rattles and drums, as well as women singers, who sat farther back. According to Riggs, the dancers "always make incisions in their flesh, in which they insert swan's down or horse hair," the usual place being on the shoulders or arms (235). "When the sacrifice is intended to be as complete as possible, an incision is made in the back, through which a cord of horse hair is passed, and a buffalo head is attached to the lower end, so that every time the body moves up and down, a slight motion is given to the buffalo head which lies on the ground behind him" (235). At the end of the dance, the dancer may drag the skull around the area. As a more severe form of torture, the dancer makes "an incision in his breast, and passing a cord through it, he draws it tight and fastens the other end to a pole which stands immediately in front of him" (235).

Riggs states that the dance ceremonies begin in the evening, remarking that he had thought that the full moon was essential but is now told that it is not. The preparations include practice by the musicians and singers, feasts, and "some dancing." The Sun Dance proper begins at sunrise and continues "without *eating, drinking,* or *resting,* until nature is quite exhausted" (235–36). He notes that some may join the dance in support of the dancer, and that these may rest. If the "maker of the dance" falls down or is exhausted, a friend may give away something valuable, which secures a rest for the dancer. He also states that some dancers last into the night, while others give out before the sun goes down.

According to Riggs, the dancer makes a song embodying his vision. The following is apparently the one for the dance he observed, in which Makpiya Sna was the chief dancer: "*Having these I come; / Having these four souls may I make my camp fires*" (236). Riggs takes this to be a prediction that the singer would take four scalps in battle (236). Riggs also quotes six other songs, including the song to the sun as it rises: "*Wacinhe wakanyan / Taninyan wahinawape*"; "With a crown of glory, / I come forth" (236). The final song is not translated, possibly owing to a typesetter's error, but it addresses the dancer by name, tempting him with a drink of water, which he ignores (236–37).

Riggs does not say so explicitly, but his location and the details of the dance indicate that he is describing a Santee dance. The first indication is the small number of dancers. Also, there is no mention of the central pole characteristic of the Teton dance, and the primary form of piercing described is that of having a buffalo skull suspended from the shoulders, which may be dragged around the circle at the end of the dance. This method of piercing is also practiced, to a lesser extent, by the Teton. Riggs notes that a more severe form of the torture involves being pierced in the chest and attached to a pole, but it seems that this is not a central pole, but an individual pole placed "immediately in front of him" (235). The dance is strongly associated with war, the object being to secure the aid of the sun in battle. Riggs also notes that a rest period can be secured for the dancer by giving away something valuable. This is the first mention of the redistribution of wealth in a Sun Dance. The dancers fast, also a feature of the Teton dance, and even the most moderate form of the sacrifice is described as fairly severe—nature being "quite exhausted." The mention of a song embodying the vision of the chief dancer is interesting. Similar songs are attested to in the Teton scalp dance, but not in Teton Sun Dances. George W. Hill attests to "kill talks," or descriptions of battle actions during the Teton Sun Dance, but not songs based on them (Paige, 105–6). It is possible that Riggs misunderstood, and that this dance was undertaken in thanksgiving for the taking of four skulls.

Several other early sources contain some information on the Santee dance. Mary Eastman, the wife of a military man, lived at Fort Snelling, Minnesota, for seven years. In 1849, she described the Santee life-style and legends from a point of view like that of the missionaries, referring to the native religion as "absurd" (76) and "odious" (267) and eagerly anticipating the triumph of Christianity among the savages (267–68). Her brief notice of the Sun Dance states that the Sioux worship the sun and describes the dance as being performed by young warriors who dance at five-minute intervals for several days. They hop alternately on each foot, blowing a whistle, faces turned to the sun. The medicine men provide the music, the drum being a keg with a rawhide cover (xxii).

Philander Prescott was a fur trader and superintendent of Indian farming. In answer to a questionnaire promulgated by Henry R. Schoolcraft for publication in his work on Indian tribes (1854), Prescott gives only this passing comment on the Sun Dance, while describing other dances: "The dance to the sun is performed by two young men, with several men beating on raw hides. They dance for two days and nights" (63).

The most remarkable early account of Santee religion was written not by a missionary, but by a fur trader, James Lynd, who was killed in the uprising of 1862. His discussion is worth considering at length both for its detailed description of sacrifice and for its unusual theoretical sophistication. The principal object of his essay is to distinguish between aboriginal and intrusive forms of religion among the Dakota. To this end, he first discusses the idea of the deity. Lynd interprets *Wakan Tanka* as a *deus absconditus,* "an exact prototype of the ancient Brahm of the Hindoos" (152n). A creator god who "sank into silence," *Wakan Tanka* takes no interest in affairs on earth: "They never pray to Him, for they deem Him too far away to hear them, or as not being concerned in their affairs. No sacrifices are made to Him, nor dances in His honor" (151–52). In his view, the missionaries revived, rather than created, the idea of *Wakan Tanka.* In support of this, he notes that when the Dakota swears by *Wakan Tanka,* it is as the god of the white man (152n). Lynd thus describes Dakota religion as pantheism, with the qualifier that it is not classic pantheism (one god in many forms) but the view that there are many things, each of which has a spirit or a god.

Lynd regards contemporary Dakota religion essentially as a degeneration, and because his project is to reconstruct aboriginal Sioux religion, the Medicine Dance, the Circle Dance, and the Brave Dance, which he classifies as intrusive forms, hold little interest for him. He comments that these intrusive forms have created an apparent diversity in Sioux religion. The intrusive forms are not universally respected, so that "one speaks of the Medicine Dance with respect, while another smiles at the name" (150). There is, however, a mutual tolerance among the native sects. On the other hand, all unite in a suspicion of the missionary religion, for it represents the revocation of all traditional belief.

In Lynd's view, *Wakan Tanka* represents a good god, but one whose force is latent or negative. He interprets all other Dakota divinities (a class into which he lumps *Wakinyan, Inktomi, Iya,* and *Anogite*) as evil, taking "especial delight in deeds of darkness" (153). His impression is thus that Santee religion is "negative," directed primarily to the propitiation of malevolent spirits. Despite this misinterpretation, Lynd understands the traditional worldview, in which every object has a spirit, and his argument is sophisticated enough to specify that the use of concrete images in worship is not idolatry, since the image itself is not worshiped but its "spiritual essence," comparing this aspect of Dakota worship with the use of imagery in Christianity.

Lynd identifies many aspects of Dakota belief that remain basic to traditional religion today. He notes that certain men profess to have "an unusual amount of the *wakan* or divine principle in them" (158), which, among other things, qualifies them as curers. He characterizes the medicine men as "faquirs," who back their claim to supernatural power through performances such as the *heyoka* feast, where *heyokas* plunge their hands into boiling water without being burned. The same function is served by a rite like the present-day *yuwipi*, where the medicine man is bound and left alone in an empty lodge to free himself. The purpose is to obtain an interview with *Takushkanshkan,* whom Lynd correctly identifies as the "moving god."

In approaching the subject of the Sun Dance, Lynd describes

sacrifice as one of the "radical bases" of Dakota religion, noting that sacrifices are made to every divinity the Dakotas worship. Indeed, sacrifice is "at the foundation of all their ancient ceremonies" (160). Sacrifices are offered on recovery from illness, when a wished-for event occurs, on the appearance of disease in the family or camp, and on other occasions.[4] Objects sacrificed range from red cloth or animal skins to a pan or kettle. Other people may take what is offered, but must replace the object with something else. Lynd notes that most hunters sacrifice a portion of the game killed, a custom called *wohduze,* and states that the more religious leave a portion of every meal for the gods. The taboo, also called *wohduze,* against a person killing or eating some animal, is assigned by a sacred war leader. It may be removed by excellence in battle. He also notes that the Sacred Feast, which he considers to exist only in a degenerate form, is a part of the sacrificial complex.

Lynd's description of the Sun Dance, which "carries with it the idea" of sacrifice (160), resolves the Sun Dance into two rites, both of which are individual, not communal, observances. The first of these is the *Hanmdepi,* which Lynd translates as "God Seeking." Lynd says this rite is practiced by "the Sisitonwan, Ihanktonwanna, Titonwan, Sioux, and by Crows, Minnitarees, Assinaboines, and other western Dakotas" (164). According to Lynd, the motive for undertaking a *Hanmdepi* is the desire for success in some important undertaking. The ritual is preceded by a period of purification and separation from society, especially that of women. *Inipi* (the sweat lodge) and fasting are part of the preparation. In its most severe form, the *Hanmdepi* involves self-sacrifice: "Some, passing a knife through the breast and arms, attach cords or thongs thereto, which are fastened at the other end to the top of a tall pole raised for the purpose, and thus they hang, suspended only by these cords, for two, three, and even four days, gazing upon vacancy, their minds intently fixed upon the object in which they desire to be assisted by the deity, and waiting for a vision from above" (165). An assistant checks once a day; if a vision has been received, the pledger is cut down. If not, the

4. Charles Alexander Eastman's sensitive description of sacrifice in *Indian Boyhood,* which centers on the sacrifice of a pet dog, provides the day-to-day context of the practice of sacrifice (1971, 87–96).

rite continues. Less severe forms of sacrifice involve attaching a buffalo head to the small of the back and dragging it through camp, cutting and piercing the flesh with knives, being attached to a pole but not suspended, and practicing the mental discipline of the rite without physical sacrifice. In all cases, the mind is fixed on the object of desire, a procedure Lynd compares with Hindu meditation (166). Lynd believes that among the eastern Dakota, the Medicine Dance, an "intrusive religious form [that] may be considered as an elevating and enlightening religion in comparison," has replaced or is replacing this ceremony and predicts its demise in fifty to one hundred years (166).

Fasting and purification also precede the Sun Dance, which commences with the rising sun and lasts three days, or until a communication of the sun is received. According to Lynd, a warrior will dream repeatedly or vividly of the sun and conceive it his duty to undertake the dance (170). The dancer faces the sun continually, constantly blowing a wooden whistle. A drum accompanies the dancer at intervals. The dancer bends his body forward toward the sun, raising one foot after the other. Rest periods are allowed. Lynd's comment on the mental state of the worshiper is revealing: "The mind of the worshipper is fixed intently upon some great desire that he has, and is, as it were, isolated from the body. In this state they are said to receive revelations from the sun, and to hold direct intercourse with that deity" (167). If the desired vision is not obtained, self-sacrifice is resorted to, in effect turning the proceedings into a *Hanmdepi*. The Sun Dance proper is thus undertaken to receive a communication from the sun; the *Hanmdepi* is a sacrifice that may be invoked to the same end.[5]

Lynd's interpretation of Dakota religion is that the Dakotas degenerated from monotheism to pantheism. His contemporary religious situation is again a degeneration, owing to the intrusion of

5. Lynd also notes other important features of Dakota religion. He believes that sexuality is important in Dakota religion, every divinity being part male and part female. He notes that the human body has four spirits, and mentions the rite of ghost keeping. Lynd asserts that contact with the dead is important, and he gives an account of a ritual in 1830 where an old woman foretold the unsuccessful return of a war party (157). The religious use of paint strikes him as significant, and he notes that red is for sacrifices. The women tend to wear blue, but may also wear red (169–70).

forms of worship not native to the people. His conclusion is that the "main base" of (authentic) Dakota religion is pantheism, its "derivative bases" are sun worship (or sun dancing) and *Hanmdepi,* and its "base forms" are purification and sacrifice. Although Lynd may be misled by his search for aboriginal religion into misinterpreting *Wakan Tanka* as a creator god who absconded, he is correct in emphasizing the importance and pervasiveness of sacrifice in Sioux religion. It is not clear whether Lynd ever witnessed a Sun Dance, and he may not be correct in saying that sacrifice is resorted to in the Santee dance only if a vision is not obtained by dancing alone. However, he is the first to point to certain recurring features of the dance, including the fasting and purification that precede the dance and the fact that persistent dreaming of the sun is interpreted as a mandate to undertake the dance.

Samuel W. Pond and Gideon H. Pond, brothers who were Congregational missionaries, arrived in Santee territory in 1834. Samuel Pond's memoirs constitute one of the finest descriptions of the material culture of the Santee Sioux, but they contain no firsthand information on the Sun Dance (S. Pond 1986, 102). Although the book was written in old age, his memories are vivid, and his unusual sense of fairness gives his account a balance that many missionary documents lack.[6]

Gideon H. Pond, on the other hand, writes in the heat of battle, and his discussions of Dakota religion exhibit due missionary zeal. His "Power and Influence of the Dakota Medicine-Men" (1854) is a polemic against the native priesthood that offers no information on the Sun Dance.[7] He does make a point essential to understanding it, the role of the holy man in war. According to Pond, the holy men claim to divine the movements of the enemy in war and serve as the young warrior's first resource, furnishing him with weapons, paint, and charms: "Every warrior feels that his success, both in war and hunting, depends entirely upon the strictness with which he conforms to the rules and ceremonies imposed on him by the wakan warrior" (649). Riggs describes the powers of the war prophet in similar terms (1971, 54).

6. Pond's tolerance is somewhat less in the case of religion (85–93).

7. This document, which is important for understanding the missionary point of view, is discussed in more detail in chapter 4.

Gideon H. Pond's "Dakota Superstitions," which was prepared at the request of the Minnesota Historical Society, is less polemic than his earlier essay, although it ends with an attack on the medicine men embittered by the Santee uprising of 1862. Despite this, and despite its overlap with information found in articles by Lynd and Riggs, it contains some valuable information on Sioux religion in the middle of the nineteenth century.

For instance, Pond's remarks on the concept of the *wakan* are an excellent introduction to this foundational Sioux religious concept. According to Pond, the concept contains "the quintessence of their religion": "The word *wakan* signifies anything which is incomprehensible. The more incomprehensible, the more wakan. The word is applied to anything, and everything, that is strange or mysterious. The general name for the gods in their dialect is this, *Taku-Wakan,* i.e., that which is wakan" (G. Pond 1867, 216–17). Pond further explains *wakan* by identifying it with the divine essence, saying that the only differences among Dakota divinities is in the degree of *wakan* each possesses. In contrast to Lynd, Pond argues that the idea of a supreme being is of missionary origin, claiming that alongside the great struggle between Christianity and heathenism is "a strife between the old system of worship rendered to the *Taku-Wakan,* and the new, which is rendered to the *Wakan-Tanka*" (218). According to Pond, all Dakota gods and *wakans* are mortal, being eternal only in the sense that they succeed themselves.

Pond discusses sacrifice in the context of his account of the Dakota gods, which begins with the *Onktehi.* The male dwells in the water and is addressed as grandfather. The female dwells in the earth and is addressed as grandmother. All sacrifices to the water or the earth are consequently to the *Onktehi.* The influence, or *tonwan,* of these gods is irresistible and is infused into the medicine sack used in the medicine dance, which is in their honor. Appropriate sacrifices are red swan's down, deerskins, tobacco, dogs, medicine feasts, and medicine dances. Pond describes the *Onktehi* as the most respected of Dakota divinities, providing a detailed description of the medicine dance, which—again in contrast to Lynd—he does not appear to regard as intrusive or of recent origin (223–28). Under the heading of divinities, Pond also discusses the *Wakinyan,* the *Taku-Skan-Skan,* and the *Heyoka,* before reaching the sun. After claiming that sun worship is universal among pagan nations, Pond presents the account of a Sun Dance by Stephen R. Riggs that is discussed above, succeeded by the first significant eyewitness account of a Teton Sun Dance, written by Maj. Gen. S. R. Curtis in 1866.

General Curtis describes a dance at Fort Sully that began on June 1, 1866. The Teton Sun Dance thus comes into the light of scholarship in the same year that Black Elk was born, if one accepts the date given by Lucy Looks Twice, rather than 1863 as given by Neihardt. Fort Sully was on the Missouri, near the mouth of the Cheyenne River, near the modern capital of South Dakota, Pierre. General Curtis commanded the army's Department of the Northwest and was also the chairman of an Indian commission charged with treating with the Indians. He had also visited Fort Sully in this capacity in the previous year (Hyde 1937, 135–37). Pond states that Curtis's letter is dated Fort Sully, June 2, 1866. Since Curtis writes "on yesterday, June 1st," his comments were apparently composed immediately after the dance.

This material exists in two versions. The first is the letter as published by Pond in 1867 in his "Dakota Superstitions" (G. Pond 1867, 237–38). A longer version, titled "An Indian Sun-Dance Officially Reported," was published in 1901 by Moses Armstrong, the secretary to the treaty commission chaired by Curtis, in *The Early Empire Builders of the Great West*. Armstrong does not credit the author, but much of the material is identical to the Curtis letter as published by Pond. The most convenient modern source for this material is an article in the *Plains Anthropologist* by Darcy Paige. There are minor differences in punctuation and wording between the letter as reproduced by Pond and Paige, but they do not affect the essential thrust of Curtis's account.

Curtis's opening remarks show vividly that the Indians were aware that the Sun Dance might alarm the soldiers: "The whole of the three thousand Sioux camped about us gave early information of their design to have their annual sun dance at this time and place, the season of the year, the trees in full leaf, having now arrived; and they wished us to inform Col. Recor, the commander of the soldiers, that however boisterous their demonstrations might be, they would all be peaceable and of a pious character" (Paige, 107).

According to Curtis, a herald rode through the camp on the evening of June 29, announcing that the ceremonies would commence on the following day. On June 30, the "poles for the tent" were brought by a procession escorted by a hundred horsemen covered with bushes, "the whole looking like a moving forest coming down from the green high hills that skirt the eastern side of the plains" (107). The procession ended with a full-speed charge by the horsemen through the camp, accompanied by singing and shouting. On the following day, June 1, more charges and riding feats took place along with the erection of the center pole and the shade. Curtis describes the center pole as being about thirty feet tall with bushes and red streamers near the top. He estimates the diameter of the entire area, including the shade, as sixty feet, with the shade being a "circle of bushes" about six feet high with a partial roof and an opening toward the east.

At about noon, fifteen singers began to sing on the south side of the circle while twenty-five dancers began to dance. The men wore feather headdresses, strings of fur, blue body paint, and a skirt of antelope skin. The men blew bone whistles. The women were "more modest in their costume, but all were painted hideously in the face" (108). The dancers faced the sun, keeping time by raising their heels to the beat. Occasional rest periods included smoking, but no food or drink.

At intervals, the dancing was delayed for piercing. Curtis first mentions piercing of both arms, and, in some cases, also the breast and back. An awl was used to lift the skin; about a half inch was cut out. Setons (sticks the size of a lead pencil) were inserted into the cuts and the dancer was connected to the pole with cords or ropes. According to Curtis, the dancers strained until the seton pulled out both "flesh and skin": "We saw one with two setons thus attached to· his breast, pulling till it seemed to draw the skin out three inches, and finally requiring nearly his whole might to tear out the seton" (108). Another dancer was painted black and had four ropes attached. Another dancer had four buffalo skulls attached, one per seton, which were suspended three feet off the ground. Another danced with four dry buffalo heads attached, which could not be torn loose except with the assistance of a horse. As the men were being tortured, their female relations gave flesh offerings.

Curtis states that a large number of spectators from the fort and nearby steamboats "rather embarrassed" the dancers, who "concluded the performance at twelve o'clock, having only danced twenty four hours instead of forty eight, as they usually do" (108). At the end of the dance, the pledgers gave away horses and other items and their wounds were dressed. A feast of dog soup and buffalo meat ensued.

At least as George E. Hyde describes him, Curtis was not a man of great cross-cultural sensitivity (1937, 103, 109–13), and his account focuses on the things that would impress a military man—the charges, the piercing, and the courage required to complete the sacrifice. As the earliest firsthand account of a Teton dance, it is still extremely valuable, especially because it was written contemporaneously with events. In evaluating this account, it is important to bear in mind that the Indians who danced at Fort Sully in 1866 were the "progressive," or friendly, Indians, who, according to a letter by Moses Armstrong, were awaiting the arrival of their annuity goods (Paige, 108). As Hyde has shown, the hostile Indians, including Red Cloud's Oglala band, were dancing elsewhere, on the Tongue River (Hyde 1937, 141). According to Olson, this dance was held on July 16 as a preparation for war with the whites after Red Cloud walked out on the Fort Laramie Treaty talks (42). If Black Elk was born in 1863 as Neihardt reported, it is possible that he was present at this dance. If he was born in July 1866, as his daughter reported, it is still possible that he might have been present—on a cradle board.

Although Curtis clearly saw a Teton dance, it is not clear which band sponsored the dance, which leaders were present, who officiated, or to which band(s) the pledgers belonged. Paige believes that the dance had "few Oglala participants," basing this on a letter written on March 2, 1866, by Lt. Col. John Patee, which states that about 1,896 Sioux were present at that time. Patee estimates that the following number of persons were present from each band: "Brule (420), Yanktona (240), Two Kettle (231), Minni Kon-jhu (126), Blackfeet (147), Sans Arc (140), Unk-pa-pa (84), Yanktonis (84), Ogellala (84), Sauntee (40), Ogelala [sic] widows and children (300)" (Paige, 101). (Since Patee also expresses these figures in "lodges," there is clearly some imprecision involved in his estimate.) On the other hand, Curtis's letter states that there were about 3,000 Sioux present at the dance some four months later. Although either man might have been mistaken, such swelling of the ranks might not have been unusual, especially if annuity goods were to be distributed. In any case, Patee's estimates are irrelevant to the question of which band sponsored the dance, for any of the Teton bands present might have sponsored it and conducted it according to their own rites. Thus there is insufficient justification for Paige's statement that the dance was not an Oglala dance. The fact is that we simply do not know who sponsored the dance.

Although Curtis's account is brief, the characteristic features of the Teton dance are mentioned—its communal nature, the center pole, the sacrifices, the style of dance, and the flesh offerings. One unique feature of this dance is that—according to Curtis—the pole was erected on the same day that the dance began, the dance beginning at noon rather than sunrise. Since Sun Dances at this time continued during the night, a forty-eight-hour Sun Dance was the norm, rather than the four-day, sunrise-to-late-afternoon schedule of the contemporary dance. The fact that this dance was cut short owing to the attention of spectators—which is also unique in the literature—attests that early on, the Sioux were not comfortable with exposing the Sun Dance to outsiders, an attitude that is widely shared by traditionalists today. The charges and the riding exhibitions mentioned by Curtis are characteristic of the early dance, as is the function of the dance as a means of redistribution of wealth. Curtis seems to have had a clear view of the proceedings, but it seems unlikely that he was permitted inside the mystery circle, for his account makes no mention of the activities of the intercessor or the presence of other holy men or officials. Although we might wish for more detail, Curtis's account is of great value in establishing a baseline description of the classic Teton Sun Dance.

Besides Curtis's report, another account of a Teton Sun Dance that took place at (or near) Fort Sully in either 1866 or 1867 was written by another military man, Capt. George W. Hill. Darcy Paige, who published this account, believes that Hill is describing the same dance as Curtis (Paige, 100). This conclusion is reasonable, for Hill states that the Sioux were waiting the arrival of the Indian commissioners (103), and that fits the circumstances of the dance described by Curtis. However, serious discrepancies between these accounts make this conclusion doubtful. Since Hill arrived at Fort Sully on

May 29, 1866—the day on which Curtis states that it was announced that the ceremonies would begin the next day—it is likely that he did see the dance described by Curtis. He remained there until February 1867, however, and so it is also possible that he saw other Sun Dances and described one of them. Since it appears that his account of the dance was not written contemporaneously (Paige, 99), it is also possible that he consciously or unconsciously incorporated details from other dances he observed.

In any case, Hill's account is of a similar Teton dance. Although it is impossible to determine who sponsored the dance, one reason to doubt that Hill's account is of the same dance that Curtis describes is that Hill states that white men are seldom allowed to witness the dance—while there were apparently many white witnesses at Curtis's dance—and that he was permitted to observe only because he was "on good terms with a chief of one of the bands" (105). Paige takes this as an indication that Hill "made a useful friend rather quickly" (109, n. 9), but his words seem to be an unlikely description of a friendship that would have been only two days old. Also, Hill states that the shade was woven up to the top with willows "so close that you could not see through them" (103) and that preparation of this enclosure occupied "two or three days" (105). As we have seen, Curtis reports that the pole was erected and the shade was built on the same day that the dance began at noon.

These discrepancies alone seem to indicate that Hill is describing a different dance and raise the possibility that these more elaborate preparations were a response to the situation at the dance described by Curtis, where a large crowd of outsiders apparently observed the dance. Certainly, from the point of view of the participants, ending the dance when it was only half over would have been unsatisfactory. In the modern dance, some sacrifices take place each day, but more—and many of the more severe sacrifices—take place on the final day, and intensity tends to build as the dance progresses. The same was probably true of the classic dance. Even if ending the dance early was not perceived as in itself offensive to the sun and the other spiritual powers, it is likely that an early end to the dance meant that many pledges went unfulfilled. The curiosity of the white people at the fort was, under the circumstances, simply unavoidable. From the point of view of the holy men, an adaptation to secure privacy may have seemed well worth the additional effort, and Hill may well be telling the truth—rather than resorting to artifice—when he implies that he was fortunate to witness the dance. In his account of a dance (to be discussed below) that was held by the Brulé in 1875, Frederick Schwatka mentions a "wattling of willows" around the shade. This might be taken as an indication that this feature, if it was an innovation, may have been retained for subsequent dances. For the same reason, it might also be taken as an indication that the dance Hill is describing was also a Brulé dance.

Hill was apparently not at leisure to observe the entire dance, for he says, "I therefore gave all the time I could spare from my duties to satisfy my curiosity" (105). It seems, however, that, unlike Curtis, he had the benefit of an informant, and therefore had some inside information. Hill mentions that his informant, apparently the interpreter assigned to the fort, told him that the dance was undertaken as part of the initiation into the Strong Heart Society, as a vow in war, or as a vow undertaken to effect healing (Paige, 103). Apparently he was also told that the timing of the dance was tied to the presence of the full moon (103). In another discrepancy with Curtis's account, Hill reports that the preparations for the dance began about a week before, when he "heard a great outcry and noise in the Indian camp," which was occasioned by the recruitment of the youths by two old men with switches to gather materials for the shade (103). The bringing of the pole and any charges that took place are not mentioned. Hill estimates that the entire circle, including the shade, was fifty feet in diameter and that the center pole about thirty feet long. A bundle of grass was attached to the top of the pole. Despite the differences in construction, Hill's circle, like Curtis's, was open to the east.

Unlike the dance described by Curtis, Hill's dance began at sunrise, with a medicine man stationed to signal the first appearance of the sun over the horizon. The dance was accompanied by "some half a dozen Indians with their tomtoms" (105). He states that the dance was kept up continuously for two full days and his informant told him that no one who began the dance was allowed to eat or drink. Several dancers fainted and did not return to the dance, although Hill's statement to this effect does not make it clear whether this was by rule or inclination. The dancers sang along with the singers, with the women joining the singing at intervals.

According to Hill, speeches punctuated the dancing: "As the

dance proceeded the bucks would get excited over the incidents over which they were doing penance or paying their vows and break out in a speech (when all dancing would cease for the time, and thus gain a rest) detailing the scene of the war party or hunt, brandish their weapons and pipes in wild gesture, and sometimes mark out the position of the parties on the ground and end with a hi yi taken up by all" (105–6). Hill also witnessed the severe form of the sacrifice in which the pledger is attached by four skewers to four posts driven in the ground. Two skewers were attached to the chest and two to the back. Hill states that this piercing took place at 10:00 A.M. and that the pledger had not broken free from any thong by dinner time, despite strenuous efforts. When he returned in the afternoon, the pledger had broken free from the right breast and shortly after that was free from the left breast. The increased freedom of movement thus afforded permitted him to "lunge with the ferocity of a maddened bull" (106). Hill did not see the end of the sacrifice, but was informed that the pledger freed himself in the early evening, and was carried exhausted to a tipi, where he died. As Paige notes, this is the only reported death in the literature of the Lakota dance (110, n. 18). If this death occurred, it was probably not because of the severity of the wounds, but because of exhaustion. The sacrifice is usually described as painful, but it is not normally life threatening, although one account of the Battle of the Rosebud on June 17, 1876, states that Sitting Bull could barely ride owing to the wounds received in a recent Sun Dance (Hyde 1937, 263–64).

Hill also mentions that one pledger danced with three buffalo skulls attached to the skin on his loins above his belt. The buffalo heads were suspended just above the ground. After dancing for more than an hour and breaking out only one skewer, two ponies were given away to secure his release: "By their laws or customs he could not detach then only by dancing or running till they broke out, but he could hire some one to cut them off, so he called two friends, and gave each a pony in the presence of the lookers on to cut them off which they did" (107). In addition, he mentions cutting and scarring of the arms and legs and says that he was informed that the more severe forms of the sacrifice were rarely enacted "as few are found with courage enough to brave the ordeal" (107). Hill does not mention the form of piercing described by Curtis where the arms or shoulders or both and backs are pierced, unless he includes these in his mention of "cutting and scaring [*sic*]" of arms, legs, and thighs (107). This description seems more likely to refer to the taking of flesh offerings from these areas of the body.

The discrepancies between Curtis's and Hill's accounts on the starting time and duration of the dance, along with the other discrepancies noted above, seem sufficient to establish either that Curtis and Hill are describing different dances or that Hill synthesized details from several dances in his account. In effect, however, the accounts complement each other, for they describe Teton dances that could have occurred at most a year apart. Since Hill's account was apparently not written contemporaneously—and no field notes are known to have survived (Paige, 99)—Curtis's account must be conceded pride of place as the earliest eyewitness account of a Teton Sun Dance and, as contemporaneously written, must be considered more reliable. Nonetheless, Hill's longer account adds a wealth of detail to our knowledge of the Teton Sun Dance of the 1860s.

Both accounts agree that the dance normally lasts for two days and nights and both describe sacrifices of roughly equal severity (although the death Hill reports is certainly a more severe consequence). Their estimate of the size of the circle is roughly the same, as is their description of the ritual space, which comprises a circle, open to the east, about fifty or sixty feet in diameter, with a tree about thirty feet high in the center. Both Curtis and Hill mention a bundle at the top of the tree, although only Curtis mentions red streamers. Spectators and singers are mentioned by both, as is fasting. Both mention the redistribution of wealth at the dance, although Hill's is the earliest mention of horses or other wealth being given away to secure a release that could not be secured by the dancer himself. Although subsequent Teton Sun Dances in the classic period would involve a larger ritual space, the basic outline of these dances remains as Curtis and Hill have described it.

Frederick Schwatka, better known as the Western artist Frederick Remington, observed the Lakota Sun Dance—apparently in 1875, since he mentions that within a year, Custer's command had been wiped out (759). It seems likely that Black Elk was at this dance, for he mentions a Sun Dance that took place near Fort Robinson, which Neihardt places in June 1875 (DeMallie 1984, 160;

Neihardt 1979, 80).[8] Schwatka identifies the location by referring to the Spotted Tail Agency on Beaver Creek, Nebraska, but reports that the dance was held between that agency and another encampment of Sioux forty miles west near the head of the White River. This location was near both Fort Robinson and the Red Cloud Agency. Schwatka reports that 8,000 Brulé from the Spotted Tail Agency and another 6,500–7,000 Sioux (presumably Oglalas from the Red Cloud Agency) held a joint celebration. Although Schwatka's informants estimated the crowd at 20,000, his own estimate is thus 15,000. If either figure is accepted, this is the largest Sun Dance attendance reported in the eyewitness literature. According to Schwatka, the actual site was midway between the camps, on a plain between the forks of the Chadron Creek.

Schwatka knew he was lucky: "In general it is almost impossible for a white man to gain permission to view this ceremony in all its details" (754). Chief Spotted Tail and Standing Elk, the head warrior, assisted him in gaining access to the dance: "Their promise that I should behold the rites in part slowly widened and allowed me to obtain full view of the entire proceedings" (754). Schwatka reports in some detail on the preliminaries. The people began to assemble "for many days" before the dance, and Schwatka provides a vivid description of the movement toward the site—which is the subject of one of his plates—and mentions that many visitors arrived from distant bands and locations to participate in this important festival.[9] He discounts the native crowd estimates, but "it was easier to believe the statement of the Indians that it was the grandest sun-dance within

8. Unfortunately Black Elk does not give enough details of the dance to confirm his presence, saying that "only two men danced this sun dance" one of whom had lost a leg and the other an eye (DeMallie 1984, 160). DeMallie rightly questions this remark, and it must be remembered that Black Elk was very young in 1875. This Sun Dance would have been one of those unreliable "childhood memories" even if he did attend. On the other hand, we can regard his presence at the Sun Dance on the Rosebud in June 1876 before the Custer fight as confirmed. Standing Bear describes the dance (DeMallie 1984: 173–74) and Black Elk comments on the Custer fight (180–84).

9. The chaos occasioned by this gradual arrival makes obvious the reason for establishing a ceremonial camp immediately before the dance. Those arriving earlier would have taken the best spots, without regard for rank.

the memory of the oldest warriors; and as I became fully convinced of this assertion, I left no stone unturned that would keep me fast in the good graces of my friends, Spotted Tail and Standing Elk" (754).

After the preliminary camp was established, a date was set for the dance. The tree was selected, "a handsome young pine or fir, forty or fifty feet high, with the straightest and most uniformly tapering trunk that could be found within a reasonable distance" (754). According to Schwatka, an old woman, the oldest if possible, selects the tree. The involvement of women at this point is indicative of the communal focus of the Lakota dance, and women play the leading role in the ensuing tree-cutting ritual. The chosen woman led a procession of virgins, who were subject to public challenge, to the tree. They stripped the tree of limbs as high as they could reach. (Schwatka also states that the tree was stripped of limbs almost to the top, which would be considerably higher than could be reached from the ground.) The tree was not felled. Rather, the ground was cleared around the tree for a considerable distance to prepare the tree for the charge. This procedure, in which a standing tree is charged, is unique in the literature. The charge—which is the subject of another plate—took place at dawn, an old medicine man mounting a hill to signal the moment when the sun was visible. The warriors were lined up facing the east, five hundred to six hundred yards from the tree. They were naked and wore "gorgeous warpaint and feathers, with rifles, bows and arrows, and war-lances in hand" (754). When the signal—depicted in another plate—was given, the charge ensued: "The morning sun had sent its commands to its warriors on earth to charge" (754). According to Schwatka, when the leaders in the charge approached within a hundred yards of the tree, rifles were fired: "A moment later the rushing mass was a sheet of flame, and the rattle of rifle-shots was like the rapid beat of a drum. . . . Every shot, every arrow, and every lance was directed at the pole, and bark and chips were flying from its sides like shavings from the rotary bit of a planer" (755–56). Schwatka's informants said that if the tree had fallen, another would have been chosen and subjected to a charge another morning. Although this rarely happened, it was feared that the tree might succumb on this occasion because of the large number of warriors assaulting it. The tree "looked like a ragged scarecrow, with chips and bark hanging from its mutilated sides" (756). There were some casualties. A great warrior was trampled and another man was shot: "The bruises, sprains, and cuts that might have been spoken of in lesser affairs were here unnoticed, and nothing was heard of them" (756).

After the charge, the tree was cut and transported about a mile to the site of the dance. Its bushy top was gone. The tree was set in a shallow hole, supported by ropes of buffalo thongs tied about seventy to eighty yards away to the vertical poles supporting the shade. The shade itself was constructed of elk skins, buffalo robes, canvas, blankets, and "a wattling of willows and brush" (756). During the dance, the shade was augmented by throwing various materials on the supporting ropes, to form an awning. From a distance, "the affair looked not unlike a circus tent, the top of which has been ruthlessly torn away by a cyclone" (756).[10]

According to Schwatka, the construction of the dance lodge occupied the rest of the second day. The third day was occupied mostly with singing, dancing, and other ceremonies. Horses were brought into the circle and blessed, being painted red. This is the subject of another plate, "Making Medicine Ponies." Schwatka is not certain whether the dance proper begins this day or the next, but he does report that about a dozen young warriors in battle dress, fists clenched over breasts, "jumped up and down in measured leaps to the monotonous beating of the tom-toms and the accompanying yi-yi-yi-yis of the assembled throng" (756). Bone whistles were also employed. Male and female dancing seems to have been sequential, since Schwatka reports that at intervals, women would dance and sing. The dancing lasted all day, at ten- or fifteen-minute intervals.

The first piercing took place on the fourth day (counting from the day the tree was chosen). Schwatka was informed that the pledgers had observed a fast from "food for seven days and from water for two" but is skeptical about its extent: "While their condition did not indicate such abstemiousness as this, I think it true that some fasting precedes the more barbarous ceremonies" (756).[11] The

10. Although the top of the lodge is still open, this does provide some analogy to the otherwise unprecedented closed lodge described in *The Sacred Pipe* (Black Elk, 80–81).

11. This is the first mention both of fasting and of a recurrent skepticism about its extent and severity.

dancers of the previous day were the pledgers who pierced on the fourth day and so forth throughout the "four or five days" of the dance. The dance began at sunrise, the tortures taking place about nine or ten. Schwatka's description of the piercing is detailed, indicating that he was probably inside the mystery circle: "Then each one of the young men presented himself to a medicine-man, who took between his thumb and forefinger a fold of the loose skin of the breast, about half way between the nipple and the collar-bone, lifted it as high as possible, and then ran a very narrow-bladed but sharp knife through the skin underneath the hand. In the aperture thus made, and before the knife was withdrawn, a stronger skewer of bone, about the size of a carpenter's pencil, was inserted" (757). A figure-eight knot was made fast to the skewer. Both breasts were thus pierced, the leads being mated to a rope, which in turn was attached to the top of the sun pole. The piercing in 1875 was a rigorous affair. To break loose was "a horrible task that even with the most resolute may require many hours of torture" (757). The first attempts are "very easy, and seem intended to get him used to the horrible pain he must yet endure before he breaks loose . . . his shouts increase, huge drops of perspiration pour down his greasy, painted skin, and every muscle stands out on his body in tortuous ridges, his swaying frame, as he throws his whole weight wildly against the fearful fetters, being convulsed by shudders" (757–58). Schwatka writes that he has seen the skewers stretched nearly an arm's length from the dancer's chest. The amount of time necessary to free the dancer is the longest reported in the literature: "Generally in two or three hours the victim is free, but there are many cases where double and even triple that time is required" (758). Schwatka reports that a half dozen may be attached to the pole at once, and that forty to fifty dancers were pierced overall, the largest number reported as being pierced in the period before the ban.[12] Schwatka also mentions the severe form of piercing reported by Hill, in which the dancer is attached to four poles arranged in a square, saying that

12. This number was almost reached in a dance I observed at Three Mile Camp in 1983, which is described in chapter 5. Mails reports that at a dance at Crow Dog's in 1974 "something like *eighty* pledgers took part" (1978, 11) and piercing was generally mandatory at AIM-associated dances during this period.

the one attempt that he witnessed ended in a faint. Schwatka writes that fainting is not unusual, and can discover no loss of respect because of it. The dancer who faints is taken to a nearby lodge. Apparently such dancers do not return to the dance, for he remarks that he does not know whether they are ever allowed to dance in another Sun Dance.

The dance ended with the warriors who had been pierced walking to a point just outside the "doors" to the inner circle. They knelt on an area of painted buffalo skins and watched the sun set, arms crossed. This is the subject of a plate, "Facing the Setting Sun." Schwatka was told that "no two of the ceremonies were alike" (759) and mentions several things that he did not witness, including the form of piercing where the dancer drags a buffalo skull and the drawing of a fainted dancer aloft by the rope until his weight tears the skewers loose. He was informed that some aspects of the ritual were optional or could be replaced by other rites, including the consecration of the sun pole, much of the dancing and singing, and "the double efforts of ambitious youths" (apparently the four-pole form of the sacrifice). Despite his colorful prose, Schwatka explicitly claims to have described the dance faithfully: "I describe it only as I saw it" (759).

With Schwatka's dramatic account of the Brulé dance of 1875, we have the first Sioux Sun Dance that can be identified by band and by named participants. Spotted Tail was the greatest of the Brulé chiefs, and Standing Elk was an eminent warrior, so Schwatka had excellent informants. Since they were able to gain him admittance, the Brulé evidently sponsored the dance, and the ritual probably took place according to their customs. Among the points of interest in Schwatka's account is the first description of the cutting of the pole and the first mention of the role of women in the ceremonies except as dancers and givers of flesh. His account of the charge is extremely colorful, and, as noted before, it is the only charge in the literature in which a standing tree is attacked. His description of the ritual area is the first to mention ropes between the tree and the shade, and his estimate of the height of the tree, fifty feet, as well as the diameter of the circle, seventy to eighty yards, indicates a very large ritual area. As mentioned above, the "wattling of willows" around the shade might be taken as a clue that the dance previously described by Hill was in fact a Brulé dance. While Schwatka sounds the first note of a recurring skepticism about the extent of the fasting, the duration of the sacrifices he reports is the most severe in the literature.

One of the strengths of Schwatka's account is that it emphasizes the communal nature of the festival, the bringing together of all of the Brulé bands as well as visitors from other bands. It was not necessarily a completely peaceful affair. According to George E. Hyde, the Sioux followed their old custom of forming a large war party after the dance, and set out after the Pawnees, who had been removed to Indian territory without their knowledge (Hyde 1961, 233). According to Hyde, this was one of the last times for this custom, as they were prevented from doing so after the dance of 1877 (Hyde 1961, 282).

The next accounts of the Lakota Sun Dance are from the early 1880s, immediately before the enforcement of the general ban against the Sun Dance that ended the era of the classic dance. Stephen R. Riggs's *Dakota Grammar, Texts, and Ethnography* (1893) contains a grammar, apparently based too closely on the Ponds' work,[13] texts in interlinear Dakota and English, including translations of Christian texts, and some ethnography. The last item of the ethnography is an abstract of an anonymous account reprinted from the *Daily Journal* of Sioux City, Iowa. Riggs recommends it as a "very trustworthy and more than usually vivid description of a ceremony which is becoming rarer under the influence of Christianity." According to Riggs, the article describes a dance held in June 1880 by the Teton under Red Cloud (229). Black Elk was apparently not at this dance, since he mentions being at a dance at Fort Keogh (Montana) in June of this year, and he apparently remained there all winter (DeMallie 1984, 213–14). This large dance began at 5:00 A.M. on June 24, 1880. The ceremonial circle contained seven hundred lodges and was six miles in circumference. The author identifies the location as near White Clay Creek, Nebraska. The author estimates that four thousand took part in the initial charge. The charge, which served to clear the area of evil spirits, lasted an hour. A rain ensued, which

---

13. The issue of authorship is mentioned in Gary Clayton Anderson's introduction to Samuel Pond's *The Dakota or Sioux* (xxvii–xviii).

delayed the proceedings. When the rain lifted, the tree was cut within a circle of spectators regulated by a marshal. Six men struck the tree, which was finally felled by a woman. A charge was made on it. Both men and women carried it into the circle, a distance of two miles, and another charge ensued. That evening and the next morning the tree was erected and the shade constructed. The circle was five hundred yards in circumference and the shade was twelve feet tall. This is the largest reported Sun Dance circle. The center pole was decorated with red, white, and blue flags, "gifts to the Great Spirit" (230).

The author estimates there were a thousand spectators and three hundred dancers, with twenty-five men on horseback riding around inside the enclosure (probably inside the shade but outside the mystery circle proper). There were seventeen pledgers. The dancers were painted and wore breech cloths and cartridge belts. They spent two hours dancing, singing, and shooting up at the pole. The ear-piercing ceremony ensued. At 8:00 P.M. the pledgers entered the circle. The author states that they had been fasting without water for three days previous and remarks that after making a Sun Dance vow the pledger was compelled to fulfill it: "After making such a declaration they lose all control of their own wills. They are obliged to fast, and are placed on buffalo robes in a sweathouse until they become as gaunt as greyhounds" (231). This testimony thus tends to contradict Schwatka's skepticism about the severity of the fasting. Each pledger had a whistle and a banner on a long staff. Ten bass drums were beaten by sixty men, the drumsticks having horsetails "instead of the scalps which would have been used in earlier days" (231). The dancing continued until the morning of the third day.[14]

At 11:00 A.M., seven men were pierced. Horses and calico were given away. The piercing was of both breasts with the holes being about an inch long: "This operation was performed by raising the skin of the right breast and then that of the left, cutting a hole about an inch long through the skin at each place. A round wooden skewer

14. The author apparently decamped occasionally, relying on informants for details, since he states in one place that the "white visitors" reached the grounds at 10:00 A.M. (Riggs 1893, 231).

was inserted through each hole, fastened by sinews, the sinews tied to a rope, and the rope to the pole" (231). One pledger had his arms pierced and fastened to a horse. The first two dancers broke loose immediately. The third—evidently the one mentioned above—broke away from both the pole and the horse: "This feat pleased the Indians, who shouted lustily." It also moved Little Big Man to shoot an arrow into the air, which landed on a woman outside the circle. Although the arrow was removed, "Little Big Man was obliged to part with three horses to satisfy the woman" (232). The remaining four dancers could not break loose, so they gave away horses and were cut loose. One of them, recovering from a faint, became unruly and ran from the circle. He was brought back and put to dancing while a man wearing a buffalo skull on his head attended to him with a mirror.

An old man administered the "mysterious anointing," for which women were eligible if they had borne arms in battle or held a horse (presumably in battle). A hole was cut in the right arm and something was put under the skin. The author states that the man wearing the buffalo skull dismissed the crowd at 6:00 P.M., when the sun went behind a cloud, and that an hour later the lodges were down and most of the people were departing.

This account again confirms the large communal nature of the Lakota dance, and emphasizes what seems to be the normative style of piercing at this time, that of being pierced above each nipple. The redistribution of wealth is mentioned both as a normal feature of the dance and in the special case of the Little Big Man episode. This account is the only one of men on horseback riding in circles in the ritual area.

James Owen Dorsey's *Study of Siouian Cults,* which was published in 1894, is a compendium of various sources, including the familiar Lynd and Pond. Dorsey also incorporates two texts that discuss the Teton Sun Dance. The first is George Bushotter's Lakota account, which was written during the ban, and is considered in chapter 3. The second is an eyewitness account of a Lakota dance written by Capt. John G. Bourke, a member of General Crook's command. In 1890, after hearing Dorsey read a paper based on Bushotter's work, Bourke introduced himself. He was eventually to furnish Dorsey with his impressions of a dance held in June 1881 at the Pine Ridge

Agency. If the dating of the dance described immediately above at White Clay Creek is correctly given as 1880, this dance would be the Pine Ridge Oglala dance for the subsequent year. Black Elk would not have been present at this dance, for he returned to Pine Ridge from Fort Keogh only after performing the Horse Dance in September 1881 (DeMallie 1984, 226). He was presumably present at the subsequent dance or dances held at Pine Ridge before the onset of the ban.

Although Bourke's discussion is organized primarily as a list of differences with Bushotter's account, there are many interesting points. He must have had an excellent opportunity to observe the dance, since he provides a detailed account of the piercing and can even determine that the wailing of the pledgers before the piercing was not accompanied by tears (Dorsey, 466). Since these actions take place at the foot of the tree, Bourke must have been inside the mystery circle at the time of the piercing. He also provided Dorsey with a number of ritual objects used in the dance, including effigies of a man and a buffalo that hung from the tree, again indicating the position of respect he must have been held in as a military man by the intercessor.

Bourke reports that the Sioux were having difficulty obtaining buffalo skulls and that only two were employed, placed erect and leaning against the framework of the pipe rack, which held pipes decorated elaborately with quills, beads, and horsehair. Bourke also states that pipestone was hard to obtain, apparently in explanation of why there was not a pipe for each dancer. In 1881, the cutting of the tree was preceded by a charge undertaken by the young warriors. At the tree, there was singing, dancing, and giving of presents to the poor. The four warriors selected to cut the tree gave kill talks, "each reference to the killing or wounding of an enemy, or to striking *coup,* being corroborated by thumping on the skin" (465). Using a new ax, each of the men cut a gash in the tree, starting at the east and proceeding sunwise around the tree. A maiden of good character, dressed in a beaded robe of white antelope skin "almost completely covered with elks' teeth," felled the tree (465). The tree was carried to camp on skids. A charge ensued as the procession neared the camp.

Bourke does not mention the shade but says only that the tree was erected. He takes note of the following officials: an attendant for each pledger, a force of armed men, criers, heralds, and "water-carriers armed with long staves tipped with bead-work and horse-hair" (465). The pledgers were not allowed to drink, but Bourke states that the medicine men would spray mouthfuls of water on any dancer who happened to faint. Bourke mentions no preliminaries to the piercing, saying only that all male dancers were pierced and tied to the tree by ropes of hair or thongs. The one woman dancer did not pierce but was scarified from shoulder to elbows on both arms. The flesh offerings were taken by the same man who had pierced the babies' ears. The piercing was preceded by a symbolic capture of the pledgers: "Their attendants . . . seized and laid them on a bed of some sagebrush at the foot of the sacred tree. A short address was made by one of the medicine men; then another, taking up as much of the skin of the breast under the nipple of each dancer as could be held between his thumb and forefinger, cut a slit the length of the thumb, and inserted a skewer to which a rope was fastened, the other end of the rope being tied to the tree" (465). Although this seems to imply that the skewers were placed below the breasts, this seems unlikely. Bourke is probably only describing how the flesh was raised for the usual piercing above the nipples.

Bourke mentions the use of the eagle-bone whistle, saying that it is to be sounded continuously while dancing. He characterizes the dance as a "buck jump, the body and legs being stiff and all movement being upon the tips of the toes" (465–66). The dancers look at the sun, dancing either with their arms at their sides (palm forward) or upward at a 45° angle, fingers apart, "inclined towards the sun" (466). The pledgers approached the tree clothed in blue "petticoats" and buffalo robes, fur side out (indicating that they were sacrifices). The pledgers were laid on a bed of sagebrush to be pierced, the robe having been discarded. They wailed before being pierced.

Bourke reports that one pledger could not break loose, fainting four times in an hour and seven minutes. The medicine man put seeds of *Dulcamara* in his mouth, and presents were given: "costly robes, blankets, articles of beadwork and quillwork, and others of the skin of the elk and antelope [were thrown] upon the rope attaching him to the tree, in the hope of breaking him loose" (466). According to Bourke there was "any amount of this giving of presents at all stages of the dance" but at this point the criers exhorted the crowd strongly to give to the poor: "'So and so has done well. He is not afraid to look the poor women and children in the face! Come up some more of you people! Do not be ashamed to give! Let all the people see how generous you are!'" (466).

In an interesting note, Bourke states that "one of the prime movers in the organization of this particular dance," Rocky Bear, declined at the last moment to be pierced: "He explained his reasons to the tribe, and was excused. He gave presents with a lavish hand, and it was understood that on some subsequent occasion he would finish the dance" (466). Bourke could detect no sign of disapproval. In closing, Bourke notes that there was much singing by the women and drumming by the medicine men. A feast ensued after the dance, Bourke giving his opinion that dog stew with wild turnips "tastes very much like young mutton" (466).

In this valuable account, Bourke provides the first mention of a pipe rack and—implicitly—of a pipe ritual. He mentions the role of a woman in felling the tree, and takes note of the charges. He also provides the first listing of some of the minor official participants, including water carriers. Bourke is the first to report a symbolic capture of the pledgers before the piercing takes place. According to Bourke, the dominant style of dance was rising to tiptoe, and the normative style of piercing was apparently above the nipples. The shortage of buffalo skulls noted by Bourke would have made it difficult to enact the styles of piercing involving buffalo skulls. Bourke also provides a particularly vivid and explicit account of the role of the dance in the redistribution of wealth among the tribe.

Alice C. Fletcher was the first professional anthropologist to report on the Lakota Sun Dance. Fletcher describes the 1882 dance at Rosebud, and she also observed a Sun Dance at the Pine Ridge Agency, which may have been the same one observed by Bourke.[15] She describes the Sun Dance in general as an annual tribal festival, coinciding with the budding of *Artemesia ludoviciana* (a variety of

15. Fletcher does not give the location of the dance that she describes, but De-Mallie states that it took place at Rosebud (Walker 1980, 56). Fletcher's attendance at a dance at Pine Ridge, which was apparently also the dance described by Bourke, is mentioned in *McGillycuddy Agent* (172). The problem of dating this dance is discussed in chapter 4.

sage) in late June or early July. According to Fletcher, attendance is compulsory. In 1882, the ceremonial camp circle opened to the east and was ¾ mile in diameter, containing more than nine thousand people. She points out that the Sun Dance takes place in the context of a great communal gathering, with many other ceremonies surrounding its performance. She describes the Sun Dance pledge as a voluntary fulfillment of vows "made in sickness or trouble in order to secure health and prosperity" (580). Although this definition does not rule out war-related vows, she does not mention them (perhaps because she is speaking only of the present dance). She describes the pledgers' "mental characteristics" as "thanksgiving and a desire for future benefits." The "religious characteristics" are recognition of and dependence on supernatural powers, along with a sense of performing a religious vow. She further points to the necessity for "exact observance of certain forms and rituals," which is the obligation of the holy men, whose cooperation is required "to secure the full blessing sought" by the participants (580).

Fletcher states that each Sun Dance has only one "Leader," whose obligations are to procure articles for the ceremony, abstain from certain behaviors, fast, dance, give away property, and be scarified and tortured. This constitutes the "first degree" of the dance, through which, by definition, only one can pass. The second degree involves the same obligations except for providing the equipment for the dance. The third degree involves all the obligations of the second degree except torture. The fourth degree involves the same obligations as the third degree except for scarification. In 1882, there were twenty-two dancers. The leader danced the first degree, one man danced the second degree, seven men and a woman danced the third degree, and eleven men and a boy of eleven or twelve danced the fourth degree. In other words, only two pledgers pierced. None of Fletcher's informants could remember a woman having been pierced.

The leader, who is also described as the "Leader of the Dancers," having made his vow, spends the winter assembling the necessary gear, while living under a strict discipline.[16] In June, he chooses an

16. The account of the Sun Dance by J. R. Walker, which is summarized in the next chapter, contains the most elaborate account of the winter period of preparation and instruction in the literature.

assistant, and they visit one of the holy men and "offer him the charge of the dance" (581). Fletcher calls this person "the officiating priest." The leader is under the direction of this holy man, as is his assistant. All other dancers must have a lay assistant and a holy man to guide them. This is the first mention of the extensive role of holy men in the dance and, implicitly, the role of the dance in the holy man's income.

The opening ceremonies center on the preparations tipi. The intercessor and the leader enter the tent with their attendants. All are painted red and wear a buffalo robe with the hair outside. An ax is purified by passing it through sweetgrass burned on a fire and is used in the preparation of an area of mellowed (or pulverized) earth. All equipment to be used in the dance is rubbed with sage and passed through the smoke from the sweetgrass. This is the first mention of the use of sweetgrass in a purification ritual. The intercessor faces the east as he sings the prayers specific to this yearly occasion. The sacred pipe is smoked "stem downward" (582). This is the first explicit mention of a pipe ritual in the Sun Dance literature.

Each morning the dancers gather at the preparations tipi for rituals, and in the evening they gather to dance and sing in rehearsal of the dance. Fletcher notes that the camp is under the control of marshals appointed by the intercessor. On the fourth day, the center of the circle is chosen, the pole is located, and the digger is appointed. A ceremony ensues at the tree in the morning. The "priest, leader and attendants repair to the selected tree, present the pipe, lifting the stem for the first time, after which a pipe is laid at the foot of the tree, a circle drawn on the ground near it, an offering of calico tied on the tree just below the branch which forks toward the east, and a man appointed to remain and watch the spot and suffer no living creature to pass over the consecrated ground" (582). At noon, seven holy men, the two singing societies, and the people return to cut the tree. Five men and three girls are chosen to cut the tree, with the actual felling done by the girls. The tree must fall to the west. The tree is carried to camp on a "litter of sticks." A charge ensues on horseback, skirting the camp circle. The pole is painted, offerings are attached, and it is erected. Next the shade, which is covered with tent poles and cloths, is erected. The ear-piercing ceremony ensues. Fletcher adds to the evidence that the classic Sun Dance was a major mechanism for the redistribution of wealth by noting that a giveaway takes place at these ceremonies and that "a vast amount of possessions changes hands" (583). Women's puberty rites also take place.

At noon on the next day, the shade is charged by warriors on foot. They exit through the entrance and, shortly afterward, the dancers appear. They are naked except for their skirts. They wear crowns of sage and blue horns cut from rawhide and they carry sprays of artemesia. The leader carries the buffalo skull. The intercessor is next, followed by his attendants. The dancers, their attendants, and the holy men follow. They move sunwise,[17] placing the skull opposite the entrance. Directly behind the skull is the rest area for the holy men and the dancers. The dancers have been fasting from both food and water since the pole was cut. They dance at intervals for "the rest of the day and night and until after noon of the following day" (583). A whistle made from the wing bone of an eagle ornamented by "a peculiar, soft feather used in religious ceremonies" is used in the dance (583). The singing is by the societies and is accompanied by a drum of dried hide.

The morning of the sixth day, the piercing takes place. The skull is painted with a blue sign that indicates the four winds (and thereby *Taku Skanskan,* the god of motion or release). The area behind the skull is cut of sod, which is piled to the east of the oval cut area. The skull is placed on the sod and the earth in the oval is mellowed. The figure representing the four winds is made in the earth. Tobacco is offered by dropping it in the oval, and it and the skull are painted with red ochre. A pipe rest is made behind the oval, and the bowl is set on a buffalo chip. Artemesia is spread behind the pipe rest, and another chip is placed to hold the ashes. Sweetgrass is deployed, and food offerings are made. The dancers are now painted. The scarifications (or flesh offerings) follow. After noon, the leader is "led to the pole" and pierced "a little above the nipples by a wedge-shaped knife, and a stick having one end embroidered with porcupine quills is inserted" (584).[18] A rawhide rope is used to attach the dancer to the pole. The leader is led out to the end of the rope, in an eastward

17. All Lakota ritual action takes place in a sunwise, or clockwise, direction. At the Sun Dance, all movement inside the mystery circle is thus in a sunwise direction.

18. This is another good example of the use of the "prescriptive present" and the difficulties of summarizing it that I previously mentioned.

direction. "A large amount of goods are then given away, and many ceremonies take place to insure him a speedy release" (584). A certain song is the signal for the struggle to begin, a process that requires "all his force." This leads Fletcher to a statement that can be interpreted variously: "When one side gives way he raises his hand, palm upward to the sky, as a sign of thanks for the deliverance" (484). Fletcher probably means that the style of dance in 1882 was to break loose one side at a time, but she may mean only that if this occurs, thanks is given. An indication of Fletcher's presence as an observer occurs at this point, when she notes that it took one man twenty minutes to free himself. Compared with the descriptions of the sacrifices in previous dances, this indicates a relatively light ordeal. According to Fletcher, the piercings conclude the dance.

Since this dance took place in the summer of 1882, the year before the dance was officially banned, it is the last eyewitness report of a Lakota Sun Dance until the 1950s. The pressure to ban the dance had been building for some time, and many of the agents attempted to discourage or prevent the dance before it was officially banned in April 1883. Such pressure may account in part for the small number of pledgers. At the Sun Dance described six years earlier by Schwatka in 1875, which was held by the same group of Brulés, forty to fifty pledgers were reportedly pierced; at the dance attended by Fletcher, only two were pierced. This decline might also be attributed to the fact that the motive for making a war pledge— either in prospect or in thankfulness—had disappeared.

Fletcher's professional account provides the first information about many details including the preparations of the pledgers, the construction of the altar, color symbolism, and ritual purifications. This abundance of detail seems to indicate that Fletcher had an informant or informants among the holy men, or among former participants, since this sort of "priestly" information would not have been readily available from the average spectator. In the retrospective account of the dance by J. R. Walker, which will be discussed in the next chapter, this kind of priestly information is present in profusion.

In review of the information presented by observers of the classic Lakota Sun Dance, 1866–82, we have analyzed six good accounts of the dance.

Eyewitness Accounts of the Classic Dance, 1866–1882

Date	Observer	Band	Location
1866	Curtis	?	Fort Sully
1866–67	Hill	?	Fort Sully
1875	Schwatka	Brulé/Oglala	[a]
1880	Anon/Riggs	Oglala/Red Cloud	[b]
1881	Bourke	Oglala/Red Cloud	Pine Ridge Agency
1882	Fletcher	Brulé	Rosebud Agency

[a]Between Red Cloud and Spotted Tail agencies.
[b]White Clay Creek in Nebraska.

This information clearly confirms the high degree of variability present in the Sun Dance, for even the two successive Oglala dances in 1880 and 1881 display strikingly different features. The two dances described for the Brulé in 1875 and 1882 also display many differences as do the two dances observed in 1866 (or 1866 and 1867) at Fort Sully. It may also be noted that in the three cases where timing is mentioned, there is no agreement, Curtis calling for the trees to be in full leaf, Hill calling for a full moon, and Fletcher calling for the sage to be in bloom. Despite this variation, all dances described took place in June or July.

Despite the variability, a common outline of the Lakota dance can be discerned. The dance is communal, always involving a center pole, mystery circle, and shade. The dance is associated with the buffalo through use of the buffalo skull and robes and with war by kill talks, charges, and symbolic captures of pledgers. The giving of flesh offerings and sacrificial torture are essential to the dance. The redistribution of wealth is a major function of the classic dance. The degree of fasting is variously estimated, but the sacrifices themselves are relatively rigorous in all dances under consideration except Fletcher's. The normative duration of the dance is two days, with dancing being continuous from dawn on the first day to sunset on the second day.

This completes our portrait of the classic Sun Dance as it was reported by outside observers. The reader will have noticed that although these accounts tell us much about what happens at a Sun

Dance, they provide relatively little information about its symbolism and meaning. A fuller picture of the classic dance will emerge from the next chapter, which is devoted to accounts of the Sun Dance based on interviews held during the ban with former participants and officiants. Since the dance was under ban after 1883, subsequent anthropological research was necessarily confined to interviews. Although they lack direct information on the performance aspect of specific dances, these interviews supplement and complete the portrait painted by outside observers by presenting the participants' perspective on the dance.

3

The Classic Sun Dance Remembered
1887–1911

The period of the ban produced three outstanding accounts of the Sun Dance, which were compiled by anthropologists in an attempt to preserve knowledge of a culture that was perceived as rapidly vanishing. Although based on recollection, rather than observation, these sources embody invaluable perspectives on the ritual and meaning of the classic dance. Each has a particular strength. George Bushotter's description of the dance is the first written by a Lakota, and, perhaps because it was collected shortly after the ban, it is particularly rich in details of the ritual. J. R. Walker's contribution, which focuses on the instruction and ceremonies before the dance, is of interest because his informants were eminent holy men, whose information is unique in the literature. Frances Densmore's professional account, which is based on interviews with Sun Dance spectators, participants, and officials, provides an especially clear picture of the ideology and meaning of the classic dance. These sources add a depth of detail and meaning to the literature on the Sun Dance, testifying to the great contribution Boasian anthropology made to the understanding of native American religion and culture.[1]

1. The contribution of the Boasians to the understanding of native North America was inarguably of great significance. From our present perspective, however, it can be said that their unremitting focus on the past—on "salvage ethnography"— paid a high price by largely ignoring the present. The acculturation studies produced by the later Boasians are also marred for us today because of their assumption that adaptation necessarily constituted degeneration. Another problem with the Boasian

The first significant retrospective account of the dance was produced by collaboration between James Owen Dorsey and George Bushotter, a Lakota who attended the Hampton Institute in Virginia from 1878 to 1881 and studied at the Theological Institute in Virginia from 1885 to 1887.[2] Unfortunately, Bushotter had to abandon his ambition to become a minister when his English proved inadequate to the task of learning Greek and Latin. After ending his theological studies on the advice of the faculty, he was employed in 1887 by Dorsey at the Bureau of Ethnology in Washington. He worked for ten months, eventually producing 258 Lakota texts on a variety of subjects. Bushotter's material on the Sun Dance was published by Dorsey in 1894, compiled and arranged in a series of numbered paragraphs, with commentary and comparative material interspersed. Some of Bushotter's drawings illustrate the text.

Although Bushotter was not a holy man or Sun Dance pledger, his account provides important details on the dance.[3] He is the first to mention communal goals in the context of the Sun Dance vow and the first to mention famine. According to Bushotter, the dance is undertaken for various reasons, "during any winter when the people suffer from famine or an epidemic, or when they wish to kill any enemy, or they desire horses or an abundance of fruits and vegetables during the coming summer" (Dorsey, 451).

One of the advantages of the accounts collected during the ban

---

paradigm is that it tended to produce cultural description that, in the words of Raymond J. DeMallie, was an "idealized and generalized synthesis of the past" (Deloria 1988, 237). In other words, it tended to view the Indian past as a timeless and static state and synthesize details that were collected in different ways and different times to produce an idealized culture. Humanists who need orientation to Boas and the Boasian paradigm might benefit from Marvin Harris's discussion (1968, 250–318).

2. The following biographical details are from DeMallie (1978). DeMallie reports that Bushotter was the son of a Yankton man and a Minneconjou Lakota woman. His father was killed by whites when he was still young, and his mother remarried a man from the Lower Brulé reservation. His family background was thus mixed in terms of the traditional divisions of the Sioux nation.

3. The English version of Bushotter's text is redolent of the native idiom and is characterized by short, choppy observations and abrupt transitions between subjects. In the following, I have done my best to provide a coherent summary of his account of the dance. This account provides another prime example of the "prescriptive present" previously discussed.

is that they focus to a greater degree on the social context of the Sun Dance, rather than simply the dance itself, as is characteristic of observer accounts. Bushotter, for instance, places considerable emphasis on the preliminaries to the dance. Men become pledgers by making a vow: "Well, I will pray to Wakantanka early in the summer" (451). The pledgers frequent the sweat lodge in the winter and announce their intentions at a feast. From then on, the candidate is set apart and the people treat him with respect.

The communal aspects of the dance emerge from Bushotter's description of the involvement of the pledger's family, which makes clear the increased status of the Sun Dance pledger. Bushotter emphasizes that the vow creates an obligation for the entire household to support the pledger. All members of the family must avoid certain behaviors including loud talking. The family must be supportive of the pledger in many ways, for instance by preparing his food only in the best possible way and by furnishing the pledger with a new implement for his exclusive use. His relatives must make him a new ornamented pipe. An altar is made in the tipi, which must be respected. The pledger places all the ash from pipes smoked in his tipi on this altar. The candidate treats all game he has killed in a *wakan* manner, saving each skull taken. The candidate erects a post on which hangs a tobacco pouch and a robe, both of which will be sacrificed. The pledger may not swim and cannot use a towel on leaving the sweat lodge, using sage instead. The pledger must not fight, even in defense of the camp. The financial demands on the family are also great, for they are expected to give generously at the dance: "All his female kindred make many pairs of moccasins and collect money and an abundance of all kinds of goods, in order to give presents to poor people at the time of the sun dance" (452). This earns them the right to have a child's ears pierced.

The dance is held in the latter part of June. Invitations are sent to surrounding tribes, and despite the mix of people in the camp, peace prevails. The camp circle includes only round structures, and it is made in the form of a circle opening to the north. The completion of the camp takes several days, and all men and boys are expected to help fill in any holes in the ground that may trip horses. The military associations of the dance emerge on the third day, when a party of warriors is selected to find the sacred tree (*Can-*

wakan): "These men must be selected from those who are known to be brave, men acquainted with the war path, men who have overcome difficulties, men who have been wounded in battle, men of considerable experience" (453). These men, who are also apparently those who will fell the tree, dress for battle and mount decorated horses. They race to a nearby hill and back. Bushotter writes that the custom was for women who had lost children in attacks on the camp to run out to these men, wailing and singing, but that the custom is no longer practiced. The men recount their kills three times and enact them in pantomime.

On the fourth day, the men go to find the tree, returning to camp to make an altar of mellowed earth, sweetgrass, and sage, laying on it a buffalo skull. The preparations tipi is erected, and a skull is placed in its rear for each candidate. Bushotter also mentions the use of sweetgrass and sage for purification and states that "they wear a kind of medicine on their necks, and that keeps them from being hungry or thirsty, for occasionally they chew a small quantity of it" (454). This is also tied on the feet to prevent fatigue. Dorsey identifies it as a "bulbous root."

On the fourth day, the candidates assemble in front of the preparations tipi, wearing a buffalo robe hair side out, representing the buffalo as a sacrifice. The leader occupies the *catku* (the place of honor opposite the door), and the sacred pipe is smoked. At night, the songs are rehearsed, and, apparently, the dance steps are practiced with the aid of whistles and drum. The sacred pipe is smoked again, being passed by a man who holds the pipe so that the candidates do not need to touch the stem or bowl.

The next morning, which is Bushotter's fifth day, the tree is cut. Everyone goes out. The warriors chosen to cut the tree rush it as if it were an enemy. They ride away and return, assaulting a bundle of leaves that represents an enemy. A child is brought forth and seated on a pile of robes. Each of the warriors who will strike the tree gives a kill talk, then gives away a horse. Bushotter's description of this act is detailed, indicating again the Sun Dance's function in the redistribution of wealth. In striking the tree one is "by this act considered to make a present of a horse to some one." As he strikes the tree, his father or kinsman hands him a stick, representing a horse. The striker then names the person who is to receive the horse. The crier goes to camp and sings the giver's name in a way that indicates a brave deed. On reaching the tipi of the intended recipient, the crier then says, for instance, "O Leaping High, a horse is brought to you! A horse is brought to you because Mato éuwi maza has given a blow to the mystery tree!" (456). The recipient expresses his thanks, palms extended toward the crier, taking the stick. The transaction is further announced in the camp by the crier.

Women play a significant role in the symbolic capture of the enemy, felling the tree: "After all the chosen men have told of their deeds, and have performed their parts, the women select a man to speak of what generous things they have done, and when he has spoken, the larger women who are able to fell trees rise to their feet, and take their turns in giving one blow apiece to the tree" (456). When the tree falls, there is singing and wailing. All limbs are cut except the highest one. The crown is left intact. When a limb is cut, red paint is rubbed on the wound. A bundle of wood "in imitation of that for which they have prayed" is hung crosswise from the fork (456). Above this a scarlet blanket is tied along with a buffalo or weasel skin. Under the buffalo robe are two effigies of rawhide, which represent a man and a buffalo.[4] According to Bushotter's account, the center pole, or "sun pole," is decorated before being taken to camp. No one may touch the tree, which is transported in a wagon. Formerly, the tree was placed crosswise on a horse's back, with the holy men supporting each end. The people gather the leaves and cut limbs, dropping them at camp where they will pitch their tents (the ceremonial camp has apparently not yet been established). Bushotter writes that "some of the riders make their horses race as far as they are able" (457).

The military motif continues with the ceremony of the raising of the tree, which is accomplished in four stages. When it is erect, "the men around the camping circle fire guns, making the horses flee" (457). The hole is filled and the shade is erected. The sacred pipe is smoked. The "aged men and the chief men" dance around the pole, shooting at the objects suspended from the pole with pistols, "knocking them aside suddenly" (458). They continue to dance around the

4. Dorsey states that both have erect penises and says that Bourke allowed him to examine those used in 1881.

camp until they reach their tipis. A more general charge, on horse-back, ensues. The men dress up, tie their horses' tails, and ride two abreast through the camp circle, shooting into the ground, "filling the entire area with smoke" (458). At sunset the young men and women ride in pairs, singing in a call and response fashion. The preparations tipi is reerected (probably after the ceremonial camp is established).

The candidates spend the night before the dance decorating themselves. Their skirts are red, and a design is painted on their chest, which may be a sunflower. Brave deeds, either those done personally or by a kinsman, are also appropriate subjects, as are de-signs representing an animal the dancer has killed. Other designs signify stolen horses. Animal tails are sometimes held between the teeth, to represent an enemy scalped. The hair is worn loose. Some dancers wear a buffalo head skin, horns on; others wear eagle war bonnets. Each wears a buffalo robe, hair outward. The pledgers leave the preparations tipi with a filled pipe, held with stem facing the front. The leader goes first, holding a red skull: "All cry as they march, and on the way they are joined by a woman who takes the place of her 'hakata' or cousin; and sometimes they are joined by a horse that is highly prized by his owner" (459). A line of sticks is placed from the preparations tipi to the mystery circle. Each candi-date offers tobacco pouches and four blankets, which are set on the sticks. After this, the people may no longer cross this line.[5] The can-didates move in procession four times sunwise around the shade. They raise their hands to the cardinal points as they proceed inside the mystery circle and then sit "at the back part of the lodge" and sing (460). An altar is cut into the soil in the shape of a half moon between this area and the pole. The skulls (presumably having been carried by the attendants) are placed here, while the men are painted red again. The procession marking the compass points is repeated. The Sun Dance song is begun, and the candidates hands are reddened, after which they may not touch anything. Bushotter writes that a woman may take the part of a relation who is too poor

5. Dorsey introjects that Bourke showed him a staff used for crowd control. Five feet long, decorated with beadwork and tipped with horsehair, the people fell back whenever it was extended.

to perform the required gifting or acquire the necessary equipment, the Sun Dance being a considerable financial commitment. She carries his pipe, wears her hair loose, and wears a buckskin shirt, suffering "as the male candidates do, except in one respect—her flesh is not scarified" (460).

According to Bushotter, the candidates have been fasting from the time the pole was cut. He mentions that horses may take part in the dance, by being painted red and decorated and being attached to the sun pole. He also mentions four kinds of piercing. The first is standing inside a square of poles, with ropes attached to each of the poles two in the chest, two in the back. The second is dancing with a buffalo skull attached to the back: "The blood runs in stripes down his back" (461). The third is dancing fastened to the sun pole. Apparently each dancer does not have his own rope, for Bushotter writes that there are eight, attached halfway up the tree. The candidates must look upward after being pierced. Bushotter writes that a special problem is created for the short man (apparently because all the ropes are tied at the same height, and are not long enough to allow a short man to stand). In this case, his back is pierced and he is suspended from the tree and "for a long time he remains there without falling" (461).[6] Bushotter recalls that such a short man's friends once gave away a horse to release him, whereupon the man who had received the horse recounted his kills and then jerked the pledger to the ground. His family gave away more gifts, including a horse, which was given by throwing a stick into the crowd.

The fourth form of piercing described by Bushotter involves a man and a horse. The man is tied to the horse's tail and pierced. The horse is whipped up, and the man is broken loose from the tree. In a further reference to the redistribution of wealth at the dance, he mentions that if a candidate's female relations love him, they will furnish him with quilled objects to suspend from his wounds. This is a mark of respect, which Bushotter says often leads the women to "deprive themselves of all their property" (462).

Bushotter gives the first detailed account of flesh offerings.

6. Although it is very circumstantial, this is a curious interpretation, compared with J. R. Walker's statement that this form of the dance is required to obtain shamanic powers.

When the men are pierced, those who wish to give flesh seat themselves near the pole: "With a new knife small pieces of flesh are cut out in a row from the shoulders of each of these men, who hold up the pieces of their own flesh, showing them to the pole" (462). Bushotter also states that they "cover the base of the pole with earth" and that women may give flesh.

During the dance, the spectators sing a song of praise and "the old women are walking about with their clothing and hair in disorder, the garments flapping up and down as they dance" (462). The dance is interrupted by a pipe ritual for the candidates, and dancing resumes after they are redecorated. After noon, the ear-piercing ceremony ensues. A rest is called at midnight. A circuit of the cardinal points is made, after which the dancers face east.

At sunrise, the dance ends. The shade is circled four times, as is the preparations tipi. Gifts are again placed on the line of sticks and "there is considerable disputing among the small boys" for these gifts (463). The dancers are taken to their lodges, where they are fed when they revive. An *inipi* is required, at which time the vow is considered fully discharged. After the dance, the spectators scramble for the gifts and remove everything from the sun pole, which remains in place. Camp is then broken.

Bushotter does not provide much information on the interpretation of the dance, but a remark appended at the end does point out a very important aspect of Lakota ritual: "All who participate in the dance must act according to rule for if one slights part of the rites they think he is in great danger" (463). Lack of respect or lack of knowledge of the proper ritual customs continues to be interpreted as life-threatening in the contemporary period. Bushotter also writes that the candidates think that their actions are pleasing to the sun: "As they dance, they pray mentally, 'Please pity me! Bring to pass all the things which I desire!'" (463).

As is typical of retrospective accounts, Bushotter constructs an "ideal" Sun Dance, rather than giving the details of any particular dance. However, the prescriptive tone that seems to come naturally to native speakers of Lakota when describing the dance should not be taken to imply that all Sun Dances are the same. Bushotter's account, the first written by a Lakota, adds a wealth of detail to the observer accounts analyzed in the previous chapter. Among other things, he adds considerable detail on the preparations by the dancers, and he makes it clear that dancing the Sun Dance leads to increased importance and leadership in the tribe. The pledger is treated to increased respect from his family as well as outsiders, and particularly from his female relations, who acquire considerable economic responsibilities from his pledge. This also underscores the function of the classic dance in the redistribution of wealth, and Bushotter provides an explanation for the ear-piercing ceremony by saying that the female relations who contribute moccasins are entitled to have a child's ear pierced. He also emphasizes the purification of the pledgers and their responsibility for special conduct, which is continued until an *inipi* after the dance. The associations of the dance with war are particularly clear in Bushotter's account, but he also provides the first evidence of a communal focus to the dance by mentioning its role in the prevention of famine and epidemic. As will become clear below, the theme of the communal good is especially pronounced in Black Elk's reinterpretation of the dance and in the ongoing revival of the dance in the contemporary period.

J. R. Walker's *The Sun Dance and Other Ceremonies of the Oglala Division of the Teton Dakota* (1917) is generally acknowledged as the classic account of the Sun Dance. Its fascination stems both from the material itself and from Walker's complex relationship to his informants. Although the work has long been recognized as a central source on the Lakota Sun Dance, its authenticity has been questioned because of the uniqueness of its information and point of view.[7] The recent publication of many of Walker's interviews (1980, 1982, 1983) has laid to rest the question of authenticity, but significant questions remain about his point of view as a researcher and his relationship to his informants, making a brief account of Walker's life necessary to discussion of his contribution to the literature of the dance.

Walker's first contact with the Lakota came as agency physician at Pine Ridge, a post he held from 1896 to 1914. When posted to

7. In 1937, Franz Boas sent Ella Deloria to Pine Ridge to attempt to collaborate Walker's information. She met with no success. In fact, her informants were highly suspicious of Walker's claim to have uncovered material that was known only by a few shamans, information kept secret from the rest of the tribe (Walker 1980, 44).

Pine Ridge, Walker was forty-seven years old and had been involved with Indians for eighteen years. As agency physician, Walker was an agent of the government, formally charged with combating the influence of the tribal medicine men.[8] His first interactions with the local medicine men involved the major health problem on the reservation, tuberculosis. Walker believed the disease was exacerbated by the persistence of sanitary conditions that were acceptable in a nomadic context but had disastrous effects on the reservation, where people lived on the same site from year to year (Walker 1906). The medicine men were not oriented to the Western notion of disease, and Walker at first tried to loosen their hold on the health care of the people. His belief in the superiority of Western medicine was uncompromising: "I found that they have little knowledge of disease, that the most of their medicines are inert, and that their practices consist mostly of mysticism and trickery" (Walker 1980, 10). Walker also refers to "the trick with the worm" in which a medicine man produces a worm from the body of his patient (11). He approached the medicine men, however, as rational beings, attempting to win them over by differing with them in private rather than in public, showing them the tuberculosis bacteria under the microscope, and compiling statistical data on his cures. It is a testimony to his character and to his tact that he won their cooperation; his success with this procedure also shows that the medicine men were not as intransigent as is often supposed. Walker's willingness to work with the native priesthood annoyed those who sought to repress it, and he was investigated on at least one occasion (48).[9] Winning the respect of the medicine men, however, was the essential condition for his subsequent ethnographic work. As the agency physician, Walker was a successful "medicine man" who had demonstrated his concern for the people; no better platform for ethnographic work among the Lakota could be conceived.

The second phase of Walker's evolution began in 1902, when he met anthropologist Clark Wissler, who was on a collecting trip for

8. However, according to Francis Paul Prucha, "few, apparently, made it their business to mount a frontal attack upon the traditional Indian culture" (1984, 646).

9. James McLaughlin, who became an inspector in 1895, was the investigator. He gave Walker a clean bill of health.

the American Museum, where he worked under Franz Boas. It was Wissler's policy to look for collaborators on the reservations he visited, and he realized that Walker would make an ideal field-worker. When Boas left the museum in 1905, Wissler became head of anthropology, and he quickly moved to commission work from Walker. By 1908, Walker had completed an article on Lakota games, collected samples of Lakota music, completed an extensive study of Lakota anthropometry, and turned to the study of the *Hunka* ceremony (the making of relatives). Then, in 1910, Walker began his work on the Sun Dance. Wissler apparently regarded Walker highly, mentioning him as a coworker in his 1912 monograph on the Oglala (3). In the context of the professional anthropology of the day, the Sun Dance was considered central to the anthropology of the Plains and its investigation was pursued essentially in reference to the diffusionist paradigm, which held that similarities in cultural practices were to be explained by their transmittal, or diffusion, from a common source.[10] It is clear from Wissler's correspondence with Walker that he wanted a standard ethnographic document, recording informants' names and biographies along with the information they provided, printing all supporting documents, and noting divergent points of view. Walker deflected Wissler's requests, showing that he understood them perfectly well (Walker 1980, 29–30). Instead, he pursued his own course, molding his information into a continuous narrative. If Walker's second phase involved an intellectual shift from medicine to ethnography, the narrative focus emerging in his work on the Sun Dance signaled the beginning of his third phase, an intellectual movement from ethnography to literature.

The monograph that Walker eventually produced presents an ideal Sun Dance, described from the point of view of a shaman instructing a candidate. In a footnote, Wissler, as editor, characterized this as "from the point of view of the native conductor of the ceremony rather than from that of an onlooker" (Walker 1979, 58n). Wissler goes on to say that because of this, he is omitting references to previous accounts, a fact that indicates that, although he recognized the value of Walker's work, he also recognized its essential in-

10. Leslie Spier's 1921 article summarizes this work, and John W. Bennett's 1944 article provides a critical evaluation of its results.

commensurability with the anthropology of the day. Although Walker pursues his own agenda in the monograph, he is not altogether insensitive to the requirements of science, expressing repeatedly in his letters a desire to verify his information for fear that he has misunderstood or has been misled by his informants or translators. It is clear that Walker was disturbed by what he regarded as the fragmentary nature of his knowledge of the subject, and he pressed on until he could provide a start-to-finish view of the Sun Dance. In the later stages of the project, the Walker emerging from his correspondence with Wissler is increasingly a perfectionist, obsessed with his subject and deeply concerned with literary matters.[11] Walker's letter of transmittal for the manuscript indicates that he has reached the final phase of his creative evolution, for he reserves the right to use the myths he collected as part of a literary work. In fact, Walker was to devote the rest of his life to systematizing Lakota myth, as a connected literary cycle (Walker 1983).

Walker's intellectual development from medicine through ethnography to literature is remarkable, but his unique relationship to his informants is even more remarkable. At some point while at Pine Ridge, Walker became a holy man. Based on his "Autobiographical Statement," a document compiled by Raymond J. DeMallie, this must have happened after 1898, which was early in the period during which Walker was collaborating with Wissler (Walker 1980, 45–50). This honor was, as far as we know, unprecedented. Walker states that he began his studies with the common people but found the information he obtained had many inconsistencies, which the people told him could only be resolved by the holy men. To access this information, he became a Buffalo medicine man, learning their procedures well enough to employ them in the practice of medicine: "As a medicine man I practiced some of their methods, sometimes with success, but not such as the Oglala medicine men had" (47). Walker found, however, that the medicine men eventually referred his questions to the holy men. According to Walker, he then discovered that the information he sought was in the sole possession of an order of shamans that had only five remaining members. However,

11. Walker's literary concerns are evidenced in the elegant and economical translation of the native idiom that occurs throughout the monograph.

they had not had any candidates for some years and were reluctant to accept a white man as a candidate. One of Walker's informants, George Sword, a Christian and captain of the Indian police, argued to the holy men that their wisdom would perish with them unless they instructed Walker and implied that the gods of the Lakota would be displeased if they were to pass from human memory. Short Bull, the old Ghost Dance apostle, sought a vision, and Walker was accepted as a candidate, although he was required to promise that he would not divulge what he had learned until all five were dead. Sword and Thomas Tyon were the interpreters. Walker was first instructed in the customs of the Lakotas, and was required to dance the "Holy Dance," which obligated him to hold the wisdom he would receive holy. Walker required a patron god but was considered incompetent to receive a vision, so Short Bull chose the "Buffalo God" as his patron. Walker was presented with a fetish (*sicun*) and pronounced a holy man. That this was not merely a *pro forma* initiation is indicated by the fact that Walker states that the people subsequently addressed him as such (Walker 1980, 49). It is likely that Walker had learned not to say too much about this phase of his life, for there is little direct evidence concerning the effect that it may have had on his life and work. Certainly it was in direct contradiction to the ban and to his duties as agency physician, at least as they would likely have been construed in Washington. It may be that Walker regarded his initiation merely as a heuristic device necessary to gain the information that he sought. On the other hand, the fascinating possibility exists that he came to regard himself as the last of the Lakota holy men and his cycle of Lakota myths as a primary, not a secondary, text.

In his description of the Sun Dance, Walker focuses his attention on the teachings and ceremonies antecedent to the public ritual. These preceding ceremonies are devoted primarily to purifying and instructing the candidate and preparing him mentally for the austerities of the dance as well as for the new responsibilities devolving on a Lakota who has danced the Sun Dance. It was a commonplace of the anthropology of the day that ritual in some way refers to myth, and Walker accompanies his manuscript with translations of relevant myths, reflecting the common assumption that the meaning of ritual was to be sought in myth: "In performing these ceremonies every word or movement is a formal rite that has reference to the mythology. Therefore, to understand the ceremonies, one must know the rites and something of the mythology" (Walker 1979, 56). Since ritual as such was not Walker's primary interest, his description of the dance is rather brief. It is not clear whether Walker ever had the opportunity to observe a secret Sun Dance while at Pine Ridge, an affair that would in any case have been very different from the great communal festival that he was describing. Even if he had observed the annual dance, however, it is unlikely that he would have produced a detailed ritual description, for his real interest lay in myth, not in ritual.

Despite the eminence of his informants, Walker characterizes them very briefly, although Sword is given his own short paragraph. Since Walker tells the story from the point of view of a holy man instructing a candidate, not from the point of view of an anthropologist, his informants quickly drop from sight. In his preliminary remarks, Walker emphasizes that the ritual is being described with reference to the "customs of the Oglala" and claims that the precontact form of the dance will be described.

Walker's account begins with the holy man, not the vow. The prospective dancer must choose a mentor, establishing a master/disciple relationship that Walker terms "Mentor/Candidate" (Walker 1979, 63). The Sun Dance creates considerable financial and social responsibilities for the candidate, who must gift his master and provide for feasts, presents to his assistants, an offering to the sun, and equipment. The feasts alone would have been expensive, a burden that also fell on the pledger's family and friends: "While it is expected that a Candidate will give all his possessions in making provision for the feasts, his kindred and his friends should also give liberally; indeed, the entire band should contribute for both feasts and presents" (62). The "higher forms" (those involving piercing) cost more than the "first form" of the dance, so the poorer people were in effect restricted from piercing: "If he cannot comply with these conditions in an abundant manner, he should undertake only the first form of the dance, and then little will be expected of him or his people" (62). The highest form of the dance was used to make a shaman by bestowing a vision of the sun, and anyone completing this form of the dance could claim to have demonstrated the four cardinal virtues, bravery, generosity, fortitude, and integrity. The Sun Dance scars were themselves marks of distinction. Walker notes that because the dance benefits both one's self and the people, the prospective dancer should carefully consider his qualifications and his ability to meet the requirements for the dance, for it is possible that the people will not support his aspirations (62).[12] Walker distinguishes four forms of the sacrifice: (1) gazing at the sun, (2) gazing at the sun carrying buffalo skulls, (3) gazing at the sun staked (attached to four posts in the shape of a square), and (4) gazing at the sun suspended (60). The first form of the dance, which may involve women and children, requires a "wound to cause the blood to flow" that must be at least the size "made by cutting away a bit of skin as large as a louse" (61). These are the flesh offerings mentioned previously. The three higher forms of the dance involve torture, and women and children are excluded. Walker notes that the wounds should be made alike for those dancing each form.[13] There are two variations of the fourth form. In the first, the pledger is "suspended" by being attached to the tree by a rope. In the second, the pledger is fully suspended from the tree. To become a shaman by dancing the Sun Dance, it was necessary to dance the fourth form, and to gain shamanic powers, it was necessary to appear before the people suspended—that is, in full shamanic flight—dancing the "fullest" form of the Sun Dance.[14]

According to Walker, the dance takes place when the buffalo are fat, the new sprouts of sage are a span long, the chokecherries are ripening, and the moon is rising as the sun is going down (61). As

12. Although Walker mentions that the dance benefits the people, he does not mention this as a reason for undertaking the dance. The four purposes he does list are to fulfill a vow, to secure supernatural aid for another, to secure supernatural aid for self, or to secure supernatural power for self (1979, 60).

13. The modern dance exhibits much more individuality in styles of piercing, and the idea of "degrees" is not attested in the literature on the modern form of the dance. Walker probably means that those dancing the same degree should be pierced both in the same way and with comparable severity.

14. Walker notes that it was not necessary to dance the Sun Dance to become a shaman, but that those who did were more highly regarded. Only the shamans who had danced the Sun Dance could possess a fetish with the potency of *Wakan Tanka* (1979, 58).

Paige points out, this last condition requires a full moon (109n). Considerable time, however, is required for instruction of those dancing the higher degrees. Walker reports that one wishing to dance the higher forms of the dance should contract the mentorship in winter or at least no later than the return of the wildfowl in spring. Those dancing only the first form of the dance must find a master before the establishment of the preliminary camp. The master/disciple relationship is contracted when the person making the vow chooses a mentor. He offers the pipe to the mentor, who may refuse it. If it is accepted, the relationship is announced at a feast held for the purpose. A helper is appointed by the master. The master/disciple relationship is a public matter and must be ratified by the council of the band.

Since a large Sun Dance is desirable, other bands are invited as early as possible. The candidates begin their preparation with the sweat lodge, which Walker states is undertaken before all rites concerned with *Wakan Tanka,* which he translates "the Great Gods" (66).[15] The candidate must seek a vision and must be governed by his master's interpretation of it. It is possible that the vision will disqualify the candidate from participation in the dance. Walker mentions that one receiving a vision identifying him as *heyoka* (a sacred clown) must behave as one at the dance, appearing to enjoy the tortures and making fun of the others (68). The master prepares an altar in the candidate's tipi that must remain until the dance is completed. The altar, a smaller version of the altar in the mystery circle, is four-sided. It is made by removing everything living from a square of mellowed earth. The altar has four horns, and its centerpiece is a buffalo skull. The skull and the candidate are painted with red stripes, indicating that they are relatives. The candidate "smokes in communion" with the skull by blowing the smoke from the pipe into the skull's nostrils, harmonizing his spirit with that of the buffalo.

15. Walker's comments on the sweat lodge (*inipi*) are revealing. The purpose of the rite is "to stimulate the *ni,* or vitality, so that it may increase strength and purify the body" (1979, 66). The "spirit-like" of the water is released in a confined space so it may enter the body. This vitalizing may be also for refreshment or to cure disease and may last only as long as is necessary to smoke two pipefuls. On the other hand, it "may be a complex ceremony supervised by a Shaman, and prolonged for a day and night or even longer" (67).

Outside the candidate's tipi, a meditation bed is made of sage. The pledger should occupy this bed most of the time when he is not with his master. At its foot stands a rack of cedar, painted red, with the bottom end stripped of bark. The candidate's hunting and war equipment is consigned to the rack for the duration of the preparation period. The rack also holds gifts given to the pledger, who may have one by his tipi for the rest of his life. The candidate is then consecrated by being painted. His hands are painted red, so that he may touch sacred things. He is given a bunch of sweetgrass in the shape of a scalplock, painted red, to ensure the favor of the feminine god. An insignia is painted on him in red, indicating the degree of the dance he has chosen. All his clothes and implements are reserved to him alone until the dance is over. A sacred space is thus created and the candidate is singled out and set aside by this consecration, which limits even the things he can use and touch. Walker gives the following rules as governing the conduct of the candidate: The candidate must be subordinate to his master; meditate constantly; speak little, except with his master; use only his consecrated utensils; show no anger; indulge in no dirty jokes; stay out of the water; and have no sex. Provision is made for penance and reconsecration if rules are broken.

Walker then turns to the instruction of the future shaman, which is in two parts. The first part comprises a thorough instruction in the laws and customs of the Lakotas, which the shaman must know because it is his office to instruct others. Also, because his discretion to change and override customs and usages is broad, the candidate must know when a shaman may not interfere (78).[16] The second part comprises the secret instructions concerning the supernatural, or *Wakan Tanka*. One of these doctrines forms the immediate background of the Sun Dance: *Wakan Tanka*'s aid can be secured through sacrifice. Walker's remarks on the sun are particularly relevant. The sun is a god whose "favor may be secured by appropriate offerings and ceremonies and He may grant a communication to one who dances the Sun Dance" (81). The sun's symbolic color is red. Since the sun is the chief of the gods, red is the sacred color generally.

16. Although the holy men were given considerable latitude, this indicates that they were also subject to community control.

When applied alone, it symbolizes consecration. The buffalo is the sun's companion, and his potency prevails in ceremonies relating to the sun, particularly in giving success to hunters. His potency inheres in his skull and can be imparted to anything that was part of a buffalo. Walker also notes that the bear is the patron of magic, medicine, and wisdom and that his aid should be sought by one who seeks to learn the lore of the Lakota. Instruction is given the future shaman in offering the pipe, in mythology, and in the medicine bag. Walker notes that the sun, like the Great Spirit, has no fetish (88). The instruction of the shaman ends on a practical note, with the observation that the shaman receives an honorarium for his services.

The instruction over the Sun Dance tortures is particularly rich in meaning. The sacrifice is the guarantee of the dancer's sincerity: "Such torture should cause the blood to flow, for when the blood flows as a token, it is the surest guarantee of sincerity, and without such a guarantee the people or the Sun may doubt the professed purposes of the dancer" (93). The pain that the pledger experiences is for the accomplishment of a purpose, and it thus demonstrates fortitude, the greatest virtue that must be exhibited when one appears before the face of the sun in the dance. The pledger also shows bravery through his suffering and endurance at the flow of blood. The dancer gazes at the sun, so that no one might say that he failed to look the sun in the face when making his request. Indeed, this request is for a vision of the sun. Walker concludes the section on the instruction of the candidate by noting that the formal relationship between the mentor and his candidate ceases when the instruction is over.

Walker then turns to the community, whose duty it is to provide the feasts, offerings, presents, and equipment for the Sun Dance.[17] The community's direct involvement with the dance begins with the journey to the site, which initiates a holiday that lasts until the dance is done. (The candidates themselves stay aloof from the merrymaking.) A preliminary camp of four days precedes the ceremonial camp, which also lasts four days. On the first day at the preliminary camp, the superior of the ceremony is chosen along with the head of the ceremonial camp. On the second day, the Council of the Bear is

17. Walker lists the equipment required in full (93–94).

held, to which mothers who want their children's ears pierced apply. The female attendants are also chosen. The day ends with a feast. On the third day, other appointments for the dance are announced—the hunter of the tree, the digger of the hole, the group that will escort the tree, and the musicians. A buffalo head is decorated and the god invoked. The feast of buffalo tongues ensues. This feast is the last for the candidates and they should get a tongue apiece, at least (98). On the fourth day the women who are to chop the tree are announced. In Walker's account, they are virtuous mothers, preferably those who have lost kinsmen in war, not virgins. The feast of the maidens ensues, during which the intercessor and the mentors go to a nearby hill to pray for four blue days and ask the favor of the sun as it sinks. That night, the merrymaking is curtailed.

The second four-day period begins with an imposition of the intercessor's authority, which is announced by the "red herald" (100). The elders go to the hill and pray to the rising sun. If the weather is bad, the unworthy, to whose presence this is attributed, are expelled from the camp. The elders pray to *Wakan Tanka* through the sun, their chief, for an effectual Sun Dance. The escort then makes a charge against malevolent spirits, shooting arrows and shouting. Because Walker is trying to describe the precontact form of the dance, firearms are not mentioned. The sacred spot is located by the intercessor, and the hole, which is associated with the buffalo, is dug. The camp is then realigned in accord with this sacred center, establishing the ceremonial camp. The lodge and other sacred places are located. At the same time, the sacred tree is found, a tree not less than two spans in circumference and forked at "four times the distance from hand to hand when the arms are outstretched" (102). The Sun Dance lodge (the shade) is then built. The Buffalo Feast ensues. Since the buffalo is associated with fertility, the young people may court aggressively. The Buffalo Dance is danced. The buffalo is the god of generosity, so the old, needy, and poor are fed. Tidbits are carried to the pledgers before the people are served. The intercessor and his company pray to the sun at sunset, but social affairs and the courting continue far into the night.

On the second day, the sun is again greeted, and the attack on the malevolent spirits is repeated. (If the sun does not appear, it is

not counted one of the four days.) The tree is captured and sub-
dued. It is felled by a woman. The tree is trimmed and the bark is
stripped to the fork. It can be touched only with red hands. As the
tree is brought in, a race ensues back to the camp, which is dangerous to those involved. The tree is painted, the west being red, the
north blue, the east green, and the south yellow. These are the respective colors of the superior gods, the sun, the sky, the earth, and
the rock (82). The fork will be oriented east/west when the tree is
erected. Images of a man and a buffalo, both with exaggerated penises, are attached to the tree. Another feast and dance ensues. The
"procession of sex" takes place (108). The Sun Dance pole is raised,
whereupon the buffalo prevails in camp, as his fetish is attached to
one fork. This fetish is a chokecherry bundle, which includes sage,
sweetgrass, shed buffalo hair, and other "trinkets or ornaments"
(109). On the other fork is the red banner of the shamans, four
arm's lengths long. A *heyoka* attaches the images of the man and
buffalo, and the pole is raised in four stages. The "obscene gods"
then prevail, and a period of licentiousness begins, which ends when
the escort arrives and kills the obscene gods. The war and victory
(scalp) dances follow, which level the area. The intercessor scorches
the obscene gods and touches the buffalo image's penis to the tree
(110). These actions end the indecency. The feast of this day is the
feast of the shamans.

The fourth day, midyear day, everyone dresses up to greet the
sun. The shamans on the hill pray for endurance for the candidates
and invoke the bear god. Another charge is made, which obligates
everyone taking part to do the sun's duty as a warrior. The candidates are dressed, prepared, and painted. Their feet and hands are
painted red, they are painted according to their degree, their personal insignia are attached, a wreath of sage is placed on their heads,
and a wisp of sage is given them to carry. They are dressed in red
skirts, otterskin capes, buffalo hair armlets, and rabbit skin anklets
(112). Those dancing to become shamans are also equipped with a
four-sectioned hoop. As the procession comes out of the preparations tipi, it is taken down. The dancers follow the "sun trail," wailing as if in mourning, and circle the shade four times. A buffalo
head is placed on the altar. The candidates then recline on sage
beds. At this point the intercessor may address the people about the

dance, and all in the lodge smoke. Buffalo chips are burned, and all are harmonized with the spirit of the buffalo god, who prevails during the dance. The candidates stand, becoming dancers, and are issued whistles and instructed to blow them continually. The people cheer. The mentors then instruct their candidates in the symbolism of the hoop, mentioning the sky, the four winds, time, all that grows, and all circular things. This ceremony ends the mentor/candidate relationship. The leader of the dancers is now placed in charge and the Buffalo Dance and the Sun Gazing Dance alternate. Completion of the Buffalo Dance while looking continuously at the skull makes one a Buffalo Man, meaning that one is inducted into the people of the sun, having to pay no price for a bride, ensuring many children, and making a vision of the sun possible. A buffalo tail is placed on a stick, and the children's ears are then pierced.

The Sun Gaze Dance, the Sun Dance proper, begins with the pledgers being captured, thrown to the ground, and prepared for torture. The maidens encourage and exhort the dancers as the musicians sing a war song. The female relatives of the pledgers grieve while the captors sing a victory song. The women ululate, and emotion is high. The captives are bound, and the fork of the tree is used to draw the dancers who are to be suspended up into the air. The maidens wipe the wounds with sweetgrass, making an effective love charm (117). There are twenty-four Sun Dance songs, which may be repeated as necessary. The first is always a song of the captive, the last a song of victory. In Walker's account, all are suspended at once, and those dancing suspended are lowered to the ground for the rest periods (indicating that they were suspended for much longer than is usual today). At the end of the second period, the captors discover that the captives are buffalo men, at which point they become friends, remaining by the dancers and offering encouragement and aid (118).

The dance continues into the night, and none break loose until the fourth period. Those dancing far into the night may get a drink from their lovers. Walker reports that it is best to tear loose or dance until the dance is over, which is a "rescue" and is as meritorious as an escape. Second best is to require assistance to break free. Worst is to swoon. On breaking free, the pledgers return to their tipis (119). Those who have previously danced the dance to completion may cut themselves and join in the dance of the first form. The scalp-staff dance takes place in the fourth intermission, along with the "women's dance." The dance is continued all night, either until the next day dawns or until all are free. At the end of the dance all tipis are taken from the ceremonial circle. The tree is left undisturbed. According to Walker, the expected vision of the sun comes later, but before the dispersion of the next winter camp (120). Those who danced to become shamans should apprentice themselves to a shaman for further instruction, and the others should fit themselves to the purpose for which they danced. Walker's account ends with the observation that the shamans are the sole authority and may alter any feature of the dance.

Walker's account provides almost an embarrassment of riches for the interpreter, providing insight as it does into the point of view of the holy men on the dance. Among the items of special notice are the fullest explication of the buffalo symbolism in the dance, from the feast of the buffalo tongues, in which the pledgers are harmonized with the buffalo, to the burning of buffalo chips in the dance and the information that it is the spirit of the buffalo that prevails during the dance.[18] The role of war symbolism in the dance is also clear in Walker's account, with his mention of kill talks at the tree-cutting ritual, the performance of the scalp dance, and the symbolic capture of the pledgers. Walker is especially valuable in presenting a full account of the preparations of the pledger, and the instruction of the candidate in the norms of Lakota culture, which makes clear the function of the dance in the transmission of the culture. Walker is also the only source to mention that the intercessor may use the dance to instruct the people (a function taken over in the contemporary dance by the announcer). Walker also emphasizes the importance of the blood sacrifice in ensuring sincerity, which is also emphasized in Frances Densmore's account, to be discussed below. As is to be expected in a priestly account, the power and responsibility of the holy men is fully emphasized—as is their payment. Walker is especially frank on the financial aspects of the dance, making it particularly clear that the poorer simply cannot afford to

18. Julian Rice's reading of the buffalo symbolism in Walker's account of the dance is insightful (1991, 125–36).

dance the higher degrees of the dance. Walker also ranks the various means of obtaining release according to their prestige, from fainting, to outlasting the dance (a rescue), to breaking loose (a release), and provides the important information that full suspension is necessary to make a holy man. Although it seems unlikely that Walker ever saw or danced a Sun Dance, his account is one of the fullest and most revealing in the literature.

Besides Walker's monograph, other primary materials collected by Walker bear on the Sun Dance. These materials provide various details and points of emphasis that supplement the information in Walker's monograph. Thomas Tyon, writing in 1911–12, explains that the goal of the race back from cutting the tree is to strike a symbolic enemy, the first to strike it being assured of killing an enemy in the future (Walker 1980, 178). In a document attributed jointly to Little Wound, American Horse, and Lone Star, the holy men emphasize the inclusiveness of the Sun Dance, saying that "anyone may dance the Sun Dance if he will do as the Oglalas do" (181).[19] The financial obligations of the pledger are that the dancer must give feasts and presents, and is expected to give away all he possesses. In corroboration of Walker, these informants state that to become a shaman of the highest order, it is necessary to dance fully suspended. They also state that no Oglala will doubt the word of one who can show Sun Dance scars, and that such a person is eligible for leadership of a war party or for chieftainship (182). In a document from 1909, Sword informs Walker that according to Lakota customs, he is his grandfather, for Walker has chosen him for instruction on the Sun Dance (182). Bad Heart Bull mentions that the crown of leaves on top of the pole is its scalp, which must be left intact, since it will thus serve those who have captured it (183).[20]

The most remarkable documents collected by Walker on the Sun Dance are paintings of the third and fourth days of the dance by Short Bull. In notes translated by Walker, Short Bull explains the

19. This universalism has given way to a certain amount of exclusionism in the contemporary dance, especially in dances associated with AIM. Paul B. Steinmetz provides some perspective on these tensions in his account of a dance at Porcupine, South Dakota, in 1979 (1990, 31–35).

20. Since the crown was removed in the Brulé dance observed by Schwatka, it is possible that this reflects an Oglala custom only.

details of the paintings, mentioning among other things the dragging of buffalo skulls, the chokecherry bundle, the man and buffalo
effigies, and the flag of red flannel at the top of the tree. Short Bull
emphasizes the courting by showing two couples courting in a single
painting. Short Bull also mentions the sage wreaths, the eagle-bone
whistles, and the fanning of the weary dancers with feathers. The
notes state, "Should be only two dancers. When one breaks loose, the
other dances" (185). This presumably indicates that only two dancers
are pierced at a time, dancing in succession. Short Bull also mentions
that after the first night, the men are tempted with water.

Walker also collected a longer manuscript by Sword on the Sun
Dance, which has been presented by Ella C. Deloria in three versions—Lakota, literal translation, and free translation (Deloria
1929).[21] Sword's manuscript presents explicit information on two aspects of the dance that are touched on lightly by Walker, the relationship of the Sun Dance to war and the piercing. Sword describes
the primary context of the Sun Dance vow as the desire to kill an
enemy in war, but says that the vow may also be taken in the context
of "threatening danger" (389). The public declaration of the men
who are to pledge is made before a holy man, who prays to the sun,
saying that "when these sprouting grasses change their appearance,
these youths of proper age promise to meet you face to face" (389).
He also expresses their desire to meet the animals face to face, that
is, to enjoy good hunting. Sword stresses that the vow is expected to
bring success in war, but that the dance must be made no matter
what the outcome: "If it should happen now that those who pledged
themselves in return for a favor in war do not get an answer in
exactly the way they wished, they are still bound by oath to carry out
their promise" (390). Sword mentions on several occasions that the
crying that the pledgers do at various points in the ceremony is "crying for the enemy," that is, crying because they want an enemy to kill
(394). The theme of war asserts itself especially with the search for
the tree, which is scouted like an enemy (395). After the tree is cut

21. An analysis of the relationship between Sword and Walker—and their ac-
counts of the Sun Dance—is best deferred until the appearance of Raymond J. De-
Mallie and Elaine A. Jahner's final volume in the Walker series, which is to focus on
Sword.

and raised, and the shade erected, the dance for smoothing the ground is performed, with the men performing the "missing aim dance," shooting repeatedly at the image of the enemy man on the tree, but contriving to miss it (399). After this takes place, about eight men who are "being trained to become brave fighters" are chosen to be honored. Those not chosen react aggressively: "Some stand by, hoping they may be taken for this honor, but when they find that they are overlooked, then they pout, and dance angrily, shooting their guns more frequently than is necessary" (399). Additional shooting ensues when a warrior who has killed an enemy leads a dance with a scalp tied to a long stick. As the dancers assemble in procession, they cry for an enemy. The intercessor also cries for an enemy at the sacred tree: "At dawn when the world is beautifully still, the sun dance leader stands leaning against the sacred tree, crying for the enemy" (400). These and other details indicate that Walker's relative lack of stress on war is certainly not because of its absence from his sources.[22]

Sword also mentions the role of the Sun Dance in love, saying that the young women bring water surreptitiously to the dancers at night, the dance being for two days and two nights (400). Sword also mentions that "his girl, if he is yet unmarried, stands by weeping silently in great sorrow" (405). Deloria's informants confirmed that sometimes a man would undertake the dance to make an impression on a girl, a tactic that was apparently successful, there being many elopements after each Sun Dance (405n).[23]

Sword's account of the piercing is especially rich. The Sun Dancer who is to be pierced presents a pipe to someone who has previously been pierced. This evidently entails a gift: "But at such times, now and then such a man will refuse the pipe for some time pretending he dreads to perform the act until the thing he wants is offered in return for the service" (404). At the piercing, two braided ropes are attached to the tree, and the one who is to perform the

22. Stanley Vestal's account of White Bull's participation in the Sun Dance in *Warpath* casts additional light on the role of the Sun Dance in war (1984, 95–97).

23. This aspect of the annual festival has received relatively little emphasis, except in Ella Deloria's *Waterlily*, which describes the dance through the eyes of the protagonist, a young woman (113–34).

piercing grasps the dancer by the waist and lays him on the ground. The pledger cries for an enemy. Sword is unequivocal about the severity of the piercing: "Holding the flesh stretched out far, the piercer pierces the chest down to the quick through the muscle under the skin, and runs a sharpened stick through the holes like a pin" (405). His relatives stand by watching, suffering at the sight. According to Sword's account, it was apparently not usual for a man so pierced to be able to free himself: "When the sun dance songs are being sung, the man dances, pulling hard on the wounds, trying to break away. He pulls hard on the skin and on the muscles, trying to pull himself free, but failing, he dances from side to side, pulling away backwards, with a mighty effort, hoping thus to tear himself free. But still he is not able to do so" (405).[24] At this point, a relative may intercede, giving the dancer a stick to throw to the crowd. The stick represents a horse to be given away to the poor. Then if he chooses, the piercer may come to his victim and dance from side to side with him, pulling on the wounds. Or he may add his weight to the dancer's, pulling him free. On breaking loose, the dancer apparently feigns death: "At first, the one who pulled him free falls down with him, and then the pierced one lies as one dead. Like a fish, he gasps several times and then he lies motionless as death" (406). Deloria appends remarks from another informant that also testify to the severity of the piercing, referring to the piercing of Lone Man, who pulled "the whole flesh off his chest," stating that winter counts refer to the year when "Wiskeha's whole chest was torn off" (412). Except for this last incident, Sword provides unequivocally the most severe estimate of the piercing, which is today through the skin only, not through the muscle. This makes comprehensible the longer struggles noted in the literature, as well as explaining why it was often impossible to obtain release. One explanation of this severity may be related to the role of the dance in the redistribution of wealth. Clearly, it was not in the interest of that redistribution for the pledger to break free on his own, without the necessity of gifts being given to obtain release.

24. Edward S. Curtis, who describes the piercing of the chief dancer as being under the muscles, states that if he has not broken free after four tries, his relatives give presents, which allows the partial cutting of the flesh to allow the dancer easily to break free (97–98).

Sword also mentions the four-post form of the sacrifice, saying that it "is harder for it takes longer for the victim to free himself, and the wounds are very painful" (406). At times, some of the dancers lie as if dead from thirst, and "to all appearances they are dead" (406). Sword mentions horses accompanying their owners in the dance. The horse is tied to a post and stands without water and food until nightfall, when he is watered. When a man who is pierced in four places dances with his horse, the reins of the horse are tied to the two wounds in his back. According to Deloria, the horse was not cut. Sword mentions the suspension of four buffalo skulls from the shoulders (407). He also provides an interesting detail in his remarks on full suspension. When the dancer hangs by his wounds, they are made in the small of the back, which is "pierced deeply." "Having so pierced him they lift him up and hang him suspended. No part of his body not even his feet, touch the ground, and during the singing of the sundance songs, the one who pierced him, comes and swings him by pushing him from behind, at which times, fearing that he will go over head-first, he kicks about with his feet to hold his balance. It is Dakotas who practice this, but the Hukpapaya alone do not have it" (407). Sword also mentions the giving of flesh by both the dancer and his female relatives (407). Sword's manuscript thus shows that Walker had available a much more detailed account of the piercing than is apparent from the brief treatment of the subject in his monograph.

Frances Densmore's *Teton Sioux Music* (1918) contains an authoritative, professional account of the Lakota Sun Dance that might be described as the equivalent of Alice Fletcher's firsthand account for the period of the ban. Densmore was an anthropologist who specialized in ethnomusicology. Her work on Sioux music was a continuation of her work on Chippewa music and is, to some extent, comparative. Besides recording songs for translation and transcription, Densmore employed interviews to establish the context for the songs and to aid in their interpretation, providing a full account of many aspects of Sioux culture, belief, and ritual.

Densmore collected her information on the Sun Dance at the Standing Rock Agency in 1911, James McLaughlin's old agency, which was populated primarily by the Hunkpapa band. Her inquiries, which were probably perceived as official, caused some concern in the community. Before deciding to participate in the interviews, the elders discussed the matter thoroughly.

When we heard that you had come for the facts concerning the Sun dance we consulted together in our homes. Some hesitated. We have discarded the old ways, yet to talk of them is "sacred talk" to us. . . . When we decided to come to the council we reviewed all the facts of the Sun dance and asked Wakantanka that we might give a true account. We prayed that no bad weather would prevent the presence of anyone chosen to attend . . . [and] Wakantanka heard our prayer. (Densmore 1918, 92)

This statement underscores the fact that in 1911 the Sun Dance was still a very sensitive subject. The informants were carefully chosen. Densmore was obliged at one point to drop an informant whose morals were offensive to the community and to expunge his statements from the record (5–6). The fifteen primary informants were unusually well qualified. Most had made a Sun Dance vow, and most had also witnessed or participated in the dance of 1882, the last public dance on the Standing Rock before the ban. Despite the passage of nearly thirty years, this dance looms large in Densmore's account. The informants included two practicing medicine men, a man twice chosen leader of the dancers, a man in training for the office of intercessor when the dance was discontinued, a survivor of the Battle of the Little Big Horn, and several men prominent in public life, including John Grass, a principal in the treaty-making process. Densmore had also the honor of interviewing Red Weasel, the intercessor at the dance of 1882. Densmore states that all but one of the fifteen—the Little Big Horn warrior—had been friendly to the white man during hostilities and reckons that "six of the men have steadily refused to be influenced by the missionaries and still retain the native religious beliefs" (87).

The interview was a staple of Boasian anthropology, and Densmore's interviews were carefully structured, care being taken that "the form of a question did not suggest a possible answer by the Indians" (93). Densmore's intent was to obtain an authoritative communal statement on the Sun Dance, not merely to collect individual interviews, and so her informants played a significant role in the arrangement and interpretation of the data. The process was complex. Densmore first conducted interviews to collect individual statements. These statements were then read to a council convened to discuss and clarify them, and a final draft was prepared and approved by the council. The council also visited the site of the 1882 dance. Some forty additional interviews were held with ordinary people in the community to secure their impression of the material presented by the council and to assess the reputation of the primary informants. (Densmore allowed more weight to some statements than to others, based on the informant's status in the community.) Densmore held further interviews with Red Bird, an eminent elder, and others who wished to insert additional information into the record. Densmore also met with five others who were concerned about the conclusions of the original council. At that point Red Weasel was invited to give his opinion on the material and to add details of his responsibilities and actions as intercessor. Chased by Bears, the council member who was twice leader of the dancers, was then solicited for statements pertinent to the meaning of the Sun Dance, its "theology." These interviews with Chased by Bears were evidently quite sensitive, for it was necessary for the interpreter, Robert Hightower, to conduct them personally while driving to and from the councils. Finally, Chased by Bears returned to the site of the 1882 dance and reconstructed the altar as it was then arranged. The process was thus carefully controlled by both Densmore and her informants, making the account a true collaboration. Densmore explicitly assures the reader that the process issued in consensus.

> Throughout this series of conferences the principal points of the account remained unchanged. Each session added information, placed events in the proper order, furnished detail of description, and gave reasons for various ceremonial acts. The councils were not marked by controversy, a spirit of cordiality prevailing, but the open discussion assisted in recalling facts and nothing was recorded which was not pronounced correct by the council as a whole. (94)

This careful procedure produced a document of unusual authority.

Densmore's informants associate the Sun Dance strongly with war. About half of the lyrics she collected mention or concern warfare (nos. 5, 7, 8, 11, 12, 23, 27, and 28). No. 28, "I Have Conquered Them," reads "[W]ell, a war party / which was supposed to come / now is here / I have obliterated every trace of them" (142). For Densmore's informants, the Sun Dance vow is always uttered on the warpath. The four informants who mentioned a context for their vows all specified the warpath, and one who had never performed a Sun Dance vow had made a similar vow while on the warpath. The dancers wore their hair on their shoulders in the manner of one who had recently killed an enemy (125) and several of the songs (8, 11, 27) mention the black face paint worn in the victory dance: "Wakan-tanka / when I pray to him / black face-paint / he grants me" (141). That is, *Wakan Tanka* answers the warrior's prayer by assisting him in the killing of an enemy. The context of the vow is the mortal danger faced by the warrior who is about to encounter the enemy, and the prayer is for individual survival and triumph. It is hoped that *Wakan Tanka* will respond, but there are no guarantees, and the vow must be performed whether the warrior is successful or not. The community took an active interest in ensuring that vows were performed. Persons failing to carry through on their pledge were prone to accidents. "More than one man who disregarded his vow to the sun had perished in a lightning flash; or if he escaped punishment himself, it was known that disaster had befallen his family or his horses" (101). In most cases, the entire war party would make a vow, a man who had performed a previous vow speaking it for the whole party. The individuals did not necessarily specify the form that their sacrifice would take, vowing only to take part in the dance. Chased by Bears gave Densmore an account of this procedure, including his prayer preparatory to combat.

> Wakantanka, these men have requested me to make this vow for them. I pray you take pity on us and on our families at home. We are now between life and death. For the sake of our families and relatives we desire that you will help us conquer the enemy and capture his horses to take home with us. Because they are thankful for your goodness and will be thankful if you grant this request these men promise that they will take part in the next Sun dance. Each man has some offering to give at the proper time. (97)

Densmore reports that there were six forms of the pledge. (Walker and Fletcher refer to four forms, reflecting the statements of informants from the Oglala and the Brulé respectively.) The first was simply to dance. The second was to give flesh by cutting from ten to two hundred small pieces of flesh from the arms with awl and knife, or cutting similar numbers of gashes in the arms. (The larger numbers of cuts or gashes might be divided with a male or female relative.) The other four forms of the sacrifice involved insertion of a stick, painted blue, into the flesh, which was then placed under strain until the skin broke, releasing the stick.[25] Densmore notes that the most common form was being pierced in both sides of the chest and attached to a cord running to the crossbar of the tree. In Densmore's dance, the men stand on tiptoe in this position and cannot place their heels on the ground. They thus dance in place until the time comes to break loose from the tree (133). The fourth form of the sacrifice was to have from two to eight buffalo skulls attached to the back, and, in the case of six or more skulls, to the upper arms. The buffalo skulls were suspended and did not touch the ground, making it necessary in most cases for a stick to be used for the pledger to stand (133). The fifth form of the sacrifice was being pierced and fully suspended from the tree by the lower back. On one occasion reported to Densmore, the pledger rode to the tree on a horse and was suspended when the horse was led away. The sixth, most severe, form of the sacrifice was being pierced in both the chest and the back and hung from four poles in the shape of a square so that only the toes touched the ground (134).

Although her informants state that the stick was "put through the skin," Densmore believes that "probably it pierced also the subcutaneous fascia" (131). The exposed portion of Chased by Bears's knife, which appears to be about an inch to an inch and a half long, gives a good idea of the depth and severity of the piercing (pl. 21). Densmore noted that a horse might be attached to the thongs to hasten release. If release did not come soon, the wealthy or their relatives could give horses. In that case, the flesh was cut to make release easier. The less well-to-do were simply jerked down (133). While suspended, the men faced the sun, blowing an eagle-bone whistle and praying for the welfare of the tribe (134).

Women did not dance the Sun Dance, although they might fast and dance alongside a relative (135). They could, as noted above, assume a portion of the cuts or gashes undertaken by a male pledger. They were also involved in the gifting and feasting that was integral to the dance.

25. Blue probably indicates *Taku Skanskan,* the spirit of motion or release.

Densmore describes the dance as lasting two days, the men dancing all night long on the first day. On the second day, the men were
allowed to return to their lodges for a rest. Since those who had
made sacrifices were returned to the dance, the dancers began to fall
from exhaustion on the second day, at which point they were carried
to the shade until they revived, which appears unique to Densmore's
account, for most accounts state or imply that those who faint have
completed the dance and are released from further obligation to
dance. In a parallel to the Ghost Dance, Red Bird stated that the
intercessor once flashed a mirror into his face, whereupon he
swooned and had a vision of the sun (149). After the dance was over,
the pledgers returned to the sweat lodge and then were permitted to
eat or drink. The final ritual action of the dance was the smoking, in
the intercessor's lodge, of the leader of the dancers' pipe. Densmore's informants stated that camp must be broken before nightfall
by the entire tribe.

Densmore's account presents major statements that touch on the
meaning and interpretation of the Sun Dance by Red Bird, Red
Weasel, and Chased by Bears. Red Bird, who was training for the
office of intercessor when the dance was banned, contrasts the Sun
Dance religion with Christianity, emphasizing its authenticity and
validity: "There is a great deal in what a man *believes,* and if a man's
religion is changed for the better or for the worse he will know it.
The Sun dance was our first and our only religion" (86). Red Bird
says that with the ascendancy of Christianity, the people have lost
faith (and hence power) and do not live as long. In explanation of
the dance he says: "We believed that there is a mysterious power
greater than all others, which is represented by nature, one form of
representation being the sun. Thus we made sacrifices to the sun,
and our petitions were granted" (86).

In his statement, Red Weasel, the intercessor at the 1882 dance,
emphasizes his lineage and authority: "I am not boasting; I am telling you what I myself know and I must speak for myself as there is
no man living who can vouch for me" (88). His master was Dreamer
of the Sun, who taught him the Sun Dance; he knows only what was
taught by Dreamer of the Sun, who taught him as he was taught. His
training began at an early age when he was selected by his master as
being unusually gifted. Dreamer of the Sun's first teaching was that

he must have the utmost reverence for *Wakan Tanka*. Dreamer of the Sun advised him that if he did his work well he would be a help to the people and taught that if he was well prepared, the correct actions would come naturally at the ritual and that he need not fear the unexpected. Dreamer of the Sun also taught that a prayer reached *Wakan Tanka* more quickly if it was sung. Finally, and most significantly, Red Weasel emphasizes that all his prayers were taught to him by his master and that he can still recall them all. The import of this is evidently that Red Weasel could still do the Sun Dance. Densmore surreptitiously recorded Red Weasel's prayer before giving the above statement, which indicates clearly that traditional religion was for him a present reality: "Wakantanka, hear me. This day I am to tell your word. But without sin I shall speak. The tribe shall live. Behold me for I am humble. From above watch me. You are always the truth, listen to me. My friends and relatives, sitting here, and I shall be at peace. May our voices be heard at the future goal you have prepared for us" (95).

Chased by Bears, who was twice leader of the dancers and assisted frequently at the Sun Dance, was solicited by Densmore particularly for a statement on the meaning of the dance. His statement, which shows considerable awareness of Christian criticism of traditional religion, emphasizes the greatness of the sacrifice, contrasting it with both the cutting of flesh during mourning and the giving of horses and other gifts.

> A man's body is his own, and when he gives his body or his flesh he is giving the only thing which really belongs to him. We know that all the creatures on the earth were placed here by Wakantanka. Thus, if a man says he will give a horse to Wakantanka, he is only giving to Wakantanka that which already belongs to him. I might give tobacco or other articles in the Sun dance, but if I gave these and kept back the best no one would believe that I was in earnest. I must give something that I really value to show that my whole being goes with the lesser gifts; therefore I promise to give my body. (96)

Chased by Bears emphasizes the sincerity and humanity of the Sun Dance pledge and stresses the spiritual maturity that is necessary to understand the idea of sacrifice: "A child believes that only the action of some one who is unfriendly can cause pain, but in the Sun dance we acknowledge first the goodness of Wakantanka, and then we suffer pain because of what he has done for us" (96). Chased by Bears also mentions repentance and suggests that the Lakotas cry when they pray in the Sun Dance because they are like children who wish to show that they are sorry for what they have done and know that "a request is more readily granted to a child who cries" (96). Although Chased by Bears states that he has never joined a Christian church, his concept of *Wakan Tanka* includes a role as a creator and regulator of nature, a nature to which man is closely related, as is shown by the belief that some men can understand the language of the birds. Chased by Bears admits some difficulty (apparently raised by the missionaries) in explaining prayer to *Wakan Tanka*, for Lakotas talk to him but admit that they cannot hear his voice in reply.

Densmore herself places the Sun Dance in the context of sun worship in general, something "widespread among the Indians of North America" (84). She also views it in the context of its culture area as a Plains Indian phenomenon. Her remarks stress that the misunderstanding of the Sun Dance can be traced to its sacrificial aspect.

> In the Sun dance, the Indian considered that he offered to Wakantanka what was strongest in his nature and training—namely, the ability to endure physical pain. He did this in fulfillment of a vow made in time of anxiety, usually when on the warpath. Strange as it may seem, the element of pain, which ennobled the ceremony in the mind of the Indian, was a cause of its misunderstanding by the white man. The voluntary suffering impressed the beholder, while its deep significance was not evident. (85–86)

She goes on to quote reports of the agents at Rosebud and Pine Ridge, Wright and McGillycuddy, who condemned the dance as "aboriginal and barbarous" and "heathenish." Without directly criticizing them, she contrasts their remarks with the statement of Red Bird, whom she characterizes as "thoughtful." In this way, though stopping short of advocating the dance, Densmore implies that the agents and others who condemn the dance lack a thoughtful appreciation of cultural relativism.

Yet it is clear that Densmore's perspective on traditional religion is firmly retrospective. Boasian anthropology was oriented decisively to the concept of assimilation, setting for itself the task of reconstructing the aboriginal past. From this perspective, traditional religion was at best a survival, not a viable and functioning part of the religious situation on the reservation. This is especially clear in Densmore's comments on Red Weasel's opening prayer, when she says that he used "the same gestures which he would have used when filling his ceremonial office" (95). Given the overwhelming orientation of the anthropology of the day to the past, it is not surprising that Densmore failed to see that Red Weasel *was* "filling his ceremonial office" when he prayed to *Wakan Tanka* before discussing the dance. Albert H. Kneale, the agent at Standing Rock in 1913 and 1914, remarks in his memoirs that "July was devoted to the Sun Dance" (265). Since Densmore collected her information in 1911, the possibility exists Red Weasel was still active as a Sun Dance intercessor at the time of his interview. It may be that Densmore simply assumed it was extinct, and failed to ask about the possibility of its persistence. Certainly it would have been in no one's interest to bring it up, and it is possible that a direct question might not have yielded a forthright answer. The participants would have been admitting to a crime, and the agent would have been guilty of permitting it. Densmore's translator, Mrs. James McLaughlin, would hardly have mentioned it, for her husband had declared the Sun Dance extinct some thirty years previous. So it is not necessarily Densmore's fault that she failed to discover that the dance persisted underground.

But the fact remains that for the Boasian anthropology of her day, traditional religion had a highly interesting past, but no future. Since it never engaged the present on its own terms, the persistence of traditional belief did not come into its sphere of investigation. This focus on the past had the effect of limiting its vision; the social science of the day would never have predicted the revival of the Sun Dance in modern times.

4

The Sun Dance under Ban
1883–1934/1952

The Sun Dance was officially banned from 1883 to 1934, and piercing was not permitted until 1952 or later.[1] The ban has received surprisingly little attention in the literature on Lakota religion, perhaps because it is not a pleasant subject to contemplate from the perspective of religious tolerance. Although studies of Lakota religion typically mention the ban, the literature contains no thorough investigation of its genesis, methods, and results. Instead, studies of Lakota religious acculturation typically note that traditional religion "withered," "declined," or "died out" in the years after the great Sun Dances of the 1880s. Intentionally or not, these usages tend to obscure the real situation. Traditional religion did not "wither away" among the Lakota, it was vigorously repressed. The ban must be seen clearly to understand both the development of the dance and the lives and motivations of religious leaders such as Black Elk, whose livelihood and position of leadership in the tribe were endangered by it. In Black Elk's case, the ban was the context of nearly his entire life as a holy man, since it began only two years after he announced his vocation with the Horse Dance in 1881 and persisted in a de facto form until at least two years after his death in 1950. Accordingly, this chapter discusses the ban, the means em-

1. The ban officially began on April 10, 1883, with the appearance of "Rules for Indian Courts." As discussed below, the closing date is a matter of interpretation. As discussed in chapter 5, various dates have been given for the resumption of piercing. Black Elk's *The Sacred Pipe*, which appeared in 1953, is also discussed in chapter 5.

ployed to effect it, and the effects of the ban on the holy men and on the dance itself.

After the end of the Civil War in 1865, the attention of the country turned to western expansion, and the attention of the U.S. Army turned to Indian fighting. The history of the running skirmishes between the Lakota and the army in the 1860s and 1870s is a fascinating study that lies outside our present subject. However, it is extremely important for our subject to grasp that, in the context of the Indian wars, the effort to confine the Indians to reservations and civilize them was the response of the era's liberal humanitarians to the army's ongoing slaughter of them. Gen. William T. Sherman's orders to Gen. Philip St. George Cooke after the Fetterman massacre on December 6, 1866, were probably an accurate reflection of the majority sentiment in the army: "Of course, this massacre should be treated as an act of war and should be punished with vindictive earnestness, until at least ten Indians are killed for each white life lost. . . . It is not necessary to find the very men who committed the acts, but destroy all of the same breed" (Olson, 52). Since Sherman specified that the war should be carried to the "Indian camps, where the women and children are," it is clear that the campaign was to include noncombatants. Indeed, Sherman instructed Gen. Christopher C. Augur in February 1867 that all Sioux near the Powder River and Yellowstone should be considered hostile and that he should "punish them to the extent of utter extermination if possible" (Olsen, 53). Gen. Philip H. Sheridan was apparently in full agreement with these tactics, writing as late as April 1872: "Should Red Cloud and his people not be appeased with our humility and submission to his insolence, but still make war, I will . . . make it lively for the squaws, papooses, ponies and villages" (Olson, 144).

Although not "politically correct" in today's relatively enlightened context, the so-called peace policy that led to the ban on the Sun Dance was formulated in direct opposition to the army's "war policy" by men who clearly had the interests of the Indians more at heart.[2] Reform efforts had gained some ground earlier, but the com-

2. One of my prepublication reviewers pointed out that post–Civil War Indian policy was complex—not all military personnel looked to slaughter and not all reformers saw eye-to-eye. This is certainly the case. In the following discussion, I pre-

pletely gratuitous Sand Creek massacre of 1864 provided the impetus necessary to effect reform. This massacre was widely interpreted as an epitome of the government's treatment of the Indians, and it quickly became a focal point of efforts for reform. The peace policy formulated in response was the outcome of determined lobbying by a group of Christian reformers that included Episcopal Bishop Benjamin Whipple and philanthropist William Welsh. In response to their efforts, President Grant appointed a Board of Indian Commissioners in 1869. The board, which was controlled by the reformers, was to act as a watchdog over procurement of supplies for the Indians. This area was of considerable corruption and scandal, and it was hoped that an independent board would clean it up. Once created, however, the board demanded a wider role. The first annual report of the board, in 1869, argued passionately for a new beginning in Indian policy, based on the principle that the Indians should be confined on reservations and civilized.

As this report makes clear, it was not incidental that the reformers were churchmen. In their view, civilization necessarily entailed conversion: "The religion of our blessed Savior is believed to be the most effective agent for the civilization of any people" (Prucha 1975, 133–34). The peace policy was thus essentially a religious policy, the idea being to replace extermination with Christianization. Although the original members of the board resigned in 1874, attenuating its influence, the policies proposed by the board effectively dominated subsequent Indian policy. The board favored concentration of the Indians on small reservations, eventual allotment of land in severality, abolition of the treaty system, abandonment of money annuities, establishment of schools to teach English, and Christianization.

The churches also gained direct control over the reservations in 1872 by the apportionment of the agencies among various church groups, whose missionary boards controlled the appointment of the agents and other employees. Among the Sioux, the Episcopal influence was very strong. Cheyenne River, Pine Ridge, Rosebud, Lower Brulé, and Crow Creek became Episcopal agencies; Standing Rock and Devil's Lake became Catholic agencies. Although this policy was

---

sent the reform agenda in broad outline simply to provide part of the background necessary to understand the ban.

revoked in 1881 by Secretary of the Interior Carl Schurz, largely in response to Catholic dissatisfaction with the system, it gave the churches an enduring involvement in reservation affairs. Catholic influence on the reservations increased considerably with the demise of apportionment and the creation of the Catholic Bureau in 1874 (Prucha 1984, 707–11). Red Cloud had apparently lobbied for a Jesuit presence on the Pine Ridge Reservation for many years (Olson, 251, 308) and subsequent Catholic presence among the Lakota included sizable and enduring missions on the Rosebud Reservation (St. Francis) and on the Pine Ridge Reservation (Holy Rosary).

The essential program of the reformers was acculturation. They proposed to solve the Indian problem not by eliminating Indians, as the army had done at Sand Creek and elsewhere, but by eliminating Indianness. They regarded it as obvious that if all Indians were fully assimilated, the Indian problem would disappear. Since their proposal was essentially to replace genocide with cultural genocide, repression of the native religion and its priesthood was an obvious strategy. The churches had always been deeply committed to the acculturation of the Indians as an essential element in the conversion process. The missionaries in the field who confronted the task of civilizing and Christianizing the Indians as a practical problem had struggled for years against traditional culture and the medicine men, whose influence and interests were necessarily opposed to the missionaries.

As Gideon H. Pond's "Power and Influence of Dakota Medicine-Men" shows, missionary frustration with the medicine man was extreme. Pond's essay is essentially a plea for the destruction of the entire native priesthood.

> Each in particular, and all together, as wakan-men, they are not only useless, but a decided and devouring curse to their nation, on whose neck, mentally and morally, they have firmly planted the iron heel of priestly despotism: and until they are put down by the mighty operations of the Divine Spirit, through the word of Christ, they will effectually baffle any effort to elevate and civilize the Dacotas. "O Lord, how long!" (1854, 651)

Note that Pond is not attacking the medicine men proper, saying that some employ roots "often with very beneficial effects" (641n). His real target is the "*wakan* man," whose primary role is addressing the existential ills of Indian life "in the chase, in the lodge, and on the battlefield" (641–42). Although the holy men were also healers, in Pond's view this is a secondary function, which merely bolsters their claim to supernatural power. Since science easily reveals that the *wakan* man is a fraud, his power can be sustained only through a conjunction of ignorance and deceit: "No absurdity is too great to be heartily received by an ignorant savage, when proposed by one of artful cunning" (646). Hence the holy man's desperate opposition to progress, which exposes his bogus claims to power.[3] Among other devices, the medicine men exploit the ignorance of their people by appearing to be in control of the social and natural world.

> They assume great familiarity with whatever astonishes others; they foretell future events, and often with a sufficient degree of accuracy; those at one village affect to be familiar with that which is transpiring at another village leagues distant; persons who are almost reduced to a skeleton by a disease, in a day or two are as suddenly restored to perfect soundness, by their agency. (647)

They also hedge their bets by attributing their failures to corporate or individual sin. In war, they pretend to divine the movements of the enemy. They also eat raw flesh, consume whole fish, and (according to Pond) "quaff considerable quantities of human blood!" (648). In Pond's view, such performances are intended simply to deceive an ignorant public. Unfortunately these performances are successful: "I do not know an individual Dacota [*sic*] who does not yield full credence to the claims of some of these impostors" (648). The medicine men are thus the chief factor opposing the civilization of the Indian, and, as such, they are a factor that must needs be eliminated.

The considerable influence of Henry Hobart Hare, Episcopal Missionary Bishop of Niobrara (the missionary district that included the reservations in South Dakota), was also brought to bear against traditional religion and culture. Hare not only insisted that his "Christian Indians" boycott traditional rituals, but also attempted to actively repress traditional religion and culture, as indicated by Wil-

---

3. Pond sees *wakan* merely as a substitute for scientific explanation, criticizing traditional religion not as a competing religious system, but as a pseudoscience that stands in the way of progress.

liam E. Dougherty's report from the Crow Creek Agency: "Dancing was wholly stopped for a time on the reservation, at the instance of Bishop Hare, but it resulted in rancorous disputes and enmity between the heathen Indians and the Christians, and to keep peace and good order I was obliged to compromise the case." (Commissioner of Indian Affairs [CIA] 1880, 26). In his sermons, Hare characterized the progressive, Christian Indians as a tribe set apart from the heathen Indians in the same way the Jews were set apart from their neighbors in the ancient Near East. "The Jews were the chosen people of God in the midst of a heathen world. . . . So of all Christian peoples, and so too now of those Dakotas who had embraced Christianity. . . . They also were a people of an Oath. When urged to join in heathen dances and customs as of old, their reply was: 'No, we cannot, we have taken an oath to give up all these things and follow Christ'" (Howe, 88–89). For Hare, the decision for Christ thus entailed a commitment to Christian culture. The Dakota converts were to leave both their religion and their culture behind to follow the Christ.

The mood of the times is aptly illustrated by the debate initiated by Catholic dissatisfaction with apportionment of the agencies, which tended to favor the Protestant churches. In their attacks on the system, Catholics argued that apportionment violated Indian religious freedom. The debate, however, actually centered on the right of Christian denominations to freely proselytize, not on the right of Indians to freely choose among religions. Freedom of religion for the Indian in this sense was seldom advocated.[4] A Catholic statement makes the situation clear: "The Indians have a right, under the Constitution, as much as any other person in the Republic, to the full enjoyment of liberty of conscience; accordingly they have the right to choose whatever Christian belief they wish, without interference from the government" (Prucha 1976, 58).

The missionaries had labored for years to persuade the Indians to abandon their traditional culture and accept Christianity, but

4. Thomas A. Bland, founder of the National Indian Defense Association, was one of the few exceptions. Bland became Agent V. T. McGillycuddy's bête noir because of his support of Red Cloud. McGillycuddy expelled Bland from Pine Ridge in 1884 (McGillycuddy, 221–25; Hyde 1956, 96–99).

their efforts had met with indifferent success. With the capture of Indian policy by the reformers, persuasion quickly gave way to coercion. The program of the reformers placed a new burden on the Indian agents, who were now required not only to maintain order but also to administer an ambitious program of cultural genocide. The creation of the Indian police provided the means to execute this program. As Cheyenne River agent Capt. Theodore Schwan pointed out, without an appeal to force, the reform program would necessarily fail.

> An agent may order parents to send their children to school, he may admonish men and women to abstain from practicing the sun dance or other cruel or barbarous ceremonies, he may inveigh against polygamy, he may refuse to grant leaves of absence or order renegades from other agencies to return, but being without physical backing, his authority is ever liable to be openly and successfully defied and set at naught. A more potent stimulus than moral suasion is frequently needed and used to bring white men to their senses, and it is therefore not surprising that coercion and punishment are sometimes indispensable in the management of a people who only a few years ago were savages. The Indian respects and readily yields to physical force, but is sometimes hard to move by arguments, however cogent, or advice, however well meant. This want of power is in a measure supplied by the police. (CIA 1879, 23)

The effectiveness of small numbers of Indian policemen in executing unpopular policies might seem questionable. In fact, the Indian police were probably the most effective innovation of the period.[5] Among the Sioux, the military societies had long performed a police function—ironically at the annual Sun Dance—so the institution had ample precedent. It must also be remembered that reservation politics, then as now, was highly factionalized. The "progressives" were aligned with the agent, essentially supporting the Christianization and cultural change that the "non-progressives" opposed. There was thus a higher degree of indigenous support for reform policies than is immediately obvious from official reports and other contemporary sources, which tend to focus on conflict between the agent and the

5. For general discussion of the ban, the courts, and the Indian police, see Hagan (esp. 107–13), Utley (31–33), and Prucha (1976, 208–11).

traditionalists. Also, as Gen. Oliver O. Howard notes, the chief of the Indian police was the de facto tribal leader: "Probably—under the reservation system—there never was a better or more conservative method than the organization and use of Indian police, for the chief of police, when well selected, was soon recognized as the strongest chief in the tribe" (459).

The Indian police were a godsend to the agents, who required force to execute the reform agenda. The annual reports of the agents to the commissioner of Indian Affairs show that the Sun Dance was affected as early as 1879, when Schwan employed the Indian police at Cheyenne River to enforce his refusal to let his Indians attend the annual Sun Dance at Rosebud (CIA 1879, 20). The year before, in his annual report, the Episcopal missionary at Cheyenne River, Henry Swift, had recommended repression of Indian dances.

> Dances are being repressed by the sentiment of the Indians themselves; a minority still endeavors to keep them up. Their continuance tends to keep Indians wild and idle and extravagant. The rations furnished by government for support of their families is wasted, and the children suffer for food while the men feast. I think that now dances could be repressed without exciting any ill feeling. (CIA 1878, 23)

Perhaps Schwan was influenced in part to take his action in response to lobbying from Reverend Swift.

In 1880, the year after Schwan reported his action against the dance, Capt. William E. Dougherty, the agent at Lower Brulé, called for the repression of the Sun Dance.

> These Indians appear to have abandoned the "Sun Dance," and it is rarely spoken of except when there is to be one at another agency. On these occasions a large number attend. This atrocious feature should be interdicted and the military forces employed to prohibit the practice. This would be at least as consistent as the enforcement of laws preventing cruelty to animals. (CIA 1880, 37)

Later in his report, Dougherty recommends that "tribal sovereignty, chieftainship, the sun dance, all superstitious practices, and polygamy should be abolished by a prohibition by force" (39). In the same set of reports, J. A. Stephan, the agent at Standing Rock, called for the abolition of dancing, saying that it "stimulates the young men of their tribe in their disposition to 'run wild,' declining and disdaining instruction in the manners and customs of the white man" (57) and causes consumption.

It is worth pausing a moment to consider the charge that dancing per se was an unhealthy practice. In his report for the previous year, Stephan made his charge more explicitly: "Also their dances are a source of consumption, as they are nearly in a nude state when dancing, and in cold weather they cool off suddenly, which produces lung fever and consumption. All that can be done is done to break them from dancing and exposures, but it will take time to subdue a deeply-rooted custom" (CIA 1879, 48). He reiterates the charge in his report for 1880: "Excessive Indian dancing has been the cause of many of the unnecessary ills that have prevailed among them for years. Frequent cases of incipient consumption and lung diseases has [sic] been the result of this most pernicious practice" (CIA, 58). J. S. Murphy, an agent at Fort Berthold, later made a similar charge against the *inipi* (sweat lodge): "The practice of indulging in enervating sweats, cages for which are nearly a universal adjunct to every house, is undoubtedly conducing to the continuance of pulmonary consumption, which is a prolific cause of mortality. As much as possible the practice is discouraged and its evil effects are taught" (CIA 1890, 32). Whether or not these claims have any medical basis, they indicate that the agents did not perceive any benefit whatsoever from dancing or ritual purification, quite aside from the sacrifices in the Sun Dance.

The reports of the agents for 1881 indicate that dancing in general and the Sun Dance in particular continued to occupy their attention. At Crow Creek, Dougherty reports that although he permits the Grass Lodge dance, an attempt to revive "an immoral dance" was broken up by the police with "a characteristic 'knock down and drag out' of the principal offenders." He calls for a general prohibition of this "barbarous festival," which was probably the Sun Dance (CIA 1881, 29–30). At Devil's Lake, James McLaughlin reports that the Sun Dance and Medicine Dance are no longer practiced, although the Medicine Feast continues and the Grass Dance is allowed, but regulated (35). At Lower Brulé, W. H. Parkhurst reports that dancing is indulged in to a lesser extent than in the past. Parkhurst also states that this year's Sun Dance was a "miserable failure," apparently because he withheld rations, obtaining by this means a promise that it would not be attempted again (43).

In 1882, at Crow Creek, George H. Spencer reports that he suppressed "objectionable dances" imported from Standing Rock (CIA 1880, 25). Parkhurst reports that there was no Sun Dance—"the most barbarous of all Indian dances"—at Lower Brulé (32). At Pine Ridge, V. T. McGillycuddy reports that, among the Sioux, "dancing is diminishing, and the heathenish annual ceremony, termed the 'sun dance,' will, I trust, from the way it is losing ground, be soon a thing of the past" (39). In contrast, he complains that the Northern Cheyenne, never his favorite population, "spend most of their time in finding fault, loafing, and dancing" (35). At Sisseton, Charles Crissey states flatly that "barbaric dances are a thing of the past" (43).

These agents anticipated official policy; the time to ban the Sun Dance had come. In December 1882, newly appointed secretary of the interior, Henry M. Teller, wrote to Hiram Price, the commissioner of Indian Affairs, asking that active measures be taken against the Sun Dance, other traditional dances, the giveaway, polygamy, and the medicine men.[6] Teller claimed that Indian dances "stimulate the warlike passions," but the thrust of his letter was directed toward acculturation, as is indicated by the inclusion of polygamy and the giveaway. Teller's directive was brisk.

> I desire to call your attention to what I regard as a great hindrance to the civilization of the Indians, viz, the continuance of the old heathenish dances, such as the sun-dance, scalp-dance, &c. These dances, or feasts, as they are sometimes called, ought, in my judgment, to be discontinued, and if the Indians now supported by the Government are not willing to discontinue them, the agents should be instructed to compel such discontinuance. (Teller, xi)

Teller was similarly disposed toward the native priesthood, echoing Pond's diatribe against the holy men.

---

6. Hagan oddly attributes this directive to "a random reform impulse" (107). This is hardly an apt characterization, for active repression of native culture and religion was essential to the peace policy.

> Another great hindrance to the civilization of the Indians is the influence of the medicine men, who are always found with the anti-progressive party. The medicine men resort to various artifices and devices to keep the people under their influence, and are especially active in preventing the attendance of the children at the public schools, using their conjurers' arts to prevent the people from abandoning their heathenish rites and customs. While they profess to cure diseases by the administering of a few simple remedies, still they rely mostly on their art of conjuring. (xi–xii)

Commissioner Price's response was to establish a Court of Indian Offenses, promulgating protocol for these courts on April 10, 1883. These "Rules for Indian Courts" closely followed Teller's directive. They provide that "any Indian who shall engage in the sun dance, scalp dance, or war dance, or any other similar feast, so called, shall be deemed guilty of an offense, and upon conviction thereof shall be punished for the first offense by the withholding of his rations for not exceeding ten days or by imprisonment for not exceeding ten days" (Prucha 1975, 187).[7] Subsequent offenses draw ten to thirty days of withheld rations or imprisonment for ten to thirty days. The Rules also prescribe punishment for the practices of the medicine men.

> Any Indian who shall engage in the practices of so-called medicine men, or who shall resort to any artifice or device to keep the Indians of the reservation from adopting and following civilized habits and pursuits, or shall adopt any means to prevent the attendance of children at school, or shall use any arts of a conjurer to prevent Indians from abandoning their barbarous rites and customs, shall be deemed to be guilty of an offense. (187)

First offenses draw ten to thirty days imprisonment and subsequent offenses not more than six months. Besides outlawing the major dances and suppressing the native priesthood, the Rules proscribe polygamy, the giveaway, prostitution, intoxication, and sale of alcohol on the reservation.

At first, the judges were to be chosen from the Indian police, since no salary was provided for judges. The police, appointed by the agents, were thus in charge of both arrest and conviction. To the

7. The version quoted is the revision of August 27, 1892.

lack of salary, rather than the lack of due process, should be attributed the slow start of the Indian courts. In 1886, Standing Rock was the only agency with a functioning court. In 1888, three agencies, Crow Creek and Lower Brulé, Sisseton, and Rosebud had no courts, and at Pine Ridge, H. D. Gallagher dissolved his court (CIA 1888, 48). Although Congress authorized payment of the judges in 1888, the effectiveness of the courts, at least in the early years, remains questionable. The effectiveness of the courts, however, was largely irrelevant, since with the promulgation of the Rules, the agents acquired a mandate to ban traditional religion and to harass the medicine men, with or without a functioning court to try offenses. As William T. Hagan points out, the legality of the courts was also questionable: "It was recognized then and later that there was at best a shaky legal foundation for these tribunals in the generally acknowledged authority of the Department of the Interior to supervise Indian affairs" (110). Legal or not, the reforms introduced by the Rules were sweeping. In one stroke, the secretary of the interior outlawed native religion and in another the commissioner of Indian Affairs invented a court to try offenses![8]

The Rules greatly strengthened the hand of both the missionary and the agent. The missionaries could hardly have desired more than the Rules provided. The agents, who certainly could have desired more, had at least a mandate to harass the medicine men, always a troublesome element, and another means to advance the program of civilization. Since the acculturation process was tied closely to Christianization, the missionaries had a large role to play, which was increasingly shared by teachers. The key figure in the process, however, was the agent, who was expected to implement an intensified program of cultural change. The progress of the agents in enforcing the Rules for Indian courts is recorded in their annual reports. In addition, two Sioux agents, James McLaughlin and V. T. McGillycuddy, left substantial independent accounts of their actions and motivations during the early days of the ban.

The Rules appeared on April 10, 1883. Since the annual reports for 1883 were submitted in August, the agents had only three months to respond to the ban before the reports were filed. At

8. The Five Civilized Tribes were exempt from the Rules.

Cheyenne River, William A. Swan was the first agent to report banning the Sun Dance.

> The "sun dance" was not held this year. They, however, asked my permission to have one. I explained to them that their "Great Father" was very much opposed to the "sun dance," and would be displeased with them if they persisted in holding it. I further told them that I would not permit it, and that in case they attempted it I would punish the leaders. They seemed perfectly satisfied, and abandoned their purpose entirely. (CIA 1883, 22)

Swan also moved to halt dancing at a house near Pierre, where whites were encouraging dances by monetary contributions: "I determined to put a stop to these dances at this place, which purpose I accomplished by tearing down their dance-house and confiscating their drums" (22). At Pine Ridge, McGillycuddy reports that the Northern Cheyenne continue to dance, but among the Sioux, "dancing is diminishing rapidly, and the attendance on church increasing" (34). At Rosebud, James G. Wright reports that dances are held less frequently and states that the Sun Dance is losing ground, as there were only three piercings this year as opposed to thirty or forty the year before (43).

By 1884, the agents had had a year to apply the Rules. At Cheyenne River, Swan reports problems with whites who encourage Indians to resume native dress and give dances for their amusement (CIA 1884, 21). Henry Swift, the Episcopal missionary, states in his attached report: "It is the constant effort of the church to break up Indian customs, encourage industry, educate, purify the marriage relation in conjunction with and as a part of its [C]hristianizing work. In the sphere of our influences dancing and conjuring have ceased" (22). The missionary report attached to John W. Cramsie's report on Devil's Lake states that dancing has been abandoned, the Indians adhering to Christianity "with greater tenacity than they did to their former mode of worship" (33). McGillycuddy states that, for the first time, the Sun Dance was not held: "The abandonment of such a barbarous and demoralizing ceremony, antagonistic to civilization and progress, as it has been proved, is a bright and promising event in the tribe's struggle toward advancement in the white man's ways. . . . It is to be hoped that a firm stand on the part of the

Government in the future will prevent the reappearance of the sun dance" (37). In this report, McGillycuddy also gives his opinion of the medicine men.

> With the American Indian, as with other savage nations, the native medicine-man combines the calling of physician, priest, and prophet. He is, above all others, barbarism personified, and is through his influence over a superstitious following, one of the principal obstacles in the way of civilization. Therefore no effort or means should be neglected to destroy his influence and himself in his peculiar capacity. (40)

However, he reports no actions taken against the medicine men. At Rosebud, Wright reports that objectionable practices have been kept from sight, at least at the agency, although he notes that it would be difficult to say "how far this extends outside among the camps and villages" (42). Wright was successful in preventing the tribal Sun Dance, but apparently not without difficulty: "The aboriginal festival of the sun dance was not held here this year. By a strenuous adherence to my decision of last year (when I told the Indians the one then held must be the last), it was reluctantly yielded. I do not expect it will again be revived" (48). In a revealing comment on missionary work, Wright also notes the expulsion of the Catholic missionary, Father Francis Craft. In his previous report, Wright had implied, without naming him directly, that Craft was demoralizing the Indians by teaching them that what they were taught previously (by the Episcopal Church) was in error (CIA 1883, 43). According to Wright, Craft was also officially reported for using his influence to oppose Indian industrial schools. Wright himself reported to his superiors that Craft held himself "above all civil law" and the authority of the agent, thus securing his expulsion by order of the secretary of the interior (CIA 1884, 48).[9] McLaughlin reports that he allows only

9. Mary Ewens, associate director of the Cushwa Center for the Study of American Catholicism, has brought to my attention a photocopy of a letter to Secretary Teller, signed by R. H. Pratt, the superintendent of the Carlisle Indian School, that states that Craft participated in the Sun Dance: "I had it from a halfbreed at Rosebud who claimed to be an eyewitness that Father Craft solicited the privilege from the Indians of opening the ceremonies of the Sun dance last summer with prayer, and from many sources, that he wore eagle feathers in his cap throughout these ceremo-

the Grass Dance, and claims that all other dances are things of the past.

> Three years ago the "tom-tom" (drum) was in constant use, and the sun dance, scalp dance, buffalo dance, kiss dance, and grass dance, together with a number of feast and spirit dances, were practiced in all their barbaric grandeur; but all these are now "things of the past," the grass dance alone excepted, which dance is their simplest amusement and the least objectionable of any, and this is only tolerated on Saturday afternoon of each week. (CIA, 54)

In a comment on missionary work, McLaughlin gives this apologetic, yet optimistic, explanation of the situation.

> The [C]hristianization of the adult Indians of this agency, with their pagan superstitions so deeply rooted, is but very slow, and, notwithstanding that some of them have been under missionary influences and religious instructions for several years past, yet it will require some additional years of patient missionary labor to convince the middle-aged and older persons of the absurdity of their early beliefs, or to bring them to accept the teachings of Christianity. (56)

At Yankton, J. F. Kinney complains that his predecessor (William M. Ridpath) permitted weekly dances at a house near the agency and recommends strong measures. Kinney had been at the agency only a month, so his inaction is understandable (60).

In 1885, McGillycuddy's report comments sarcastically on efforts to defend the Sun Dance: "No decided attempt was made by the Indians to attempt the sun dance this the second year of its discontinuance, although the agent came in for his usual share of abuse from these self-same 'philanthropists' for arbitrarily putting a stop to this so-called religious ceremony, with its attendant 'Christianizing' torture" (CIA 1885, 34). McGillycuddy also regrets to report that Red Cloud and his followers are still dancing in the villages (35). At Rosebud, always a center of the Sun Dance, Wright had trouble preventing the dance.

---

nies, and entered into them to the full extent allowed by the Indians, so I have no doubt Agent Wright's last information is entitled to full credit." The letter is dated November 25, 1883, and is shown as received by the Office of Indian Affairs on December 31, 1883, #23595.

I had every reason to feel assured that the assent given last year to yielding up by the Indians to them the time-honored annual festival of the sun dance, though given reluctantly, was understood by all its abandonment for all time. In this I was mistaken, and when the usual time for preparation came this year it was again agitated, first by the elders. By a firm persuasion these gracefully yielded. Later, the younger element took it up, and were discovered traveling the camps, "presenting the pipe," committing all to a participation in this barbarous ceremony. It required prompt and decisive action to prevent its consummation. Finally a very reluctant abandonment was secured. Since then the agent is held responsible for all ills and misfortunes that have occurred or have visited this people. Sickness, death, hail or other storms would have been averted if the sun dance had not been prevented. His removal is consequently demanded. I am satisfied renewed efforts will be made each successive year for this demoralizing custom, and will require a firm and decisive stand to prevent. (44)

At Cheyenne River, Swan reports that all dancing has been discontinued (18). At Crow Creek, John G. Gasmann reports more modestly that the Christian Indians do not dance (22). At Sisseton, Thompson reports that the "district which contributes the majority of the *dancers* has not an acre of new land broken and very meager crops" (48). At Yankton, Kinney reports that the Christian Indians often appeal to the heathen Indians to give up the dance (59). Kinney also admits that he cannot break up the Saturday night dance at a dance house a half mile from the agency, which was tolerated by his predecessor. Kinney charges it, among other things, with corrupting the women (61). The commissioner himself paints a more positive picture of the program, quoting from various agents' reports to show its effectiveness (xxi–xxiii).

Subsequent annual reports until the time of the Ghost Dance show a similar pattern, the Sun Dance being mentioned only by the farmer at Turtle Mountain Reservation, reporting to Cramsie at Devil's Lake (CIA 1888, 41). In 1886, however, both Charles E. McChesney at Cheyenne River (CIA 1886, 51) and Kinney at Yankton (99) admit that their police are not strong enough to break up certain dances. At Crow Creek and Lower Brulé, W. W. Anderson admits that he tolerates some dancing, claiming that the Sun Dance is defunct (66). This claim is also made by Wright (82), but Wright's

1890 report indicates that dancing is still a serious problem at Rosebud (CIA 1890, 62, 64). Given this evidence, it seems likely that the agents tolerated some dancing, including Sun Dancing, throughout this period, concentrating their attention on the annual public Sun Dance near the agency, which seems to have been completely repressed by 1885.

Although not contemporary with events, the retrospective accounts left by James McLaughlin and V. T. McGillycuddy supplement the information provided in their annual reports. McLaughlin, probably the finest Sioux agent, was a career official in the Indian Service. When posted to Standing Rock, McLaughlin had ten years of experience with the Sioux. At Standing Rock, his long tenure, nearly fourteen years, easily surpassed the other Sioux agents, most of whom were fortunate to survive their four-year appointment. He may have succeeded in part because he was politically astute, as is indicated by his remarks about his relationship with one of the tribal leaders.

> I had come to know Crow King and to regard him as a man of influence who might be depended upon to exert that influence in the right direction. . . . I found him to be a man who could be depended on to do what he agreed to. We had an understanding, and I was easily content to do nothing that would affect his standing or influence with his people; for although the government no longer recognized the tribal authority of the chief, still it was easier to deal with one man of influence than to have to deal with many irresponsible ones. (90)

In contrast, V. T. McGillycuddy seems to have left no stone unturned in his efforts to subvert the authority of Red Cloud and the other chiefs, so perhaps it is not surprising that his tenure was quite stormy in comparison to McLaughlin's.

As a Catholic, McLaughlin had a very negative attitude toward the Sun Dance. At his first post, Devil's Lake, he stopped a Sun Dance without the mandate provided by the later Rules. Although McLaughlin's chronology is not completely clear, this action probably took place in the summer of 1881, immediately before he moved to Standing Rock. McLaughlin was thus ahead of his time in interfering with the dance and was presumably in full sympathy with the Rules. McLaughlin introduces this episode with the remark that the

Sun Dance was "the most baneful of the old-time practices of the Sioux people" (30). According to McLaughlin, the primary purpose of the Sun Dance was to propitiate the Great Spirit and the pernicious spirits of the earth, in the hope that the community would be blessed in the harvest or some other important undertaking. McLaughlin says that piercing was through the muscles of the breast or back and states that at a dance he attended in 1872, two dancers remained suspended, their toes barely touching, for an hour. According to McLaughlin, one of the deleterious consequences of the dance was that the eyes "invariably became terribly inflamed" from gazing at the sun (31).

When he learned that a Sun Dance was in progress, McLaughlin took his clerk and an Indian policeman to the scene of the dance at Wood Lake. "The Indians were in the midst of this barbarous ceremony when we broke through their ring and stopped the affair. It was good evidence of their subjection that they stopped without protest when ordered to desist, an outcome that would not have been possible a few years previous, when such an attempt would doubtless have resulted seriously to the sacrilegious interloper" (32). Unfortunately, he gives no indication of the size or importance of this dance, and so the extent of his bravado cannot be accurately estimated.[10] According to McLaughlin, his action on this occasion stopped the Sun Dance at Devil's Lake permanently.

He also provides additional remarks on the Sun Dance in the context of a long account of how a chief, Crow King, broke the influence of the medicine men at Standing Rock. This account portrays the Sun Dance as a "fearful ordeal" for prospective warriors.

> With prayers and offerings the medicine men cut gashes in the breasts and shoulders of Crow King, and they picked up with cruel knives the hard muscles that lay under the red skin, and beneath these muscles they thrust strong little skewer-sticks; and to the ends of these sticks they fastened the split end of a lariat, and the other end they fastened to poles and drew tight, so that Crow King, by standing on his toes, might escape being suspended from his shoulders and his breasts. And there Crow King danced and whistled,

10. Physical courage was essential to the successful agent. McLaughlin's autobiography presents several examples, including his daring of Long Soldier to stab him with a knife (33) and his winning of a race initiating the buffalo hunt of 1882 (104–6).

that the people who sat in the great circle about the medicine lodge and watched the dancers might know that his courage was great and that he disregarded the torture. While the sun made a day's journey Crow King and the other young men danced and bore the pangs of suffering, which was so great that their muscles stood out rigid like the sinews of the buffalo and their throats were parched so that they could not utter a sound, for it was not permitted that they might drink during the dance. (79)

In this account, McLaughlin's enmity for the medicine man is fully expressed. In an effort to cure his brother High Bear, who was dying of tuberculosis, Crow King engaged the "big medicine man" of the band, who "attacked High Bear with as much vigor as though he were a white medicine man and the patient the possessor of a vermiform appendix and rich relatives" (85). That High Bear was "the most profitable patient in the Sioux nation" attracted medicine men from other bands, whom McLaughlin characterizes as bunco men, quacks, and faquirs (87). The upshot was that, despite their efforts, High Bear died. McLaughlin implies that it would have been appropriate to kill the offending medicine men, but Crow King confined himself to giving a feast, during which he obtained and burned the fetishes of all the medicine men.[11]

McLaughlin later had the opportunity to play medicine man himself, manipulating an illness of Crow King to good result. Placing the old chief, who was painted and prepared for death, under house arrest, McLaughlin hoped to establish himself as a man of power: "I had taken a rather desperate chance. If Crow King died, the Indians would be lost to faith in my 'medicine,' but if he lived I might be certain of the event having a great influence" (95). Fortunately for the cause, Crow King lived, doing his part by campaigning for white medicine after his recovery.

Although generally considered an effective agent, V. T. McGillycuddy was a controversial figure.[12] An autocratic personality,

11. McLaughlin claims that for years afterward, this was recounted with awe, an acknowledgment that the story seems unlikely (90). The "wild west" diction of the chapter indicates that McLaughlin may have taken some liberties in the telling of the story.

12. George E. Hyde's account of McGillycuddy's tenure, which is sympathetic to

McGillycuddy was also a hothead, responding with anger to events on the reservation and to criticism of his policies in the press. His annual report for the Pine Ridge Agency in 1883 contains a wonderfully sarcastic retort to his critics.

> It might be well, perhaps, for members of Congress and the superior officials of the service, to realize the fact that occasionally, after an agent has lived for several years among the Indians, he may have gained nearly as sound a knowledge of the Indian question as the visionary and theoretical cranks that hang around the Department and lobbies of Congress, trotting antiquated and superannuated chiefs around as samples and representatives of the Indian as he is on the reservation. . . . In the mean time the agent remains patiently awaiting another investigation, or that threatened indictment before the grand jury. He feels lonesome without an inspector or two camping with him. (CIA 1883, 37–38)

This diatribe was admittedly a high point, McGillycuddy's other reports being somewhat more restrained, but it gives some idea of his personality and style.

McGillycuddy's attitude toward religion seems to have been more pragmatic than McLaughlin's. Under the terms of Grant's peace policy, Pine Ridge had been assigned to the Episcopal Church. An instructive episode in *McGillycuddy: Agent,* probably taking place in 1879, turns on Catholic frustration with agency allotments. A Catholic priest, Meinrad McCarthy, arrived to establish a Catholic mission on the reservation. McGillycuddy admitted to Father McCarthy that he personally felt Catholicism best met the needs of the Indian: "It had an appeal for the red men greater than any other form of worship. They liked the chanting, the burning of incense, and the bell-ringing; it was like medicine-making to the Indian"

Red Cloud, scoffs at McGillycuddy's effectiveness (1956, 87, 99). Nonetheless, Hyde admits that McGillycuddy's "bookkeeping was perfection; his probity above criticism; and not a thing could be found that might be employed as a hook on which to hang charges" (105). Robert M. Utley considers McGillycuddy to have been a "good agent" (39). Doane Robinson, suggesting that McGillycuddy handled Red Cloud well, characterizes him as a "bad man to fool with" (449). In his discussion of the Ghost Dance, Robinson also characterizes McGillycuddy as a man of "unflinching courage, determined will and splendid executive ability" who could have averted the Ghost Dance disturbances (469).

(106). However, Pine Ridge was an Episcopal agency. So informed, McCarthy stated that he would establish a mission anyway. McGillycuddy's characteristic response was that he would put McCarthy off the reservation. McGillycuddy pointed out that this might cause violence, since Red Cloud was sympathetic to the Catholics. In turn, this would create negative publicity for the church: "Would you like to read in the press that a priest of the Church had caused an outbreak among the Sioux while opposing the government?" (108–9). Faced with this logic, McCarthy desisted.

McGillycuddy's response to the Rules for Indian Courts was similarly pragmatic. *McGillycuddy: Agent* does not mention the Rules but speaks as though the ban were McGillycuddy's own idea.[13] Seemingly recognizing that the Rules were on shaky legal ground, McGillycuddy says that

> according to the treaty of 1868 they were guaranteed the right to worship in their accustomed manner, [but] that same treaty provided that after proper agencies had been established and schools and churches built the Indians should adopt the customs of civilization in consideration of food and annuities. The subjection of the Sun Dancers to physical torture was contrary to the ideas of civilization and retarded the progress of the red men. (167)

McGillycuddy thus issued a proclamation banning the Sun Dance. He did permit one more dance, so that pledges already made to *Wakan Tanka* could be fulfilled. After that last dance, McGillycuddy directed that no more vows should be made—or else, they must be fulfilled privately: "If they did make them after this last Sun Dance, they must go to some secluded spot in order to execute their promise—it must not be done in public" (168). McGillycuddy promised to withhold rations from any full-blood and imprison any half-breed who danced. Any white man who attended a ceremony would incur expulsion. Red Cloud and Little Chief threatened to rebel against

---

13. In assessing *McGillycuddy: Agent*, Hyde says that the author, Julia B. McGillycuddy, "is far from reliable" (1956, 88–89n). As McGillycuddy's second wife, she did not witness the events described during this period, and her attitude toward her husband is quite worshipful. For all that, the book is a useful guide to McGillycuddy's attitudes and interpretation of events.

the edict, but McGillycuddy characterizes these threats as "but a last bid for authority" (168).

McGillycuddy describes this "last Sun Dance" as a cause célèbre, remarking that after years of having been performed in secret, the Sun Dance had become a tourist attraction, "a spectacle for all who reveled in human torture" (168). According to McGillycuddy, letters poured in protesting the ban and asking for permission to attend the last dance, "in spite of the fact that it was a torture dance as well as a stimulus to war" (168). When the dance took place, McGillycuddy played host to distinguished visitors including Capt. John Bourke of Crook's staff and "several ethnologists from Eastern institutions," including Alice Fletcher.

Unfortunately it is not clear exactly when the dance McGillycuddy describes took place. The account in *McGillycuddy: Agent,* which states that the dance took place in 1881, is inconsistent with McGillycuddy's annual report for 1884, which states that, "for the first time" the Sun Dance was not held (CIA, 37). The dance Fletcher described in "The Sun Dance of the Oglalla Sioux" was held in 1882, and, according to Raymond J. DeMallie, it was held on the Rosebud Reservation (Walker 1980, 56). Capt. John G. Bourke, however, described a dance at Pine Ridge in 1881 that appears to correspond to McGillycuddy's "last great dance" (Dorsey, 464–66; Porter, 89–94). George E. Hyde believes that this dance took place in 1881, "although McGillycuddy's failure to refer to the matter in any of his reports has caused some doubt whether the event fell in 1880 or 1881" (1956, 75). It seems that Mrs. McGillycuddy has conflated several events—the "last great dance" of 1881 and the ban—either for literary reasons or because of a defect in McGillycuddy's memory. If McGillycuddy had issued his ban in 1881, he would have anticipated the official ban by two years. The most probable explanation is that the "last great dance" occurred in 1881, substantially as reported by Bourke, but that this was not the dance held after McGillycuddy's proclamation, which was probably issued in 1883, immediately after receipt of the Rules. This would explain McGillycuddy's tolerance of the 1883 dance for which plans would have been well under way when the Rules were received, better than the supposition that McGillycuddy banned the dance in 1881 and tolerated it for two more years.

As we evaluate the work of McLaughlin and McGillycuddy from our present perspective, remember that these men devoted substantial portions of their lives to effecting a policy that they, in agreement with the recognized experts, believed was in the best interest of the Lakota. The reform agenda was a genuinely humanitarian response to the army's slaughter of the Indians, and its shortcomings must be attributed to lack of vision rather than to ill will. However, the reform agenda itself required considerable force. Since, in the context of the day, civilizing and Christianizing meant the same thing, the reformers believed that to save the Indians, they had to destroy their religion and culture. The Sun Dance, as the "most savage expression of savage religion," was the most obvious target, and the agents used methods ranging from direct intervention by the Indian police to the threat of withholding rations to prevent it. Since Christianization was to be accomplished by the vigorous repression of traditional religion, the Lakota were in effect driven to the Christian churches as the only available alternative for religious community—entailing the acceptance of the gods of the nation that conquered them in return for that sense of community necessary to their survival as a people.

The effectiveness of the ban is a matter of emphasis. As a blow to the medicine men, it was undoubtedly quite effective, since the status and pecuniary rewards of the holy man were closely tied to the Sun Dance and to healing. In purely economic terms, the Sun Dance was probably the more profitable activity. Each dancer required the services of a holy man, which provided employment for as many as fifty holy men in the larger dances. It may also be assumed that, as the masters of the dance, the holy men received more than their share of the massive redistribution of wealth that took place at the dance. Participation in the Sun Dance also conferred higher status on the holy men, not all "medicine men" being qualified to assist with the dance. The banning of the Sun Dance thus abrogated not only their position of leadership in the tribe, but also their primary source of income. The collateral ban on native medicine, which was necessarily more difficult to enforce, endangered their only other source of income. In economic terms, the holy men were undoubtedly hit hard by the ban, and in this sense it can be termed effective.

But as McGillycuddy's proclamation implies and the evidence of the agents' annual reports confirms, it would be naïve to suppose that the ban completely ended the Sun Dance. What it stopped was the annual communal dance near the agencies. An offhand remark of Albert H. Kneale, agent at Standing Rock for sixteen months in 1913 and 1914, indicates that the dance persisted there, wisely unremarked in McLaughlin's annual reports. In the context of a discussion of how the Indians "fritter away the summer months" by attending the camp meetings of each denomination in turn during May and June, Kneale flatly states, "July was devoted to the Sun Dance" (265). This was some thirty years after McLaughlin declared the dance extinct (CIA 1884, 54).

With the last communal Sun Dances of the 1880s, however, the Sun Dance changed forever. Although it continued as an underground performance in the outlying areas, it was no longer the great communal festival that united all the people in the social group in an annual affirmation of their identity and solidarity. Instead, it increasingly became the property of a subgroup, the community of those who were committed to its continuance despite its illegality and the possible consequences of its performance. What had been the possession of the entire community became the province of a voluntary community, and the societal functions of the dance—including its special role in making leaders and effecting the redistribution of wealth—were necessarily attenuated.

In other words, if the dance continued under the ban, it could not prosper. Since the Sun Dance was the central communal ritual in the traditional complex, the ban was certainly "a shattering emotional blow" to the Sioux (Utley, 33). This was precisely its intention. The Rules were meant to force the Indians to adopt white ways. In reality, as Prucha says, they merely created "dispirited communities" (1985, 44). In an insightful sociological study published in 1946, Gordon Macgregor interprets the Sun Dance as a drama of Dakota culture, and holds its repression largely responsible for the widespread disintegration of Dakota society.

> The prohibition of the Sun dance took away not only much of the security which religion gave to the people but also the public rewarding and sanctioning of social life and social institutions. The

ending of this reinforcement of the Dakota custom and the instruction of young people by observation and participation contributed
greatly to the weakening of social controls and the crumbling of
Dakota culture." (Macgregor, 91)

According to Macgregor, the religious value of the Sun Dance was
the attainment of power and strength for the community and the
winning of divine favor for the continuance of the tribe and its food
supply. Its social value was to publicly reaffirm solidarity with the
tribe and band and to reward the behavior sanctioned by Dakota
culture (90). In this sense, it could be said that the ban succeeded too
well, by completely demoralizing the community. The loss of the annual communal Sun Dance was a serious loss for which its continuance underground was hardly an adequate substitute. By removing
the sanctioning mechanism for social control, the ban clearly contributed to social disintegration. By disenfranchising the holy men, the
leaders best equipped to deal with change, the ban probably retarded meaningful adaptation and social change.

Some of the psychological effects of the ban on individual persons can be discerned in Wilson D. Wallis's study of the Sun Dance
of the Canadian Dakota, which is based on fieldwork done in 1914.
Wallis reports that considerable distress and psychological conflict
was experienced by persons who had not fulfilled earlier Sun Dance
pledges. One of Wallis's informants was ill and had suffered the
death of all six of his children. After being treated by the local medicine men without result, he applied to Wanduta, a "clown medicine-
man," to treat him. Wanduta told him that his troubles were caused
by his failure to dance the Sun Dance as he had been directed, a fact
that was hidden from the other medicine men. After dancing, the
man recovered his health. Another informant recalled this dance as
having taken place about 1910, quoting the principal as saying, "If I
must go to jail for making it, then let them put me in jail, but I shall
feel better for having done it" (333). The dance, however, took place
at night.

The ceremony started at dark and was over before sunrise. The
singers wanted me to continue the dance through the day, but I
told them I was afraid to do this because it was against the law to
have the sun dance. When I danced only at night the white people

would not be apprised of it, and, as for continuing during the day, the *wakan* beings knew that it was contrary to law: So it would be all right if I performed it at night and not at all through the day. (332)

Despite this suggestion that the powers understood the ban, Wallis's informants state that the thunders are zealous to persecute those who have defaulted on their vows, a number of his accounts stressing this feature.

The demoralizing effect of the ban can also be discerned in the Sioux Ghost Dance of 1890, which expressed a deep yearning for a return to traditional lifeways. Since the Sun Dance embodied many of the same traditional values, it is unlikely that the Ghost Dance would have been as popular among the Sioux if the Sun Dance had not been banned. The acceptance of the Ghost Dance by the Sioux can thus be directly attributed to the ban. In the context of the ban, the Ghost Dance filled a void for the Sioux, as is evident from the way in which it quickly acquired the trappings of the Sun Dance, including the center pole (Holler 1984a, 31–32). However, since there was no torture involved in the Ghost Dance, the emphasis being instead on obtaining a vision of one's dead relations through a trance, the Sioux Ghost Dance cannot be regarded simply as a variant form of the Sun Dance. Rather, it replaced the Sun Dance or functioned as a substitute for it, taking on much of its function and meaning. According to a statement by Congregational missionary Mary Collins, Sitting Bull's Ghost Dance "became almost like the Sun dance and was continued from evening until morning and from dawn till night. . . . As the excitement grew, the dance became wilder and more excited. People gathered by the thousands and the dance became more and more like the sun dance which was forbidden by the government" (Vestal 1934, 65). Unfortunately Collins does not specify the behavior that led her to make this association, so we are left to speculate as to the precise nature of this dance.

In conclusion, although it was the forward-looking churchmen and humanists who banned the Sun Dance, the experiment did not turn out precisely as they had planned. On the one hand, the dance was not completely repressed, but continued underground. In addition, the Ghost Dance craze and the subsequent massacre at Wounded Knee in December 1890 might never have happened if the Sun Dance had not been banned. On the other hand, it could also be said that the ban worked too well, resulting in substantial long-term damage to the fabric of Sioux culture. By disenfranchising the tribe's spiritual leadership and driving traditional religion underground, the ban took away much of the community's spiritual strength and removed a major source of the resilience necessary to weather change. In the end, it probably also retarded religious adaptation. Denied the opportunity to adapt and develop naturally, in dialog with Christianity and outside influences, traditional religion remained in a largely static state, hidden underground where repression had relegated it. With the virtue of hindsight, it might be said that meaningful change could have been effected more quickly with a policy of religious tolerance. In the context of the 1880s, however, there was no such alternative, and the cultural genocide of the reform policy, despite its brutality, was decidedly better than the real thing.

Although the beginning of the ban can be precisely dated by the issuance of the Rules for Indian Courts in 1883, the end of the ban is a matter of interpretation. John A. Anderson photographed a Sun Dance in 1910, presumably on the Rosebud, in which dancers are shown with ropes tied around their chests as a substitute for piercing (Doll and Alinder, n.p.). This probably indicates that this dance was public, so pressure against the Sun Dance may have been subsiding somewhat at that time. Steinmetz has evidence of large, well-attended dances at Kyle in 1917, 1918, and 1919. The first two were dedicated to the war, and the third to the Allied victory. According to Steinmetz, four men were pierced in 1917 (1990, 28). However, the ban was reaffirmed in 1921 by Charles H. Burke, the commissioner of Indian Affairs, in a circular letter on the subject of Indian dances. The letter is apparently a response both to agitation for Indian religious freedom by reformers such as John Collier and concerns by others that Indian dancing retarded the progress of the Indians toward civilization. In the letter, Burke said that the dance per se should not be condemned, but he also called for the enforcement of the regulations against Indian offenses for "acts of self-torture," immorality, and sacrifice of property (Prucha 1984, 801). In 1923, Burke supplemented his letter with a "Message To All Indians" that called for the end of dances that interfered with work.

It is not right to torture your bodies or handle poisonous snakes in your ceremonies. All such extreme things are wrong and should be put aside and forgotten. You do yourselves and your families great injustice when at dances you give away money or other property, perhaps clothing, a cow, a horse or a team and wagon, and then after an absence of several days go home to find everything going to waste and yourselves with less to work with than you had before. (Prucha 1984, 802)

This directive indicates that the giveaway continued to be a major concern. Although Burke reaffirmed the ban, he encountered major opposition from Collier, and his effort to strengthen the Indian courts legislatively was defeated. Perhaps partly because of the public debate, large Sun Dances without piercing were held in 1928 at Rosebud and in 1929 at Pine Ridge. The eminent Oglala holy man, Frank Fools Crow, mentions these dances in his autobiography, and dates his public involvement with the Sun Dance from the dance in 1929 (Mails 1979, 117–18). According to Steinmetz, Fools Crow also specified that the dance was held annually without piercing from 1929 forward (1990, 28).

The official situation was to change radically with the "Indian New Deal." In 1934, Collier, now commissioner of Indian Affairs, issued a circular letter, "Indian Religious Freedom and Indian Culture," that directed employees of the Indian Service to steer a new course: "No interference with Indian religious life or ceremonial expression will hereafter be tolerated. The cultural liberty of Indians is in all respects to be considered equal to that of any non-Indian group" (Prucha 1984, 951).[14]

Consequently 1934 is often given as the date for the end of the ban, following Macgregor (91). It is not clear, however, what effect, if any, Collier's directive had on the Lakota Sun Dance. Stephen Feraca states that most Oglalas believe that the first contemporary Sun Dance was held in 1934, the entire celebration, including all other dances, being known as the first annual Sun Dance (11). Although

14. Christopher Vecsey points out that the Jesuits responded strongly to Collier's visit to Pine Ridge in September 1932, and interprets his agenda as the cause of a significant retrenchment among the Jesuits that played into the recriminations over *Black Elk Speaks*, which ultimately helped end their experiment with Lakota catechists (n.d., 36–39).

this indicates that the dance was held in 1934 and in subsequent years, the exact status and importance of these dances is unclear. Fools Crow does not mention them in his autobiography, and they went unnoticed by field workers in 1942–43, who characterized the *yuwipi* as the "only continuing cult of the old Dakota religion" (Macgregor, 98). As far as the literature is concerned, the Sun Dance completely sinks from sight in the thirties and forties, making it seem likely that Collier's directive had little practical effect. Apparently, whatever public dancing took place in this period was without piercing, since the earliest date given for the resumption of piercing in the literature is Fools Crow's statement that he was required to obtain official permission to pierce eight men in 1952 (Mails 1979, 119). Fools Crow's description of the first piercing after the ban is discussed in the next chapter, which notes that various dates have been given for this event. Since sacrifice is essential to the Lakota form of the dance, it seems best to consider that the ban on the Lakota Sun Dance ended with the first public Sun Dance performed with piercing, whenever it is deemed to have occurred, not with Collier's directive, which officially ended the ban in 1934.

5

Black Elk and the Revival of the
Sun Dance

As the previous chapter indicates, traditional religion was kept alive underground during the ban (1883–1933), which persisted in a de facto form at least until the early 1950s. But there is no doubt that it suffered a decline. During this period, the dominant reservation institutions, the Catholic Church and the government, were implacably opposed to traditional Lakota religion, but even discounting the continuing opposition to traditional religion, by 1950 the classic Sun Dance was largely an anachronism. Seven decades of reservation life, bringing vast economic and social change, had made it largely irrelevant to contemporary life. It was a case of arrested development. Life no longer revolved around war and the buffalo hunt, the primary symbolic touchstones of the Sun Dance. Denied the opportunity to develop and respond organically to cultural and economic changes, but kept alive by individual holy men as an underground tradition, traditional religion remained in a largely static state. The Sun Dance, which stood at the center of the traditional ritual complex, had lost its central importance.[1]

Many holy men contributed to the revival of traditional religion, but by far the best documented—and probably the most influen-

1. Writing in 1946, Gordon Macgregor characterized the *yuwipi* as the only continuing cult of traditional Lakota religion (98). Although, as I argue previously, this overlooks the persistence of the Sun Dance as an underground performance, it is probably accurate in estimating the popularity and influence of the *yuwipi* as much greater during this time.

tial—agent of change was Black Elk. To briefly reprise the material presented in the first chapter, Black Elk first came to tribal prominence as a leader of the Ghost Dance in 1890. In 1904, Black Elk accepted Catholicism, becoming a catechist and symbol of the Catholic Church on the reservation. Black Elk came to national prominence when he was interviewed in 1931 by John G. Neihardt, who was looking for an informant on the Ghost Dance. The outcome of their meeting, *Black Elk Speaks* (1932), greatly upset the reservation's Jesuits because Neihardt, who was clearly at pains to portray Black Elk as an unspoiled traditionalist, omitted all mention of Black Elk's conversion to Catholicism and subsequent work as a catechist. Despite its traditionalist slant, Neihardt's focus on the past in *Black Elk Speaks* itself tends to distort Black Elk's traditionalism by creating the impression that he regarded traditional religion and culture as dead. Black Elk's views are somewhat better represented by his collaboration with Joseph Epes Brown, *The Sacred Pipe*, which presents Black Elk's program for traditional religion, worked out in close dialogue with Catholicism. The premise of the book is that traditional religion and Catholicism are both valid expressions of ultimate truth and that both may be professed together by Indians. To drive home his point, Black Elk describes a seven-rite ritual complex that parallels the seven Catholic sacraments (Holler 1984b). In the process, he takes the opportunity to reinterpret and reinvent traditional religion, adapting it to contemporary reservation life. Ultimately, Black Elk's continuing influence on Lakota religion is due to his creative compromise with Catholicism, which led to an atmosphere of increased tolerance, and to the fact that the reinterpretation of traditional religion represented by *The Sacred Pipe* helped release it from the period of arrested development imposed on it by the ban.

The Sun Dance seems to have been largely quiescent when Brown interviewed Black Elk in 1948. Black Elk's account of the dance could thus be construed as an argument for its revival as a central, public ritual. Black Elk characterizes the Sun Dance as "one of our greatest rites,"[2] performed annually in June or July, coinci-

2. This is an interesting statement, since one would have expected Black Elk to characterize the Sun Dance as "our greatest rite." If it is to be taken literally, it may reflect the relatively low status of the Sun Dance at the time Black Elk spoke.

dent with the full moon. Instead of describing a historical dance, Black Elk tells how "the first Sun Dance" was received in a vision and performed by Kablaya "many, many winters after our people received the sacred pipe" (1953, 67). Kablaya is apparently not a historical figure; according to Buechel, the word means "to make level by beating, e.g. a holy place; to open, as the eyes of a young dog for its first sight" (270). This elegant story-telling device allows Black Elk to speak directly to his contemporaries, enabling him to be prescriptive without discussing or criticizing actual dances. Since Kablaya explains the Sun Dance as *Wakan Tanka*'s response to the fact that "we have now become lax in our prayers, and our people are losing their strength," it is clear that the occasion for this "first Sun Dance" corresponds precisely with Black Elk's contemporary situation (68).

Since *The Sacred Pipe* has been taken for so long as an unvarnished account of the actual state of aboriginal Lakota religion, it is worth emphasizing that it is no such thing. For one thing, it should be obvious that it is the Catholic Church, not aboriginal Lakota religion, that has a seven-rite ritual complex.[3] Since there is no mention of a seven-rite Lakota ritual complex in the literature before *The Sacred Pipe*, Black Elk has clearly conformed traditional religion to the Catholic model for the purpose of comparing and equating the two. Second, it should be perfectly clear from the foregoing discussion of the classic Sun Dance that Black Elk's Sun Dance is not a description of a historical dance. It is instead an ideal Sun Dance like Walker's. The situation and essential thrust of Black Elk's dance is the need for revival, which was hardly an issue in aboriginal times. The themes and emphases of his dance are clearly a response to his own times, and the entire exposition is put in the mouth of a "historical" figure simply as a "literary" (or storyteller's) device. No Sun Dance in the literature resembles Black Elk's dance in its emphasis on the theme that "the people shall live." Furthermore, his dance is unique in its interpretation and symbolic language. The Sun Dance presented in *The Sacred Pipe* is thus primarily a product of Black

3. The Episcopal Church, the second most influential denomination among the Oglala, also acknowledges seven sacraments, although the role of the sacraments in the teaching of the Episcopal Church is somewhat less prominent than in Roman Catholicism.

Elk's religious imagination, a traditionalist Sun Dance for his own time, described imaginatively as literature or story rather than performed as ritual.

In accord with Black Elk's imaginative framework, Kablaya received the Sun Dance in a vision. He informed the elders, who in turn called a conference to discuss the matter. They finally consulted the Keeper of the Pipe, who accepted the dance as one of the seven ways of prayer to *Wakan Tanka* promised by the White Buffalo Calf Woman. Kablaya then initiated four days of preparations, which began with the construction of the preparations tipi. The list of required equipment included red and blue paint, eagle tail feathers, and eagle-bone whistles (68–69). While instructing the singers, Kablaya explained that the cottonwood tree was the center of the dance, representing the way of the people, which stretched from heaven to earth (69).

Kablaya characterized the Sun Dance as an especially powerful way of prayer and expressed the hope that through its performance the people would receive wisdom and assistance in walking the sacred path of traditional culture. After instructing the onlookers to cry "O Grandfather, *Wakan-Tanka,* I offer the pipe to You that my people may live!" (70), Kablaya taught the singers four songs. The first and fourth were wordless. The second expressed the central theme of Black Elk's dance, "Wakan-Tanka, have mercy on us, / That our people may live!" and the third invoked the buffalo: "They say a herd of buffalo is coming; / It is here now! / Their blessing will come to us. / It is with us now!" (70). Kablaya then specified the construction and meaning of certain ritual objects: the eagle-bone whistle, an otter-skin necklace incorporating a cross and eagle feathers, a circle representing heaven, and representations of the moon, the morning star, the sun, the earth, and the buffalo. The sun was red with a blue center, the circle of heaven was blue, and the earth was red. Each dancer was to wear one of these symbols, which incidentally indicates that Black Elk anticipated relatively few pledgers. Kablaya's remarks on this occasion emphasized the communal aspects of the dance: "In this great rite you are to offer your body as a sacrifice in behalf of all the people, and through you the people will gain understanding and strength. Always be conscious of these things which I have told you today; it is all *wakan!*" (72).

On the second day, Kablaya sent his helper to locate the tree and mark it with sage so that it could be found by the war party. On their return, the scouts charged the place selected for the dance lodge, circling it sunwise. Kablaya then questioned the scouts about the whereabouts of the enemy, Black Elk explaining editorially, "for you see we are here regarding the tree as an enemy who is to be killed" (73). The scouts then dressed for war and returned to the tree, which was addressed directly by Kablaya: "When you stand at the center of the sacred hoop you will be the people, and you will be as the pipe, stretching from heaven to earth" (74). The victory dance ensued, and four men struck the tree with an ax, first having given kill talks. The final blow was struck by someone "with a quiet and holy nature" (75). The tree was not allowed to hit the ground when it fell but was carried back to camp on sticks, the procession making four stops. After the final stop, the warriors charged the camp with the tree.[4]

Kablaya, to whom Black Elk tellingly refers as the "chief priest" rather than as the intercessor, then repaired to the preparations tipi along with the pledgers. Sweetgrass was burned and a small replica of a drying rack was constructed for a pipe rack. The pipe was purified and leaned against the rack. This interpretation of the pipe rest as a drying rack is one of the many instances of Black Elk's retention of the buffalo symbolism of the dance. The other ritual objects and the pledgers were then purified in the smoke, the first of many rituals of purification specified by Black Elk. Kablaya offered the pipe, which was sealed and not smoked. Another pipe was taken to the hole, which was censed with sweetgrass. The tree was painted with red stripes and touched with buffalo fat. A buffalo skin was attached to the top of the tree along with a small cherry tree to which a buckskin bag containing fat was affixed. Images of a man and the buffalo were attached to the tree "just underneath the place where the tree forks," and fat was placed in the hole. After Kablaya prayed that the

4. These preliminary ceremonies, which are like the preliminaries observed in the classic dance, are more elaborate than those attested in the contemporary dance, perhaps because the preparations for the dance are no longer attended by the entire community. Note that Black Elk retains most of the war symbolism in these preliminary ceremonies, but not in the dance itself.

earth would always be fat and fruitful, the tree was raised in four stages. All creatures then rejoiced, flourishing under the protection of the tree, which "helps us all to walk the sacred path; we can lean upon it, and it will always guide us and give us strength" (80).[5]

A "little dance" was performed, and the lodge was erected. Black Elk specifies that twenty-eight poles are to be placed from the uprights to the center pole, making the mystery circle more of a closed space, which Black Elk describes as a model of the universe with *Wakan Tanka* at the center (80–81). This description is unique in the literature, the nearest approach being Schwatka's description of the shade as being augmented by items thrown on the ropes running between the shade and the center pole (756).[6]

Consider the construction of this dance lodge. In the first place, the radius of the inner circle would be strictly determined by the length of the twenty-eight diagonal poles. Since trees are relatively scarce on the plains, thirty feet might be regarded as the outside limit for these poles. The diameter of the area inside the uprights would thus be about twenty feet. Allowing six feet all around for the spectators, if they were to be accommodated within the structure, the danceable area would be about twenty-four feet, or twelve feet on each side of the center pole. At the very least, this would indicate that Black Elk anticipated a relatively small dance by the standards of the classic dances described in the first two chapters. Even given its relatively small size, it seems that this structure would be difficult to build, even if the timber could be found. It would necessarily be a permanent structure. The diagonals would have to be lashed to the center pole, and it might prove difficult to raise them into position,

5. In explaining his vision to Neihardt, Black Elk describes the flowering stick: "This stick will take care of the people and at the same time it will multiply. We live under it like chickens under the wing. We live under the flowering stick like under the wing of a hen. Depending on the sacred stick we shall walk and it will be with us always. From this we will raise our children and under the flowering stick we will communicate with our relatives—beast and bird—as one people. This is the center of the life of the nation" (DeMallie 1984, 129–30).

6. These supporting ropes are not structurally necessary if the tree has been dug sufficiently deep into the ground, and they have not been observed in the contemporary revival of the dance.

which would presumably have to be done after the center tree was raised. Also, as Brown's illustration suggests, this arrangement would create quite a bit of shade inside the circle. For this and other reasons, I am inclined to believe that this apparent innovation results from an error in translation and that Black Elk intended only that there be twenty-eight uprights. If the closing of the lodge was really intended by Black Elk, the resulting ritual space might be interpreted as moving the Sun Dance closer to Christianity, by imitating its closed ritual space.[7]

In any case, after finishing the lodge, Kablaya's warriors dressed and painted themselves in preparation for dancing smooth the ground inside the lodge. The leader of the dancers was selected by the chiefs. He then led a dance in the shape of a cross, inscribing a path within the circle.[8] The *inipi* (the sweat lodge ritual of purification) followed, with the pledgers' buffalo robes being placed on top of the sweat lodge for purification. Kablaya then offered the pipe and commented on the dance. A woman was present to represent White Buffalo Calf Woman. After the *inipi,* the men returned to the preparations tipi and the dancers and ritual objects were again purified, as was the drum. From this point on, the dancers were not permitted to touch their bodies, sticks being provided for the purpose. The pledgers then donned the sacred symbols, Kablaya wearing the symbol of the heavens. The men also put on rabbit skins, representing "humility, because [the rabbit] is quiet and soft and not self-asserting—a quality which we must all possess when we go to the center of the world" (85).

The dancers, led by the woman with the pipe, circumambulated the lodge sunwise, crying the theme of Black Elk's dance: "O *Wakan-*

7. If one were to conclude either that the lodge was impossible to build or that Black Elk never intended for it to be built, it might bolster Steltenkamp's suggestion that Black Elk was only indulging in a thought experiment, without intending the revitalization of the dance.

8. The addition of this cross seems to be Black Elk's innovation. It also seems to be the only possible instance of Black Elk's incorporation of Christian symbolism into the ritual of the dance (as opposed to Christian interpretation of the ritual). Black Elk does not interpret the chokecherry bundle as a cross or indicate otherwise that the tree itself is seen as a cross.

Tanka, be merciful to me, that my people may live! It is for this that I am sacrificing myself" (87). In response, the spectators—representing the people—cried. The pledgers then danced for the remainder of the day and night. Black Elk interprets this first night as symbolizing the night of ignorance. Since truth is a Christian theme, this interpretation indicates Black Elk's dialogue with Catholicism. The dance was interrupted shortly before dawn, and offerings were made outside the lodge at the cardinal points.

At dawn, Kablaya and the Keeper of the Pipe entered the lodge. Kablaya made an altar, first burning sweetgrass and praying that this offering would "make all things and all beings as relatives to us; may they all give to us their powers, so that we may endure the difficulties ahead of us" (88). The altar was a circle with a cross inscribed in it,[9] oriented to the cardinal points. A bed of sage was laid to the east of the altar for the buffalo, "who gives us our food, and who makes the people happy" (90). The buffalo skull was then laid on the sage. As offerings to the buffalo, sage was placed in the eye holes and a bag of tobacco was tied on the south horn, a piece of deerskin being tied on the north horn. A red line was painted around the skull and a red line was drawn from the forehead to the tip of the nose, associating the buffalo with the earth (91).

The pledgers assembled at the entrance of the lodge to greet the sun, dancing around the cardinal points at sunrise. The dancers then sat on beds of sage as their paint was removed with sage—another ritual of purification, a strong theme of Black Elk's dance. Wreaths of sage decorated with eagle plumes were placed on their heads. (Black Elk associates the wreaths with the stars and planets, a sign that minds and hearts were close to *Wakan Tanka.*) The dancers were then painted red from the waist up, including the face. A black circle was drawn around the face, representing *Wakan Tanka.* A black line was drawn on each cheek and the chin. The four lines together

9. The cross in the altar is not an innovation, being attested by Densmore (1918, 122, pl. 20). The figure of a square with "horns"—a solid square superimposed on a cross, so that the lines of the cross do not meet—representing the four winds is attested in the Sun Dance altar by both Walker (1979, 69) and Fletcher (1883, 583–84; 1884, 284 n. 6; see Dorsey 454).

represented the four directions. Black Elk dissociates the color black from the warpath, stating that black represents ignorance and the stripes represent "the bonds which tie us to the earth" (92). The stripes reached only as high as the breasts, where the thongs were attached. The thongs thus represent "rays of light from *Wakan-Tanka*." Since the stripes are ignorance, "when we tear ourselves away from the thongs, it is as if the spirit were liberated from our dark bodies" (92). Black Elk makes his only explicit reference to the modern dance at this point, saying that only recently has each man been painted differently, according to his vision. Unfortunately it isn't clear exactly what period "recently" refers to, for it seems clear that the dancers were painted differently throughout the historical period.

Kablaya then directed that the pledgers be purified again and that they don the sacred symbols. They stood and saluted the tree, blowing their whistles. Kablaya prayed and chanted, "O *Wakan-Tanka*, be merciful to me! / I am doing this that my people may live!" (93). The dancers then moved to the east and affirmed the sacred path of traditional culture: "Our Grandfather, *Wakan-Tanka*, has given to me a path which is sacred!" (93). At the south, the chant was to the buffalo. As the other dancers cried, Kablaya was thrown to the ground and pierced in both breasts.[10] On being stood up, he danced until breaking free, which he accomplished one side at a time. (Black Elk interprets the significance of the *two* thongs as a reminder that the many is really one.) The basic style of Kablaya's dance was that of pulling back from the tree, not dancing on tiptoe. The second dancer was pierced four times and tied to the center of four posts. The third was pierced four times and carried four buffalo skulls on his back. The fourth dancer gave twelve pieces of flesh, which were left as an offering at the foot of the tree. The fifth dancer gave eight pieces, the sixth four pieces, and the seventh, two pieces. The one female dancer gave one piece of flesh (95–96). Both the dancer carrying the skulls and the one tied to the posts were freed after break-

10. This should probably not be interpreted as a requirement that the intercessor be pierced in each dance. Because this is the first Sun Dance, Kablaya's piercing is necessary to enact his vision.

ing two of their bonds (96–97). Black Elk explained that the men showed no pain: "Our men were brave in those days and did not show any signs of suffering; they were really glad to suffer if it was for the good of the people" (95).[11] Those giving flesh offerings were taken to the tree.[12] After breaking free or giving flesh, the pledgers continued to dance.

The dance ended at sunset on the second day with the smoking of the pipe by the dancers, who asked of *Wakan Tanka* the favor "that their people may walk the holy path of life and that they may increase in a sacred manner" (97). This final prayer of the dancers expresses the essential petition of Black Elk's dance. Kablaya echoes the last words of Christ in the final ritual of the dance: "O *Wakan-Tanka*, this sacred place is Yours. Upon it all has been finished.[13] We rejoice!" (98). All ritual objects and equipment, save the buffalo robes and whistles, were left in the center of the lodge with the buffalo skull on top, returning them to the earth. The people then rejoiced, and the children were allowed to play tricks on their elders. The dancers returned to the preparations tipi to prepare for a final *inipi*. In the sweat lodge, Kablaya informed the dancers that their bodies were now holy and that they would be leaders of the people. The pipe was smoked again, and Kablaya summed up the meaning of the dance: "By your actions today you have strengthened the sacred hoop of our nation. You have made a sacred center which will always be with you, and you have created a closer relationship with all things of the universe" (99–100).[14] After the *inipi*, a feast ensued.

11. The Sun Dance is the occasion for displays of stoicism, not emotionalism.

12. It would only be practicable to have those giving flesh offerings approach the tree if the number of pledgers were relatively small. In the dance I observed in 1983, which is described later, the flesh offerings were given in the outer portion of the mystery circle proper, adjacent to the shade.

13. Probably intended to recall the last words of Jesus on the cross in the Johannine tradition (John 19:30), thus relating the sacrifice in the Sun Dance to the sacrifice on the cross.

14. As Kablaya's remarks imply, this final *inipi* should probably be interpreted as something of a debriefing session for the pledgers, giving them a chance to adjust before reentering society and giving the intercessor an opportunity to engage in some final instruction or spiritual direction.

Black Elk's Sun Dance is a contemporary interpretation of the ritual, addressed to the situation on the reservation in his own time. In his reinterpretation of the dance, Black Elk achieves in thought what he might have accomplished in ritual as the intercessor in a contemporary Sun Dance. Although he retains some of the war symbolism, especially in connection with the selection of the tree, his Sun Dance is generally disassociated from war by the interpretation of black as symbolizing ignorance. Although Kablaya is thrown down for the piercing, retaining the "capture/escape" symbolism noted by Walker and others, Black Elk interprets the release as an escape from ignorance, not from enemies. Black Elk also modifies the symbolism of the rabbit skin, which Sword interpreted as "an emblem of fleetness and of endurance" (Walker 1980, 183), interpreting it as representing humility and meekness, decidedly not the traditional virtues of the Lakota warrior. Black Elk's dialogue with Christianity is evident in his stress on the theme of ignorance and in his interpretation of the sacrifice as the liberation of the soul from the body. The mystery circle has also acquired a cross, and the closing of the dance lodge, if it is intended by Black Elk, is a significant approach to the Christian notion of ritual space. Black Elk retains the symbolic role of the buffalo as the provider of plenty, by employing the buffalo skull in the Sun Dance altar. The role of women in the dance is increased by inclusion of a representative of the White Buffalo Calf Woman. This innovation might be interpreted as an appeal to respect the dance, respect for religion being the point of Black Elk's version of the story of her bringing of the sacred pipe. Since the White Buffalo Calf Woman is so closely associated with the pipe, it might also be taken as a more explicit identification of the pipe with the Sun Dance. On a more literal level, it might be taken as establishing something of a traditional equivalent of Catholic Marian devotion, the Calf Woman functioning somewhat as the equivalent of the Blessed Virgin Mary.

The greatest changes introduced by Black Elk involve the meaning of the dance and the nature of the Sun Dance vow (Holler 1984b, 45–47). Black Elk's Sun Dance emphasizes the needs of the community, becoming a ritual that ensures the survival of the people and enhances their ability to walk the sacred path of traditional culture. Although the theme of the survival of the people is attested in the classic period,[15] it is never interpreted as the reason for making a pledge. In the classic period, pledges are made primarily for success in war. Black Elk does not mention this benefit, or the acquisition of shamanic power by the individual pledger, the power acquired in the dance accruing instead to the people as a whole. Nor does Black Elk mention pledges to effect healing. Some benefits do result to the pledger in Black Elk's dance, but these are not interpreted as reasons for undertaking the dance. Black Elk's vow is primarily undertaken to benefit the people. The pledgers thereby become leaders of the people, having created in themselves a sacred center and a closer relationship to all things. These benefits reflect Black Elk's overwhelming concern with the welfare of the community and incorporate an emphasis on spiritual development probably attributable to Black Elk's experience as a catechist. The benefits anticipated by the pledgers in the classic dance were, in comparison, direct and personal. It is highly significant that Black Elk's Sun Dance benefits the pledgers primarily by enhancing their ability to serve the people.[16]

The influence of the Ghost Dance, with its theme of revival, is omnipresent in Black Elk's dance, for his dance is essentially conceived as a revival, a response to the need to restore the center of the religious life of the people. I will have more to say about Black Elk and the Ghost Dance in the final chapter, which completes my portrait of Black Elk as a religious thinker; I emphasize here that the idea of rejuvenating traditional culture through ritual dance is pre-

15. According to H. G. Webb's account of the Sun Dance of 1883 among the Oglala Dakota, "The object of the Sun Dance seems to have been principally a religious one; first for the purpose of general prayer for the whole tribe, in which they pray the Wakantanka, or Great Spirit to 'have mercy upon all men, to give them horses to ride and buffalo to eat and to clothe themselves with, and as they are but poor lost souls, would he let them have all they could get, and let them live as long as he would allow them'" (2). Webb goes on to mention that the dance is the occasion for thanksgiving after sickness and, in its "civil aspect," for the making of warriors and chiefs.

16. As Julian Rice points out, this is the ideal of traditional leadership (1991, 126). Rice's interpretation of the Sun Dance associates the sacrifice strongly with assuming the role of the buffalo, the protector of the people (126–36).

cisely the essence of the Ghost Dance. The Sun Dance portrayed in *The Sacred Pipe* is as much a product of Black Elk's engagement with the Ghost Dance as with Catholicism.

We now know that the Sun Dance was not entirely defunct when Black Elk collaborated with Brown on *The Sacred Pipe*. It was still being performed, although Black Elk does not say so. It is possible that Black Elk feared that mentioning this fact to Brown would cause another uproar. This point is particularly important in relationship to Steltenkamp's suggestion that Black Elk did not intend to revive the dance. Since it was being performed, it did not need literally to be revived. From Black Elk's point of view, what needed reviving was its influence and central place in the religion of his people. The vehicle for this revival was his sweeping reinterpretation and modernization of the dance. In theological terms, *The Sacred Pipe* is a work of "apologetic," the branch of theology that justifies and explains the faith to outsiders. The irony of the situation is that, from Black Elk's point of view, both the whites and his contemporary Lakotas are to a certain extent "outsiders" with respect to traditional religion. *The Sacred Pipe* clearly intends to assert the validity of traditional religion to both groups, daring to compare it directly with the Christian revelation. He could hardly have done this so convincingly had it not been for his many years as a catechist.

Owing to our extremely limited knowledge of the Sun Dance during the ban, it is simply not possible to determine what form the underground dance may have had in Black Elk's time, although, as I point out later in this chapter, the strongest contemporary link to these dances is probably the dance associated with Frank Fools Crow and held at Three Mile Creek near Kyle, a well-known bastion of Lakota traditionalism. Nor is it possible to determine to what extent Black Elk was aware of contemporary dances, and to what extent—if at all—his remarks might be taken as reflecting or criticizing these contemporary dances. We do know, on the testimony of his daughter, that Black Elk attended a large public dance held on the Pine Ridge in 1928 (Steltenkamp 1993, 107). It could be speculated that Black Elk attended secret dances during the 1930s and 1940s as well.[17]

17. It could be argued that Black Elk might have escaped censure for attending the 1928 dance precisely because it was public and well attended. Remember that it

For that matter, it is even possible that Black Elk assisted with or led dances during this period, although it seems to me that this is very unlikely given the fact that there is no testimony in the oral tradition asserting it.

Since we do not know either the extent of Black Elk's involvement with contemporary dances or their essential shape and features, it is impossible to determine whether some of the elements that appear to be Black Elk's innovations might not have already been incorporated into the dance. For this reason, it is probably best to picture Black Elk as both initiating and exemplifying the kind of processes and changes that were taking place at the time. The dance he describes certainly differs substantially from the classic dances described above, and Black Elk was certainly aware of these differences, having observed the dance in his youth. If one accepts the implications of the gift of the morning star pendant to Neihardt discussed in the first chapter, Black Elk had also officiated at the Sun Dance for a number of years during the ban.

Many of his strictures have been accepted in the contemporary revival of the dance, but at least one essential feature of his dance has not been accepted. Black Elk specifies night dancing, under the full moon, which was a feature characteristic of the classic dance. During the ban, night dancing was discontinued, apparently for security reasons.[18] Although subsequent Sun Dances seem to owe much to Black Elk, night dancing has not been reinstated. As mentioned above, subsequent dances have also placed less emphasis on the scouting and cutting of the tree than Black Elk envisioned. In addition, much of Black Elk's specific symbolic language has not been adopted in the contemporary dance.

Despite the impetus that may have been provided by the publica-

---

took place before the controversy occasioned by the publication of *Black Elk Speaks* in 1932, which might have inhibited Black Elk's ability to attend the Sun Dance, assuming he were so inclined. It might be argued on the other hand that Black Elk would have found it much easier to attend secret Sun Dances held in the outlying areas without attracting notice.

18. As discussed later, Frank Fools Crow attributes the cessation of night dancing to the fact that the men would be missed if they were absent during the night (Mails 1979, 43).

tion of *The Sacred Pipe* in 1953,[19] the revival of the Sun Dance was a lengthy process, taking place against the background of the tribal politics of the fifties, sixties, and seventies. In part because of their ties to the tribal council, dances of this era tend to appear in the literature in an unfavorable light. For instance, Richard H. Ruby, writing in 1955, states that the Sun Dance was revived in 1936 "more for ceremony than for real worship" (83). According to Ruby, "the sun dance today is no longer a religious dance, with special significance. It is more like an ordinary get-together" (85).

Writing in 1963, Stephen Feraca summarizes a number of dances on the Pine Ridge, concentrating on the 1954 dance, when the dancers were led by Fools Crow, although the "director" was George Poor Thunder. This dance had four pledgers who were pierced, only one of whom was Lakota (the others being Cheyenne). Feraca reports that contemporary Lakotas viewed these dances critically, regarding "the annual Northern Arapaho modicine [*sic*] lodge ceremony held on Wind River Reservation in Wyoming as the true Sun Dance" because of the rigorous fasting and practice of night dancing (12). Feraca states that few contemporary Sioux Sun Dances have lasted more than two days and characterizes the Sioux as disinterested in the Sun Dance, which is overshadowed by the social dancing that follows it (12). Feraca points out that souvenir booklets, presumably printed by the tribal council, carried a statement to the effect that "the Sun Dance is held merely as a traditional event recalling the Sioux past, and is in no way a religious ceremony" (13). Although Feraca notes that this statement does not describe the sentiments of the participants, it indicates the spirit in which the dance was sponsored by the tribal council. Throughout this period, the Sun Dance apparently continued to be less important than the *yuwipi*, which Feraca characterizes as the most popular cult on the Pine Ridge and Rosebud (26).

Feraca's account is primarily based on the 1954 dance with details from other dances being introduced to supplement the account. According to Feraca, the selection of the pole was "quite perfunctory" in 1954 (13). The pole was simply dragged behind a truck to the mystery circle, an act that outraged traditionalists (14). Feraca

19. I discuss the influence of *The Sacred Pipe* in the next chapter.

characterizes the decoration of the pole as diverse, utilizing brush bundles, human and buffalo figures, and a red cloth banner. In 1955, the figures were omitted. He considers the brush bundle a borrowing from the Cheyenne, where it represents Thunderbird's nest, but he states that the bundle is widely perceived as a Christian symbol, which, when prominent, turns the tree into a cross. He also notes that Gilbert Bad Wound, one of his informants, considers the Sun Dance a Christian ritual, stating that "he is by no means alone in this belief, citing the similarity between the crucifix and Sun Dance pole, and equating the sufferings of the dancers with the Christian concept of penance" (15). In Feraca's view, participation in the contemporary Sun Dance offers little prestige, no longer even impressing young women. Rather, to dance incurred the censure of many members of the community (16). He describes the dance as loosely structured, noting that he was invited to dance in 1956 only a half hour before the dance began (17). He also notes that fasting is not always observed, saying that he has seen the singers eating watermelon during the rest periods. Feraca also observed dancers wearing sunglasses! (18).

Ethel Nurge provides a brief account of the public Sun Dance at Pine Ridge in 1962, with annotations by Feraca. Nurge observed parts of the third and fourth days of this dance, which had only one pledger who was pierced, Eagle Feather (William Schweigman). (Eagle Feather's considerable involvement in the contemporary dance is discussed below.) Nurge characterizes the tree as quite leafy and about thirty feet high.[20] She mentions the brush bundle at the fork and states that the banners were black at the top, then red, yellow, and white (at the bottom). Effigies of a man and buffalo were present. A medicine pouch hung at head level. Flags marked the cardinal points, although only in two colors, red and yellow. The allegiances of the spectators were apparently mixed, for Nurge states that the dance was denounced from a Christian point of view over one public-address system while the dancers were introduced on another. Sunrise was at 5:10, the sweat lodge ensuing at 6:00 and the procession starting at 6:30. The male pledgers carried pipes and wore sage head-

20. Feraca editorially characterizes the tree as a giant prayer stick (Nurge 1966, 106, n. 5).

bands. They were also equipped with eagle-wing whistles. At 7:05 the dancers left the circle and Eagle Feather was pierced. The piercing was on the left side only, which Feraca considers an innovation introduced by Eagle Feather (1966, 109, n. 10). The dancers returned to the circle and danced while Eagle Feather attempted to break free. Nurge left the dance at this point but was informed that the struggle took "an hour and a half or four full rounds" (109).

Writing in 1972, Thomas H. Lewis describes the public Sun Dances at Pine Ridge from 1967 to 1970. By this time, the Sun Dance had apparently gained ground, for Lewis states that it had "increasingly become the principal social event of the year on the Pine Ridge Reservation" (44). In contrast to Feraca's statement that dancing carries little prestige, Lewis states that "some prestige accrues to the dancer" (48). Lewis contrasts the present sponsorship of the dance by the tribal council with older practices, pointing out that the tribe turned a profit on the dance, publicizing it weeks in advance through posters and print advertising. Having obtained from his informants "few convincing descriptions of abstentions, mentors, instructions or other purificatory acts," he concludes that the ordeal was "something less arduous" than that of 1881 (46). Lewis points out that some dancers were allowed to pledge as late as the evening of the third day, including a political figure and a "partially inebriated" man. He also notes that the "main Sun Dancer" received $150 and that some others danced yearly and received renumeration (about $6 a day and meals). On the other hand, Lewis believes that most would dance without renumeration, the torture providing an "automatic selective process for certain personality types" (47). He encountered a full range of motives for the pledge, including danger, a desire for personal or group power, a desire to obtain tribal welfare, and a desire for shamanic power. Although Lewis is on balance critical of the contemporary dance, stating that "the motives of the dancers are more superficial and even trivial and their sacrifice is certainly less," he states that the sincerity of the pledgers is nonetheless seldom open to question (47). He also noted that there was considerable competition and contention over the qualifications of the intercessor. Former dancers have been known subsequently to hold their own dances, and various misfortunes, including four deaths in 1969, have been popularly ascribed to ritual improprieties.

Lewis characterizes the atmosphere of these Sun Dances as festal, but not necessarily religious, saying that there was plenty to eat and drink, that sexual license was still a feature of the dance, and that "the rate of arrests for drunkenness is quadrupled during Sun Dance days" (48). The dances started at sunrise and lasted until about 11:00 A.M., the dancers fasting only for these hours. The dances Lewis observed lasted either three or four days, the piercing taking place on the final day. He characterizes the average number of participants as six to twelve men and an equal number of women. After the piercing, a receiving line was formed, where the spectators received blessings from the pledgers and the pledgers received contributions. As is typical of accounts of the dance from this period, Lewis compares the modern dance unfavorably with Walker's, saying that "some perfunctory, some syncretistic, and some modernized Sioux religious elements are present" (46).[21] He discerned no trace of the tree being treated as an enemy and no trace of the "capture-torture-captivity-escape" concept. The man and buffalo effigies were observed, as was the chokecherry bundle, which Lewis's informants characterized as "an offering" or "a Cross." Ear piercing was not observed. The dancers were dressed "much as described by Walker" (46). The dance was followed by social dancing and entertainment.

Based on his evidence, Lewis concludes that the function of the Sun Dance has shifted. Formerly a ceremony that united the bands and passed on cultural traditions necessary for the survival of the tribe and the abundance of the buffalo, the Sun Dance now had a more social and economic function: "Much of the spiritual significance is lost in the commercial aspects of the celebration. The ritual as performed today is still awesome and colorful, but it is a mere fragment of the traditional ceremony" (47). Nonetheless, Lewis believes that the fact "that the Sun Dance was revivable at all is remarkable" and pointed out that the "nuclear ceremonial forms," among which he numbers the lodge, the pole, the dress of the dancers, the pipe ceremonies, the mentors and candidates, and the use of partici-

---

21. This is a good example of the assumption that adaptation is degeneration, which pervades the descriptions of these dances held by the tribal council. Perhaps it should be taken as representing the impression left by these dances, which were controlled not by the holy men but by the council.

pation to gain status were virtually unchanged (48). He concludes by suggesting that in a conservative culture, repressed cultural traits may be dormant and not extinct.

William K. Powers, an anthropologist who has attended fourteen Sun Dances, states that no two have been performed exactly the same (1977, 139). According to Powers, piercing did not take place until 1960,[22] although one or more dancers have been pierced each year since that time, thirty being pierced in 1972 (many of them AIM members). Unfortunately Powers fails to describe the ritual of the contemporary dance, presenting instead an idealized account of the dance derived from Walker! (95–100). From this perspective, he is critical of the contemporary dance, noting that the tribal council increases the price for admission and photography during the piercing portions of the dance, something that the [real] Oglalas regard as ludicrous. This "crass commercialism" (140) led to conflict between the tribal council and the traditionalists, making the Sun Dance an "arena in which the traditionalists and bureaucrats air their factional differences" (142). Noting that the traditionalists regard the dance as sacred despite its commercial aspects, Powers ascribes to the Sun Dance the function of a "powerful mediating force" between the traditional and the modern (143). In a later piece, Powers evaluates the modern dance very negatively, stating that "the sun dance, under the sponsorship of the Oglala tribal council, which presents it as a tourist attraction, has deteriorated to the point where it is little more than an unsuccessful side show—a flesh carnival, if you will—in which the audience is invited to watch the spectacular [sic] of self-inflicted pain" (Nurge 1970, 287).

The dances held by the tribal council were indeed an increasing source of frustration for traditionalists as the revival of the Sun Dance gained momentum. Amiotte characterizes these dances as "transitional," which is probably a correct interpretation in the light of subsequent events (75). The traditionalists chafed under the control of the tribal council and objected strongly to the presence of tourists, with their cameras and tape recorders, and the tolerance of

22. Feraca tends to confirm this, stating that Eagle Feather was "superficially" pierced in 1960. He apparently pierced again in 1961 as well as at the 1962 dance described by Nurge (Nurge 1966, 108, n. 9).

alcohol abuse. Powers reported in 1970 that traditionalists were contemplating a break with the tribal council's Sun Dance: "The problem has been in the talking stage for eight years, and if they do separate the sun dance from the powwow, it will be a major achievement" (Nurge 1970, 287). According to Thomas Mails, writing in 1978, the separation of the Sun Dance from the tribal council and the powwow has come to pass as the product of a "systematic drive to upgrade [the Sun Dance] and rid it of any appendages which degrade or cheapen it" (1978, 11). Although these statements seem to imply that the traditionalists began holding their own Sun Dances sometime after 1970, it seems more likely—especially in the case of Fools Crow—that they continued their own dances throughout the period under consideration, finally deciding to withdraw their support entirely from the public dance.

The first evidence of these dances is provided by Thomas Mails, whose *Sundancing at Rosebud and Pine Ridge* contains the most extensive pictorial representations and ritual descriptions of the contemporary dance. Although Mails was apparently not permitted to paint, photograph, or describe Fools Crow's Sun Dance for either his biography or for his book on the Sun Dance, he does provide an extensive account of a yearly dance held on the Rosebud by Chief Eagle Feather (William Schweigman), which is based on interviews and observation of the dance from 1974 to 1976.[23] Besides commenting on Eagle Feather's dance, Mails also describes a "Traditional Sun Dance" held at Rosebud in July 1975.[24]

Since Eagle Feather was a major force for the revival of the

23. The Sun Dance may have exhibited more diversity on the Rosebud Reservation than on the Pine Ridge Reservation during the 1970s, for Mails reports that at least five Sun Dances, involving some 120 pledgers, took place on the Rosebud in 1974 (1978, 13).

24. This Sun Dance was an attempt to stage an authentic traditional Sun Dance, the key feature being that the dance extended further into the afternoon than Eagle Feather's dance. The organizers were Lame Deer and George Eagle Elk, assisted by Eagle Feather, and the dance was captured on film. On Mails's account, the dance was botched. The tree was damaged and only ten feet tall, no sweat lodge was held before each day's dance, the pledgers openly drank water and went to the latrine, and "the medicine man who was supposed to be running the Sun Dance" was "really drunk, and now was crying around the Holy Tree" (1978, 223).

dance, it is worth considering his work in some detail. Eagle Feather, a convert to traditional religion, attended the Indian school at St. Francis and later studied to be an Episcopal lay reader. In a 1975 interview with Mails, Eagle Feather stated that he and his wife "have practiced the Indian religion for the last twenty years" (1978, 45). Eagle Feather participated in his first Sun Dance in 1957. In 1958, Eagle Feather asked Fools Crow to pierce him at the dance that summer in Pine Ridge. According to Eagle Feather, the piercing required a letter of authorization from Washington, the consent of the Bureau of Indian Affairs, and the approval of the tribal council. Eagle Feather was also required to execute a document absolving the reservation officials and the Public Health Service from any responsibility (46).[25] Mails reports that Eagle Feather has participated in twenty-eight Sun Dances and that "it is difficult to find a record of a dance held since 1960 that does not mention his presence" (21). Eagle Feather's own account states that he has danced at least once every year since 1957 (46) and has been pierced twenty-five times (124).

Besides a detailed account of Eagle Feather's dance, Mails provides original oil paintings and an extensive photographic record of the 1975 dance, making this dance one of the best represented dances in the literature. Eagle Feather's dance revolves around a core group of pledgers, who return every year. Eagle Feather himself is pierced every year, underscoring the individualism pervading his dance. Of the twelve pledgers in 1974, only five were not holy men. Their stated reasons for undertaking the Sun Dance entail either alcohol abuse or healing, leading Mails to state that "the major-

25. Eagle Feather's account of his first piercing is comparable to Fools Crow's account of the revival of piercing in 1952 (Mails 1979, 119), for both accounts stress the difficulty of obtaining permission for the piercing. Eagle Feather states that when he asked Fools Crow to pierce him, Fools Crow replied, "Brother, I have never pierced a man" (Mails 1978, 46), although Fools Crow states that he pierced eight men in 1952 and does not mention Eagle Feather (Mails 1979, 119). Mails does not comment on the discrepancy. Based on a conversation with Fools Crow, Steinmetz believes that the resumption of piercing most likely took place between 1958 and 1960 (1990, 29), although, as noted above, both Powers and Feraca place the first piercing in 1960. Interestingly, Steinmetz also reports that Fools Crow stated that dances were performed before large crowds in Kyle in 1917, 1918, and 1919. According to Fools Crow, four men were pierced in 1917.

ity of the modern-day vows find their impetus in the devastating liquor problem which plagues the Sioux reservations" (43). Although this generalization seems to be based on insufficient evidence, it clearly applies to Eagle Feather's pledgers. This is emphasized in the dance itself, for Eagle Feather requires each pledger to address the crowd in explanation of his vow, which Mails characterizes as a "confession of past sins, such as excessive drinking and other bad behavior" (44). Eagle Feather acknowledges the problem of backsliding after the dance (150–51).

Eagle Feather requires a vision quest of his pledgers, which is ordinarily undertaken as a group expedition, the participants camping together and dispersing to separate locations for their quest. Those unable to attend are permitted to undertake the quest individually (62). Eagle Feather also emphasizes the sweat lodge, where the darkness represents "the sinfulness of the soul and our ignorance, from which we must now purify ourselves before we Sun Dance" (92). Eagle Feather's interpretation of the darkness is thus like Black Elk's interpretation of the night as representing ignorance. Eagle Feather's sweat lodge fireplace incorporates four horns, making it the "Old Man Four Generations" fireplace (88).

The site of the 1975 dance was the Rosebud Fairground, a permanent facility in Rosebud, South Dakota. The tree, which is selected a year in advance by Eagle Feather, is painted with a single red stripe (126). Eagle Feather's altar is relatively simple. A buffalo skull with nose and nostrils stuffed with sage is placed on a bed of sage near a cherry pipe rack strung with flesh offerings, which is between the black flags that delineate the west entrance of the mystery circle (112). The skull is unpainted. The pledgers fast only from midnight until noon, when they participate in a meal served to the spectators.[26] A sweat lodge is held before each day's dance, which

26. Discussing these matters with more frankness than most, Mails provides a detailed account of the costs of staging a Sun Dance, which he estimates from $1,000 to $3,000 (1978, 78). Noting that Eagle Feather is controversial, apparently for his money-raising practices (21), Mails discusses frankly his contributions to the dances. Mails paid for the printing on one of the flyers illustrated (10), provided three head of cattle for the 1975 dance, and made other contributions (22–23, 76, 78–79). Mails makes it clear that he regards these contributions as fair exchange for the "faithful friendship and dependable information" that makes his books and paintings possible (21).

begins after the sun rises (about 8:00) and continues until about 11:00 A.M. According to Mails, a round lasts about fifteen minutes (228). Four rounds of the dance are usually danced each day. At the end of each round, a pipe is presented at the south, which is smoked only by the medicine man and the singers, not the spectators (145). At the end of each round, a pledger addresses the audience. No mention is made of smudging (censing with burning sweetgrass) the spectators or pledgers, although the use of the eagle-wing fan and whistle are evident. The pledgers who break free after piercing are presented to the spectators for congratulations. Eagle Feather prays in both Lakota and English (178), although the crowd is apparently addressed primarily in English. In 1975, Mails reported that Eagle Feather made a "long address" on the significance and tradition of the Sun Dance. In an admitted innovation, Eagle Feather honors a "Mother of the Year," who comforts the pledgers when they are pierced (148). (Recall Black Elk's innovation of a representative of the White Buffalo Calf Woman.) Eagle Feather regularly distributes healing herbs during the healing portions of the dance. At one point in the 1975 dance, water was offered the pledgers, who refused it as a gesture of sincerity (182). The ritual, which ends with the noon meal, is followed by social dancing.

The piercing at Eagle Feather's dance is almost exclusively of the basic type, although Mails mentions "feather piercing" (192–93). No dragging or suspension of buffalo skulls is mentioned by Mails, although one pledger, Robert Blackfeather, was suspended, or nearly suspended, from the tree. Mails describes this as a "stunning performance" and states that it brought forth "audible cries from the flabbergasted spectators" (192). The length of struggle ranged from minimal to twenty minutes (188, 192). Eagle Feather lays much emphasis on the piercing and flesh offerings; Mails reports that he gave two hundred flesh offerings in 1975. In explanation of the flesh offerings, Eagle Feather states that "the Indian religion is designed to be more painful than any other religion in North America" (124).

Eagle Feather is especially frank about the piercing, which he considers "proves a man's sincerity" (182). Eagle Feather makes parallel knife cuts in preparation for inserting a stick or eagle claw and speaks of piercing deeper than the skin: "Some call it skin and some say flesh—it all depends on how deep you've been gotten. I was pierced pretty deep there in 1974, and I had an awful time pulling it loose. If it was just under my skin I'd have pulled loose right away" (149). Eagle Feather describes the wounds as "very painful" and says that some of the pledgers plead with the intercessor not to pierce them very deeply (149). Apparently in reference to this pleading, Eagle Feather remarks, "This is where the great showdown is!" (150). Mails is skeptical of claims that piercing once involved the muscles but reports that in 1975, after the piercing of a man named Jerry Dragg, "I could see exposed muscle" (192). Eagle Feather rubs dirt on the wounds, but applies no medicine until the sweat lodge after each day's dance.

Despite a slow start in 1975, Mails reports that some five hundred spectators attended the fourth day of the dance. As a convert to traditional religion, Eagle Feather has clearly reinvented the dance, gathering a continuing core of supporters who meet each year to pierce and dance. As such, his ritual arrangements and interpretation of the dance incorporate many innovations. It might be considered that Eagle Feather's dance represents something of a Protestant appropriation of the Sun Dance, given his emphasis on the moral state of the individual pledger, who suffers primarily to effect his own redemption. Although this reading of the dance clearly differs from the more communal focus of the Black Elk tradition, Eagle Feather does share Black Elk's bireligious orientation, equating the Mother of the Year with Mary (148) and the pipe with Christ (90, 143). In complete accord with Black Elk, Eagle Feather says, "I sincerely believe in Almighty God in both the non-Indian and Indian ways, because we pray to one and the same God" (152).

Paul B. Steinmetz provides a description of a dance held at Porcupine from July 30 to August 2, 1979 (1990, 77–82). This dance, held in a relatively urban area of the Pine Ridge Reservation, appears to have been sponsored by the tribal council, given the presence of concession stands. Since Frank Fools Crow was the intercessor, this would seem to be one of the last such Sun Dances to enjoy traditionalist support. Steinmetz estimates attendance at several hundred. Apparently no ceremonies accompanied the selection of the tree, for it arrived on a truck at 10:00 on the evening before the first day. The dancers were camped on the grounds, and Steinmetz mentions that reveille was at 4:30 A.M., followed by separate sweat lodges for the men and women. Before the sweats, the dancers filled their own pipes and placed them on a rack near the lodges.

At 6:45 A.M. the dancers, forty-seven men and twenty-eight women, processed toward the circle. The singers were in the procession and sang the first song without the drum. The pipes were presented to helpers, who placed them on two racks. After each round, the pipes were smoked in turn by the singers. According to Steinmetz, piercing was continuous throughout the four days, twelve being pierced on the first day. On the second day, one man was pierced and a buffalo skull was suspended from his back. On the third day, two men dragged buffalo skulls. Several women were pierced, one on the right shoulder.[27] A woman and her daughter were also pierced, and Steinmetz mentions that all three successfully broke loose.

Steinmetz reported to me in a communication that he made notes on some aspects of the proceedings in his car, and he presents a fairly lengthy transcription of Matthew King's remarks as announcer (80). Because the announcer is integral to the modern dance, these comments are especially valuable, for they provide a running interpretation, not so much on the specific ritual actions that occur during the dance, but on the meaning and significance of the event. They also provide a good introduction to the traditional worldview, and the reader is urged to consult them in their entirety in Steinmetz's text.

Since all the male dancers presumably pierced, along with the three women, the total pierced in this dance would approach fifty. (Steinmetz notes that eleven boys were among the pledgers, and that at least two of these were overcome by heat before breaking free.) At least one of the sacrifices was fairly severe, for Steinmetz notes that a dancer named Dubray tried to drag eleven buffalo skulls. Three dancers could not pull him free by tugging on a rope, and he was joined by another man who pierced and was attached to Dubray's waist by a rope. With the help of other dancers, they both eventually were freed. This sequence of events indicates that Dubray was pierced fairly deeply. Although this dance seems further along in authenticity than the tribal council dances of the 1950s and 1960s, Steinmetz also notes several indications of ceremonial laxity. The number of dancers fluctuated from day to day, and on the third day

---

27. The piercing of women in dances associated with AIM is discussed in the next chapter.

he noticed two teenage boys who had pierced the day before buying sodas at the concession stand. Steinmetz ends his account with the seven Sun Dance songs of Edgar Red Cloud in Lakota and English translation.

The intercessor in several of the tribal council dances described above was Frank Fools Crow. Until his death, Fools Crow was the most respected traditional leader on the Pine Ridge Reservation, and he was probably also the most influential interpreter of the Black Elk tradition. As a central figure in traditional religion on the Pine Ridge for four decades, Fools Crow was a Catholic who remained committed both to Black Elk's concept of bireligion and to the basic tenets of his interpretation of traditional religion. Fools Crow also had the opportunity that circumstances denied Black Elk to conduct public Sun Dances. The dance associated with Fools Crow, which embodies the essential aspects of the Black Elk tradition, is the central traditionalist ritual on the Pine Ridge today. Although this is somewhat speculative, given our scant knowledge of the dance during the ban, it is likely that this dance has the best claim to continuity with the classic dance, both in frequency of annual performance and ritual arrangements.

Fools Crow was born "about the time of the tragic battle at Wounded Knee" in 1890 (Mails 1979, 33), and it is natural that his earliest memories of the Sun Dance revolve around the ban. Fools Crow emphasizes that it is a misconception that the dance was discontinued until the 1928 dance at Rosebud, confirming that the dance was celebrated with piercing at Pine Ridge "in secret nearly every year," the favored time being the last part of July (43). Fools Crow also states that dances were occasionally held without piercing, which were "not flatly outlawed so long as we Sioux did them quietly" (43). Fools Crow indicates that the shape of the modern dance as a four-day celebration with only daylight dancing emerged in response to the ban: "As I said, the Sun Dances with piercing were done in secret and with the threat of arrest always hanging over us. We were even afraid that our Indian police would turn us in, so the men who pledged to do the dance started dancing each day when the sun came up, and quit when the sun went down. They did this every day for four days, going to their homes at night and coming back the next morning" (43).

Fools Crow's vocation as a holy man emerged in his thirteenth year (about 1903), when he received his initial training from the legendary holy man Stirrup, who gave him "some instruction in how to lead a Sun Dance" (41). Fools Crow became a Catholic in 1917 and is "still a practicing Roman Catholic" who goes to mass once or twice a month (45). He accepts the compatibility of traditional religion and Christianity, saying that he and his wife "find few problems with the differences" between the two religions: "Many things we believe about God are the same" (45). He also reports a conversation with Black Elk in which he stated that "the Sioux religious way of life was pretty much the same as that of the Christian churches, and there was no reason to change what the Sioux were doing. We could pick up some of the Christian ways and teachings, and just work them in with our own, so in the end both would be better" (45). Fools Crow accepted Black Elk's position, although he admits some frustration with the set prayers in the prayer book and notes that his adherence to some of the Christian doctrines was qualified in the early days: "Some of the things the new faiths said were hard to take, especially their belief that we did not know the true God and that Sioux medicine and ceremonies were things of the Devil. So we rejected these views until their positions began to change" (45).

According to Fools Crow, in 1927 the agent requested him to lead a Sun Dance without piercing and with tourism in mind: "In other words, they wanted a sideshow without its most sacred aspects: the healing, flesh offerings, and piercings" (109). The idea tormented him, and he undertook a vision quest to clarify his feelings on the subject. Fools Crow subsequently made up his mind that he "would not lead the tourists' Sun Dance yet" (113). The idea clearly outraged Fools Crow's traditionalist sensibilities: "I could hardly believe it! The whites, who had years ago forbidden the Sun Dance, wanted now to show us off to people who would purchase tickets to see us sing and dance! We were to become a Buffalo Bill kind of sideshow . . . while we performed with sincerity what supposedly was the most important dance of our traditional and sacred way of life!" (112).

In 1929, however, Fools Crow did accede to his father's request that he return to the reservation to assist Spotted Crow in a dance at Pine Ridge.[28] The dance was modeled on the spectacular 1928 Rose-

28. This may possibly be the dance attended by Black Elk, which Lucy Looks Twice places in 1928.

bud dance, which Fools Crow says drew a thousand spectators. The dance was to include the sweat lodge, fasting, and prayer—but no flesh offering or piercing. Fools Crow continued to have misgivings about the dance: "I still did not like to do the dance without piercing, or for a crowd of white spectators, so all the while we danced I prayed from the bottom of my heart for more understanding and a change of attitude on the part of the agency officials" (118). Fools Crow says that Spotted Crow used this dance to complete his training as intercessor, and that since that time, "whenever the Pine Ridge Sioux have wished to have a Sun Dance, I have served as the intercessor" (118). By his own estimate, Fools Crow has led some seventy-five Sun Dances, which is clearly more than one per year from 1929 to 1979. This number indicates that there were many more dances during this period than is apparent from the literature on the dance and tends to support the idea that Fools Crow held his own dances during the years he participated in the tribal council's dances. Steinmetz believes that dances were held almost every year during the ban, and points out that it is significant that people remember Sun Dances as taking place throughout the reservation (1990, 28).

Fools Crow states that "after the Sun Dance of 1929, we pleaded constantly with the agency superintendents to let us pierce" (1979, 119). According to Fools Crow, the ban on piercing finally ended in 1952, when a letter was issued permitting him to pierce the male pledgers. The permission was issued on the condition that Fools Crow be responsible for "infection or any other bad effect," (119) a condition Fools Crow accepted "because I had the proper medicine" (1978, 198).[29] According to Mails, there were eight men pierced in 1952, and Fools Crow has pierced pledgers yearly since that time (1978, 198; 1979, 119).

In his statements on the meaning and greatness of the Sun Dance, Fools Crow stresses that it is "the highest expression of our religion" (1979, 44). He also emphasizes the communal nature of the Sun Dance, saying that the Sioux are raised with it and that all share in the fasting, prayer, and benefits, not just the pledgers: "Everyone

29. These details are much like the piercing described by Eagle Feather, who places it in 1958.

is profoundly involved, and because of this the Sioux nation and all of the peoples of the world are blessed by *Wakan-Tanka*" (44). He also characterizes the Sun Dance as "our religion, our most important ceremony" without which it is impossible to understand the traditional way of life (119).[30] Fools Crow stresses that the sun is not God, although it "knows everything." It is rather created by God and is, like the sacred pipe, an instrument of *Wakan Tanka* (119).

Although Mails was apparently not permitted to describe an actual dance in *Fools Crow*, Fools Crow did consent to answer questions that Mails posed about the dance, largely about points of similarity and difference between Fools Crow's practices and those of Eagle Feather, whose dances Mails had carefully observed.[31] At some points in these interviews, Fools Crow seems a bit frustrated with what he may regard as Eagle Feather's innovations, or perhaps by Mails's very assumption that their dances are comparable. For instance, when Mails asks him where Eagle Feather might have gotten the idea for "horns" on the altar, Fools Crow replies, "I haven't the slightest notion" (1978, 202).

To one question, Fools Crow states that, in contrast with the situation at Rosebud, there is only one Sun Dance on the Pine Ridge each year. This is an odd statement. For one thing, it is inconsistent with his claim to have presided at more than seventy-five Sun Dances. For another thing, the evidence suggests a diversity of Sun Dances on the Pine Ridge, a trend that appears to be accelerating, for Steinmetz has evidence of fourteen Sun Dances on the Pine Ridge in 1987 (1990, 33). One possible interpretation is that Fools Crow means that there is only one *valid* Sun Dance per year, his. As for preliminaries, choosing the tree ends when he makes the final selection of the tree and wipes it with sweetgrass, offering the pipe and touching its stem to the tree at the cardinal points. The tree is then censed with sweetgrass, and a virgin chops the tree at the four directions. Several men then fell the tree. It may touch the ground

30. As noted above, Black Elk referred to the Sun Dance as "one of our greatest rites" (1953, 67).

31. This material exists in two versions. Mails (1978, 197–219) appears to be the earlier version of the interview, which was incorporated into his biography of Fools Crow (1979, 114–38, 43–45).

but is borne on sticks to a truck (1978, 199). Fools Crow explains that the tree is regarded as an enemy, but in spiritual thought, what is killed is not the tree but its growth (199). It thus remains as it was at the time of cutting throughout the ceremony. He makes the traditional four stops during the procession of the tree to the mystery circle, but omits to howl like a coyote. There is no charge. Despite the absence of a charge, these are the fullest preliminary ceremonies reported in the contemporary period.

Fools Crow places his own flesh offerings in the hole, along with sage and a saucer of *wasna,* which is described as an offering for the people of all nations who have died leaving needy dependents. A chokecherry bundle is prepared that incorporates a medicine bag with a cherry tree root, fat or tallow, and dried meat and sage. This bundle constitutes a thanksgiving to God. The ropes are then attached, and the images of a buffalo and a man are added. The reproductive organ that was observed by Fletcher and others is absent, green being painted on one side of the buffalo to represent reproduction. The other side of the buffalo and the entire man are painted red. Four banners, which according to Fools Crow represent the ascent from sin and ignorance to purity and enlightenment, are then attached, starting with black at the bottom, then red, yellow, and white at the top.

Fools Crow requires the sweat lodge before and after each day of the dance, but does not require a vision quest. His altar is relatively elaborate. The buffalo skull is painted red on the left and green on the right. Its skull holes are stuffed with sage, and it rests on a bed of sage. The earth is cut to allow a two-foot square of sod to be removed. A cross is inscribed in this square and the grooves that form it are filled with tobacco. Red paint and mica dust are sprinkled, and sage is spread. The pipe rack is set up to the west of the altar. There are some differences, but Fools Crow's altar thus exhibits essential continuity with the altar described by Densmore, including mellowing of the earth, the buffalo skull on a bed of sage, and the cross with grooves filled with tobacco, red paint, and mica dust (1918, 122, pl. 20).

To a question about fasting, Fools Crow acknowledges that some laxity exists, which irritates him but does not impair the validity of the dance: "I neither say nor do anything. It's their problem, and

God will handle it" (208).[32] In discussing the piercing, he states emphatically that piercing was *never* done under the muscle (214). This statement conflicts with some of the evidence and particularly with Sword's account of the piercing, which at the very minimum implies that the piercing was *into* the muscle. Fools Crow uses a sharpened stick for the piercing, and does not precut the skin with a knife. Unlike Eagle Feather, he does not permit the use of eagle claws for piercing, which he considers an unsanitary innovation. As a rule, he does not dispense medicine during the healing portions of the dance (216). Fools Crow states that he shares the visions of the pledgers and occasionally interprets them, which is done in private (217).

In 1983, I attended the dance associated with Fools Crow at Three Mile Camp, near Kyle, South Dakota. This dance took place July 30–August 2, the tree having been raised on July 29. In compliance with a strict prohibition on recording or photographing the dance—spectators were stopped and questioned at the gate as to whether they had cameras, tape recorders, or liquor—it was observed informally. For this reason, the measurements and related data below are estimates. Because the dance started sooner than anticipated, I observed only the final two days. I was present at the start of the dance on both days, but I missed the final portion of the fourth day, a period estimated as an hour. I thus did not observe the end of the dance.

The site was in a rural area that comprises a primitive campground that adjoined Fools Crow's residence. Sanitary needs were provided for by a single privy, and there was no running water. The spectators and participants were quiet and respectful. No use of cameras, tape recorders, or alcohol was observed at any time during the dance, nor were there any displays of public intoxication. These characteristics of the dances sponsored by the tribal council were completely absent, although the tension with the tribal council was not forgotten, one spectator remarking to me, "I'm glad we are doing this away from Pine Ridge. The goons are afraid to come out this far, because we have guns!" As mentioned above, Kyle is well known as a traditionalist stronghold, and many of the folding chairs

32. In Ella C. Deloria's novel *Waterlily,* it is explained that the young women contrive to bring water to their lovers, and that the mentors look the other way (122).

in the sought-after location sunwise of the participant's resting area bore the family name "Means."

The day before the first day of the dance was devoted to preparations, including the raising of the tree. The same site appears to be used year after year, so it is not necessary to cut and place the uprights and stringers for the shade, leaving only the cutting and placing of the pine bough awning to be done fresh. This makes one day of preparations feasible. The tree was a cottonwood, the upper branches still fully in leaf, standing perhaps fifty feet tall. The tree was decorated with the long colored banners mentioned by Fools Crow, and its presence dominated the proceedings. The grounds, especially in the morning before the dance began, were impressive in their solemn beauty, the tree rustling lightly in the constant breeze.

The following figure presents the ritual arrangements at the dance. The mystery circle, or innermost ritual area, was about eighty feet in diameter, surrounding the tree. The mystery circle was defined by flags in the four sacred colors, which were driven into the ground in pairs at the cardinal points. The flags create a gate several feet wide, through which all entry to the mystery circle takes place. The procedure for a spectator to enter the circle, when authorized to do so, was to walk through the nearest flags and proceed sunwise (clockwise) to his or her destination. An outer circle, about fifteen feet across, surrounded the mystery circle proper. Some ritual action took place in this outer circle, notably the dragging of buffalo skulls by pledgers. The shade surrounded this outer circle, being about ten feet deep. The shade appeared to be a semipermanent structure, newly cut evergreen boughs being laid on top of substantial supports, indicating that the same general area is used for successive dances. The spectators sat on lawn chairs or on the ground under the shade. The shade was open to the east to allow the dancers to enter and exit the mystery circle in procession and also to allow a path for the rising sun to enter the circle. The portion of the shade opposite this opening, the *catku*, or place of honor, was deeper, being reserved for the holy men and pledgers. Spectators were not permitted to enter this area, which was closed at the rear and at both sides. The sweat lodges and preparations tipi were behind this portion of the shade. The camping area was to the southwest of the shade, and the parking lot to its south. A survey of the license plates in the parking lot indicated that some of the spectators—and perhaps some of the participants—were from out of state.

Certain portions of the area were reserved for specific activities. The piercing took place immediately under and to the south of the tree. The altar and pipe rack were near the western entry to the mystery circle. The area comprising a triangle between the tree, the altar, and the pledgers' portion of the shade was in almost constant use during the dance, smaller rituals taking place here during rest periods or while another portion of the circle was being utilized for more major ritual action. The area for giving flesh was to the south of the pipe rack, near the southern entry to the mystery circle. The announcer was in the southern portion of the shade and the singers in the southeast portion of the shade.

The spectators were not simply passive observers of the dance, being involved in certain ritual actions and in the continuous giving of flesh offerings. The spectators stood at various points during the dance, particularly when pledgers dragging buffalo skulls in the outer circle passed by, at which point the men also removed their hats. The crowd was regularly smudged by a holy man who carried a clam shell filled with burning sweetgrass. As the smudging proceeded sunwise through the shade, the spectators used both hands to direct the purifying smoke toward their face and chest. One attractive young woman was quietly acclaimed by the spectators for the elegant way in which she censed her entire body, turning fully around in the process. The density and enthusiasm of the crowd differed from place to place in the shade. The portion of the shade immediately sunwise of the area reserved for the dancers was always crowded, as was the portion of the shade near the announcer. The eastern portion of the shade was less crowded. During the final day, the entire shade was filled to capacity, the prime areas being occupied ten or more persons deep. The crowd increased as the day progressed and was fullest in the afternoon. The crowd was at its peak on the fourth and most important day, when the nearly five hundred spectators, many of whom carried eagle-wing fans, were exhorted by the announcer to dance in place: "They are out there dancing in the hot sun. The least you can do is dance in your places." Many of the spectators heeded this exhortation. (Not all in

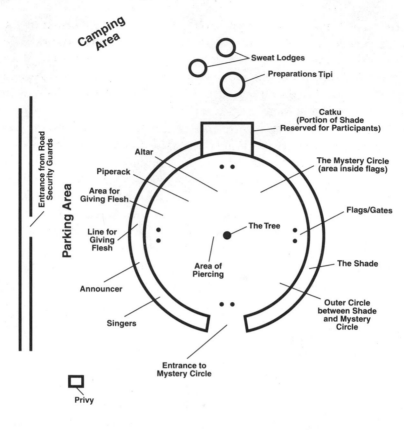

Camping Area

Sweat Lodges

Preparations Tipi

Catku
(Portion of Shade
Reserved for Participants)

Entrance from Road
Security Guards

Parking Area

Altar

The Mystery Circle
(area inside flags)

Piperack

Area for
Giving Flesh

Flags/Gates

Line for
Giving
Flesh

The Tree

Announcer

The Shade

Area of
Piercing

Outer Circle
between Shade
and Mystery
Circle

Singers

Entrance to
Mystery Circle

Privy

All movement is clockwise or
"sunwise" inside the mystery circle.

W
S — N
E

Ritual Arrangements in 1983 at Three Mile Camp

attendance approved of the proceedings, one spectator remarking to me, "I do not think it is necessary to tear a hole in yourself in order to worship God.") There were few, if any, tourists until the afternoon of the final day, when several young white men wearing shorts (which is considered disrespectful) were observed standing toward the rear of the shade immediately in front of the parking lot.

Like the spectators, the singers are essential to the dance, and their music was heavily amplified. The five or six singers sat around a bass drum turned face down on the ground. All the singers beat the drum with a drumstick as they sang. In 1983, the renowned Porcupine Singers performed on the fourth day, along with three other groups, which caused the announcer to remark "so we are loaded today." When the Porcupine Singers started their first song in the traditional high register before dropping to a lower register for the remainder of their portion of the dance, the effect on the crowd was electric. (The high register, which is very high, cannot be sustained for the duration of a round.)

The instant the singers stopped singing, the announcer began to talk. Like the singers, the announcer was heavily amplified. The announcer provided a running commentary on the dance, made necessary announcements, enforced order, and introduced the numerous religious and political leaders who clustered behind him, waiting for their chance to address the crowd during rest periods. Their remarks, which indicated that the Sioux are still very accomplished orators, were generally made in Lakota. Occasionally, English summaries were provided by the announcer "for those Lakotas present who do not even understand our language." The announcer was also responsible for enforcing a standard of traditional behavior, which occasioned an intermittent stream of censure directed toward those present who lacked sufficient knowledge of traditional ways. At several points, the announcer warned that menstruating women were to avoid the shade, "because your power is too great at this time." The suggestion was made that these women could watch the dance from their parked cars. Several young women who appeared in shorts were quickly censured, as were those spectators whose feet protruded from the shade into the outer circle. (Besides not being respectful, this behavior could expose one to mortal danger, owing to the power present even in the outer circle.) On one occasion, a new pipe had to be presented to a dancer whose pipe was broken, a misfortune that called for much censorious comment by the announcer, as did the fact that some of the pipes were packed too tightly to be lit. (Since the tip of the pipe stem is usually tapered to provide for a firm fit with the catlinite bowl, the bowl is vulnerable to breakage if excessive force is used when the pipe is assembled.) The misfortune of the broken pipe was repaired by the ceremonial presentation of a new pipe to the affected dancer. As these examples show, the announcer was responsible for both instruction and the enforcement of traditional standards, taking over to a certain extent the teaching functions associated with the classic dance.

The pledgers dressed in wrap skirts, the male dancers being bare-chested. Of the sixty or more dancers, about forty were male. Most appeared to be camped on the grounds. They wore sage headbands and blew eagle-bone whistles. Some also carried eagle-wing fans. No violations of fasting regulations were observed. Although spectators were observed to lunch in the parking area during rest periods, no food or liquid was consumed under the shade.

Fools Crow was at the dance but owing to advancing age was not the intercessor. He was observed sitting quietly in a lawn chair in the east portion of the shade in nonceremonial dress for short portions of the third and fourth days. A spectator identified the intercessor, a strong featured man who dressed in a white wrap skirt and was naked above the waist, as James DuBray. Apparently he was still associated with the dance in 1987, a situation Steinmetz describes as "Fools Crow with DuBray helping" (1990, 33). It is important to realize that, although the intercessor is in general charge of the ceremony, he does not perform every ritual action, being assisted by numerous holy men. At many junctures, the intercessor retired to the shade while the dancing continued. Unlike Christian worship, the Sun Dance often has no single focus of action, several or many rituals or ritual actions taking place in the circle at the same time. Since the ritual takes place "in the round," different points of view on the dance reveal different aspects of it. The effect is kaleidoscopic, with significant ritual action taking place even during the rest periods. The intercessor oversees this constant activity in a general way. In 1983, the intercessor was not observed to address the crowd, although he occasionally prayed aloud in Lakota.

The dance began on the third and fourth days with a solemn and impressive procession, well after the sun had arisen. The procession started by the sweat lodges, proceeding sunwise around the mystery circle, entering the circle through the gap in the shade to the east. The dancers appeared to be very well rehearsed and the singing, especially when joined by all the dancers, was electrifying. The dance began in the east, the rows of dancers proceeding to dance around the cardinal points to complete a round. All movement inside the mystery circle was sunwise, and no one was observed entering the mystery circle other than through the gates (which would expose one to mortal danger). The dancers were often smudged as they danced or fanned or both with eagle-wing fans. Each round of the dance consumed about forty minutes, followed by a rest period of fifteen or twenty minutes, when the dancers were permitted to sit in the circle or in the reserved portion of the shade. Each dancer had a filled pipe, which was rested on a pipe rack to the south of the altar. At the end of each round, the keeper of the pipes selected several spectators, inviting them into the area between the shade and the mystery circle proper, and presenting them with a pipe from the rack to be carried to an indicated elder in the crowd. The pipe was then carried sunwise to an elder, who would light the pipe and smoke it, usually passing it sunwise to the next few spectators. All pipes must be smoked by the end of the day, one or several per round, providing a rough indication of the duration of the dance. One spectator remarked to me in dismay midway through the afternoon of the third day, "Too many pipes!" This signified that the day's dance was far from over. This pipe ritual, an indication of the communal emphasis of the Fools Crow dance, thus signals the beginning of a rest period.

The piercing was continuous, taking place immediately south of the tree. The most common form of piercing was piercing above each breast, the skewers being attached to ropes that hung from the tree. Each pledger appeared to have his own rope, which was already attached to the tree. The style of dance was that of pulling back from the tree. No dancing on tiptoes was observed. Occasionally a pledger would approach the tree four times, then run quickly to the end of the rope, turning toward the tree and leaping backward to break free. Others strained against the rope in place, pulling backward a little at a time. The strain sometimes caused the flesh to pull out from the chest to a distance of four inches. On breaking free, the rope often snapped back the twenty or more feet to the tree, hitting audibly against it, such was the force of the release. Pledgers who failed to break free after an appropriate time were jerked free by one or more assistants, except one youngster, probably between the age of twelve and fourteen, who had been pierced on one side. This dancer, the son of the announcer, was released after an unsuccessful struggle. He was the only pledger whose sacrifice was introduced and commented on in public. No instances of the partial cutting of the flesh to facilitate release were observed and no instances of giving gifts in return for release were observed. The length of struggle varied from minimal to about forty minutes.

There were also other forms of the sacrifice. One dancer, identified by a spectator as a holy man, danced attached by one breast to an enormous buffalo skull staked in the northeast portion of the mystery circle. He remained attached to the buffalo skull, except during rest periods, throughout the third day, breaking free midway through the fourth day. Several pledgers danced fully suspended from the tree in a horizontal posture for up to fifteen minutes. A number of pledgers dragged buffalo skulls attached to skewers in their upper backs around the outer circle. Some of these pledgers also had buffalo skulls suspended from their backs. No pledgers danced the form of the dance in which one is suspended from four posts, dancing on tiptoe. Of the sixty dancers, nearly all the males (about forty) pierced. Many of those who were pierced bore previous Sun Dance scars.

The mood of the crowd was reverent and serious; no trace of sensationalism was evident with respect to the piercing. The pledgers who danced fully suspended from the tree elicited no gasp from the crowd, as the 1975 piercing of Robert Blackfeather reported by Mails did (1978, 192). In fact, one of the surprises for me was that the spectators did not attend very closely to the piercing, unless a relative happened to be involved, often engaging in quiet conversation or watching other parts of the dance while the struggle took place. Even the more spectacular sacrifices called for little attention and comment, perhaps indicating that for this community of spectators, the sacrifices were secondary to the religious observance taking place.[33]

In comparison with Eagle Feather's 1975 dance as reported by Mails, the 1983 dance at Three Mile Camp exhibited a more communal focus. The intercessor was not pierced (Fools Crow has never been pierced), and there were no confessional statements by the individual pledgers. There was much less emphasis on the individual pledgers and their piercing. No receiving line was formed to congratulate pledgers after dancing successfully. The altar was much more elaborate, and the rounds lasted much longer. The pipe was presented in a way that involved the spectators at the end of each round, and there was much smudging of both spectators and dancers. The piercing took place in more forms, and the dance involved many more pledgers, although the number of spectators on the final day was comparable.

The flesh offerings at the 1983 dance indicate a very high degree of community involvement in the dance. Offerings were given continuously during the dance, and it is estimated that more than half of the spectators gave flesh offerings. Teenage women were the most frequent givers of flesh, with young men being the second most numerous group of givers. The place for giving was reached through the south gate to the mystery circle. The giver stepped into the circle and knelt on a blanket facing the spectators, holding a pipe in both hands. A holy man used a razor blade to cut small pieces of flesh about the size of a match head from the upper arm. Ashes are sometimes used to stanch the bleeding, but, in 1983, none were used. The wounds often make a track of blood down the arm and leave a recognizable and enduring scar. Sage was used to purify both the arm and the razor. Four offerings made in the shape of a cross was a common configuration, although others were observed. The offerings were wrapped in cloth to be hung on the tree that stood— in imitation of the large tree—on the altar. Through these flesh offerings, the spectators participated directly in the sacrifice, helping

33. "The piercing and the breaking free should not be focused upon, however, when the essence of the Sun Dance Ceremony is being fathomed. It is the gathered tribe, the band, the gathered *Tiyospaye*, acknowledging the spiritual and physical relationship to all that is the *cante*, the heart of the Sun Dance" (McGaa, 95).

ensure personally that the goals of the community are met. Toward the end of the dance, the announcer declared that one of the women had offered free Sun Dance costumes for the first six persons to pledge for next year, illustrating one way in which the community ensures the continuity of the dance.

I would emphasize that I saw no evidence whatsoever of the ceremonial laxity reported in the dances sponsored by the tribal council that are described above. Sunglasses, concession stands, and drunkenness were completely absent, and the mood of the spectators throughout was that of religious devotion. To my eyes, there was no sense at all of a historical reenactment or a social event. I can only say that it was an incredibly moving experience, one that I hope I can have again.

In view of what transpired at Fools Crow's dance, it seems that, given the diversity of the contemporary dance, it makes much difference which dance is observed. The dance I saw at Three Mile Camp in 1983 bore little resemblance to some of the disrespectful performances noted by other authors. Since the Kyle area, which is fairly remote by reservation standards, is a stronghold of traditionalism, it may well be that the dance at Three Mile Creek has continued in essentially the same form for many years. Because of this, and because of Fools Crow's position as "ceremonial chief," it should probably be regarded as the most authoritative contemporary dance.

6

The Lakota Sun Dance—
Then and Now

The Lakota Sun Dance comes clearly into view in 1866, rather late in terms of the culture that created it. The beginning of the reservation period, which coincides with the observation of the Lakota dance by outsiders, was a time of crisis for the Lakota, who were experiencing the most severe political shock a people can suffer, the loss of self-determination and autonomy. With conquest also came the collapse of the prereservation economic system. As we have seen, in less than two decades the Lakota would suffer another severe shock, the repression of their religion and the banning of the Sun Dance, its central expression. In coming on the reservation, the Lakota eventually accepted the revocation of their old nomadic lifestyle, entering a period of change and adaptation extending until the present time. As Michael F. Steltenkamp emphasizes, it is a tribute to their resilience and ability to innovate that they continue to survive in a world that is in many ways still essentially hostile.

In assessing the degree of change in the Sun Dance over time, it is important to realize that the dances in the early reservation period were not pristine. In the 1860s, the Lakota were already being forced toward the mainstream of American culture. No matter how fresh the memories of the old life may have been, the mere fact of asking permission, as the elders apparently did at Fort Sully in 1866, indicates that the Sun Dance was already affected by change. To the extent that it was already the focus of cultural identity maintained in the face of real pressure toward acculturation and change, the Sun Dance at Fort Sully had entered the modern period.

The Sun Dance of the prereservation period thus stands behind the dance described in the literature. Not directly accessible to scholarship, it stands a little out of the light, a presence that makes itself felt in and through the dance presented in the literature. The old Sun Dance was integral to a complex culture not yet threatened with collapse. After moving onto the Plains, the Teton enjoyed a golden age. Stimulated but not yet overwhelmed by the technology of European culture, they maintained hegemony over a large area supplied with plenty of food in the form of the buffalo. The Sun Dance was a functioning part of this culture, reinforcing the warlike values necessary for survival on the hostile Plains, identifying leaders, cementing political ties among bands, and creating a common bond for the community. The Sun Dance vow, undertaken in a situation of danger in war, stimulated the warrior to courage, supported by the belief that *Wakan Tanka* would come to his aid. Its performance, in times of trouble, was a rallying point for the community. But the Sun Dance served more than a military function. It was a major mechanism for the redistribution of wealth, providing a means for the poorer people in the society to obtain the goods needed to survive the extreme Dakota winter. As Walker's account makes clear, it also served a major teaching function, inculcating and preserving the values and mythology of the society.

As a celebration of life on the Plains, the Sun Dance enshrined the central foci of Lakota life, war and the buffalo hunt. The large political unit made possible by temperate weather and the buffalo herds created the context for a month-long festival, which was a welcome contrast to the rigors of winter life with its smaller bands and difficult hunting conditions. The Sun Dance was the centerpiece, the mandala, in which many other rituals and ceremonies centered. In unifying the two themes of war and the annual buffalo hunt, the Lakota created a festival that fully expressed the central elements of their life on the Plains.[1] Because the dance ensured the return, not only of the buffalo, but also of the earth itself, the rite had cosmic dimensions. It also had very human dimensions, being the occasion

---

1. In contrast, the Santee Sun Dance, though sharing the theme of war, was not an annual, communal festival, the buffalo hunt being indigenous to Plains life.

for numerous love affairs, which were aided and abetted by the fact that the dance continued all night.

The reservation period, with its rapid cultural, political, and economic change, disrupted the intimate relationship between Lakota religion and culture. This rapid cultural change tended to make traditional religion irrelevant. Since war and the buffalo hunt were no longer the stuff of everyday life, the Sun Dance became the memorial of a life no longer lived rather than the celebration of life as it was lived. As such, it also became something else, the focus of Lakota cultural identity maintained against the pressure toward acculturation brought to bear by the dominant culture. Although the Sun Dance was always central to Lakota identity, in the old days that identity was relatively secure. Cultural identity is one thing; cultural identity self-consciously maintained in the face of an external threat is another. In the reservation period, what had been Lakota culture became "traditional culture." In the old Lakota system, religion was woven into the fabric of culture, scarcely existing as a separate entity. "Traditional religion," as one religious position among others, is purely a product of the reservation period, during which the Sun Dance, once the central Lakota religious ritual, became the central ritual of traditional Lakota religion. There is a world of difference between these two points.

The advent of the ban further disrupted the normal relationship between religion and culture. Although the ban was intended to facilitate cultural and religious change, by forcing the discontinuance of a ritual that enshrined the values of the savage past, it denied traditional religion the opportunity to develop normally in response to the new circumstances created by reservation life. It simultaneously—and not incidentally—deposed the spiritual leaders of the community, the men best equipped to deal with crisis.[2] Left to its own devices, traditional religion would likely have evolved, preserv-

2. As O. Douglas Schwartz points out, the holy man was the person best equipped to respond to crisis: "The holy man has a 'vision' of the world—its nature, its history, and its destiny—and a sense of humanity's place within that scheme. Through that vision, the holy man can hope to solve problems for which the tradition offers no ready-made solutions. The *wicasa wakan* is thus the theoretician—the theologian—of the Plains religion" (53).

ing the essential features of the cultural legacy of the past, while speaking clearly to the needs of the present. Denied the opportunity to respond to its contemporary situation, traditional religion led a shadowy existence, kept alive underground, largely away from the population centers of Pine Ridge and Rosebud.

But the reports of its demise were exaggerated. As Gordon Macgregor pointed out in 1946: "The extent of the belief and religious practice in so-called 'pagan' cults is still more extensive than most missionaries and officials are willing to believe" (93). We now know that the Sun Dance, which was declared extinct by the agents shortly after the institution of the ban in 1883, was celebrated throughout the years in which it was thought to have vanished. Although the survival of the Sun Dance was the work of many holy men, Black Elk, the key figure in the contemporary revival of traditional religion, was instrumental in increasing the awareness of traditional religion during its darker days. *Black Elk Speaks* gained a wider readership, but Black Elk's *The Sacred Pipe* called attention to traditional religion as a significant and viable presence in reservation life. This was itself a considerable accomplishment, given the extremely low profile maintained by traditionalists in 1948, when he was interviewed by Brown. Drawing on his experience as a catechist, Black Elk created a powerful argument for traditional religion, working out a compromise with Catholicism that has been widely accepted on the reservation today.[3] Whether made out of conviction or expediency, Black Elk's claim that Christianity and traditional religion are basically compatible helped create the context of official tolerance necessary for the revival of traditional religion by changing an "either/or" into a "both/and." On the Lakota side, Black Elk's "both/and" provided Lakotas with genuinely divided loyalties a means of reconciling traditional religion with Christianity in an authentic way, fulfilling a need felt by many Lakotas.

The contemporary Sun Dance is essentially in accord with Black Elk's interpretation of the dance in *The Sacred Pipe*. Although not all Black Elk's innovations and ritual directions have been accepted, his

---

3. The best accounts of the contemporary relationship between traditional religion and Christianity are in Paul B. Steinmetz and Michael F. Steltenkamp. See also DeMallie and Parks (esp. 139–47), Powers (1982), and Holler (1984b).

broad interpretation of the dance as a ritual of renewal for the tradi-tional community is the central theme in the contemporary dance. In contemporary dances, vows are still undertaken for healing and for the acquisition of shamanic power, but they are also regularly undertaken, as Black Elk envisioned, for the benefit of the people as a whole. While the contemporary dance honors the past, it is thus a thoroughly modern rite, speaking directly to the needs of the community.

Although it seems clear that the contemporary Sun Dance re-flects Black Elk's vision of it in *The Sacred Pipe*, it is worth consider-ing whether Black Elk's influence on the dance can be demonstrated. It is difficult, given the evidence, to assess the precise degree of in-fluence that *The Sacred Pipe*, and Black Elk himself, had on men such as Fools Crow and on the subsequent revival of the dance. To the extent that *The Sacred Pipe* accurately reflects Black Elk's thought,[4] we know what he was thinking about the Sun Dance toward the end of his life. We know too that the Sun Dance today is much like Black Elk's proposals, particularly in the Fools Crow tradition. This resem-blance in itself, however, does not prove that the former is the cause of the latter—post hoc, ergo propter hoc.[5]

Michael F. Steltenkamp has implied that Black Elk's books were virtually unknown on the reservation when he arrived in the early

4. We may never know the precise role Joseph Epes Brown played in shaping *The Sacred Pipe*. At this point, however, I certainly do not share the extreme skepticism expressed by one of my prepublication reviewers, who suggested that the dialogue with Catholicism in the book was "simply and wholly Brown's creation." In the first place, the text does not merely compare Catholicism and traditional religion, it cre-atively adapts traditional religion in the light of Catholicism. In my experience, it is rare for comparative religionists (or anthropologists) to possess either the knowledge of the Christian tradition or the degree of engagement with it evident in *The Sacred Pipe*. In the second place, I suspect that examination of the book by a sufficiently informed student of historical theology would reveal much that is specific to its period and milieu—reservation Catholicism. Finally—and in my opinion, decisively—Brown's angle, like Neihardt's, is to portray Black Elk as a traditionalist. The Christian perspective hardly facilitates this portrait, and the fact that the book was taken for so many years as an unvarnished ethnographic account hardly suggests that Brown was at pains to portray Black Elk as a syncretist.

5. "After this, therefore because of this"—the fallacy of relevance that results from simply assuming that earlier events are the cause of later events.

1970s (1993, xvii), and thus it might seem obvious that *The Sacred Pipe* did not influence the revival of the Lakota dance. I am a little skeptical of this conclusion. In the first place, I doubt if Stelten-kamp's circle of reservation acquaintances was quite as inclusive as his statement implies. It may very well be that Black Elk's books were not read by many of the older Lakota Catholics. We must not forget that *Black Elk Speaks* was portrayed as a very bad book by the Jesuits—one that was repudiated by Black Elk himself—and it is rather unlikely that they went out of their way to promote *The Sacred Pipe* as wholesome reading for Lakota Catholics. At the same time, *Black Elk Speaks* was—and is—a very popular book. The regularity with which Neihardt's "death of the dream" speech surfaces in native American literature and oral history indicates that this book, at least, has been widely read by native Americans. Since nothing is more characteristic of a reader than to seek out other books written by a favorite author, it seems to me likely that *The Sacred Pipe* was read as well, especially after it became widely available in paperback in 1971. Perhaps the image of the reservation community as intellec-tually isolated and aliterate is itself something of a stereotype, one that might be dispelled by regular reading of *Indian Country Today*. A personal recollection might make the same point. At the Sun Dance I attended in 1983, I was startled when the older woman sitting next to me asked me for my impression of Peter Mattheissen's *In the Spirit of Crazy Horse*, which had only recently appeared. Since she resided in the community where the killing of the two FBI agents took place and assured me that she had personal knowledge of the events Mattheissen described, it was clear that she had not read the book simply for information. This conversation led me to reevaluate my estimate of the extent to which the reservation community was aware of external perspectives on the Lakota experience.

In this connection, it is worth mentioning that competition among Lakota holy men is intense. Since the traditional sanction for a vocation as a holy man is a personal vision, no Lakota would risk ridicule by admitting that he obtained his sacred knowledge from a book. Ethnographic literature is an inadmissible source of sacred knowledge in a culture where the authority of the holy man derives solely from his personal vision and power. For this reason, an argu-ment from silence is not convincing. It may well be that the insights

Black Elk presents in *The Sacred Pipe* were read and quietly absorbed by some contemporary holy men. Since *Black Elk Speaks* clearly made quite a splash on the reservation when it was published in 1932, it seems difficult to believe that *The Sacred Pipe* sank without a ripple twenty-one years later.

In part, it depends on the decade in question. I strongly suspect that Black Elk's books were widely read on the reservation after the occupation of Wounded Knee in 1973, since Steltenkamp himself reports that at that time, "a current within the reservation milieu was an invocation of Black Elk's spirit as portrayed in *Black Elk Speaks,* along with the ignoring of the Black Elk of subsequent years" (1993, 140). Black Elk's influence on Fools Crow and the other traditional leaders of his generation, however, was almost certainly through personal contact, which is inherently difficult to trace. In a pre-publication critique of my manuscript, Paul B. Steinmetz states that Black Elk's influence on the Sun Dance was primarily through his personal contact with traditional leaders such as Fools Crow (see 1990, 185–86) and it does seem likely that the two men discussed the Sun Dance in some detail. After all, it was the central traditional ritual and Fools Crow clearly felt strongly that it should be revived. At the same time, it seems unlikely that Fools Crow was overly familiar with Black Elk's books. Thomas Mails reports that when he read excerpts from *Black Elk Speaks* to Fools Crow, he responded that the voice of Black Elk in the novel did not sound like his uncle (1991, 15). Perhaps he would have had a similar response to excerpts from *The Sacred Pipe*. But since Fools Crow's respect for Black Elk is obvious, it seems likely that he influenced the younger holy man deeply. There may also have been a mutual influence, and Fools Crow himself may be the source of some of the ideas in *The Sacred Pipe*. Despite their agreement on many points, however, the two remain different personalities as religious leaders. If I might put it this way, traditionalists such as Fools Crow innovate in a more unself-conscious way. Black Elk's innovation in *The Sacred Pipe* is clearly conscious, and it takes place on a more self-consciously theological level. Of the two, Black Elk is clearly the one most engaged with Catholicism and with the intellectual problem of its relationship to traditional religion. Although Fools Crow affirms the central tenant of the Black Elk tradition—traditional religion *and* Christianity—it is simply impossible to imagine him writing a book like *The Sacred Pipe*, which might be taken as indirect evidence that Black Elk was a more likely source of the reinterpretation of the dance than Fools Crow.

Still, a skeptic could argue that it just so happens that the dance Black Elk describes in *The Sacred Pipe* corresponds broadly with the dance that we observe today. As I said before, the ideas that Black Elk expresses may have simply been in the air. It is even possible that Black Elk's description of the dance reflects what was already happening, to a greater or lesser extent, in the secret Sun Dances of his day. In pointing to Black Elk as a likely influence on the dance, I am not intending to indulge in a "great man" theory of history.[6] Certainly the problems were obvious and the solutions were to a certain extent dictated by the situation. The survival and revival of the Sun Dance was undoubtedly the work of many men about whom we know little or nothing, although it seems clear that Eagle Feather and Fools Crow deserve the credit for leading the revival of the dance at Rosebud and at Pine Ridge.[7] There can be no disputing, however, that Black Elk was the Lakota thinker most in dialogue with Christianity and with the white world. His creative reconciliation of the two traditions is the basis for much Lakota religiosity today, whether it is styled "dual participation" or "dual religious belief." As I suggest in my conclusion, Black Elk's vision embraced the best of what he found in his own tradition, the Ghost Dance, and Catholic Christianity. His precise contribution to the revival of the Sun Dance may never be known, but there is little doubt that his vision has been the major shaper of the Lakota religious present. Black Elk's reinterpretation of the dance as a vehicle for renewal of

6. The problem with "great man" explanations is that they imply that the great man transcends his situation completely. On the other hand, I cannot wholeheartedly embrace social determinism, the theory that persons are simply the product of circumstances that are beyond their control. If apparently innovative thoughts are simply determined, why doesn't everyone in a certain situation have them? In this connection, it is worth emphasizing that the Sioux had a recognized mechanism for harnessing the power of genius—the vision quest—through which one might transcend conventional wisdom and seek innovative solutions.

7. It seems likely that Leonard Crow Dog will emerge in retrospect as a major influence on the dance on the Rosebud, although at this point there is not enough evidence to establish either the form of his dances or their major religious thrust.

the traditional community, with its emphasis on sacrifices "so that the people may live," was probably a major influence on the Sun Dance we observe today. In any case, Black Elk's vision of the dance was certainly farsighted enough to embrace its contemporary revival—another measure of his essential greatness.

Turning from the question of Black Elk's influence to the dance itself, what have we learned from the history of the dance? What changes have taken place and how do we assess their significance? By far the greatest change that the Sun Dance has undergone is the transition from its position as the central Lakota religious ritual to its current position as the central ritual of traditional Lakota religion. The old dance was a festival for the entire community, at which, if Alice Fletcher is to be believed, attendance was mandatory. Its celebration was hardly separate from Lakota camp circle society itself, taking place at the center of a ceremonial encampment of the people—the symbolic center was the literal center as well. The change from community to voluntary community is very great, meaning much more than is implied in the mere fact of competing religious systems. To participate in the contemporary Sun Dance—as a pledger or a spectator—is to choose to identify with the portion of the traditional community that is celebrating the dance. That is to say that it is a choice of identity, and since the Sun Dance is so strongly associated with traditional Lakota values, to participate in the Sun Dance is to choose to identify one's self as Lakota in the strongest possible terms.

To explore the meaning of the Sun Dance as a source of ethnic identity, it is worth pausing to consider the concept of "ethnicity as strategy" as employed in recent anthropology. In the past few years, anthropologists have discarded some of their cherished assumptions about ethnicity and ethnic populations, in part because the hoped-for and presumed-to-be-inevitable assimilation of native American populations has simply not taken place as expected. Contrary to prior expectations, native Americans still choose to be Indians, even when other choices are clearly available. What lies behind this choice, and why do traditional cultures continue to exist in the face of worldwide change?

At least since Max Weber's seminal essay, "The Protestant Ethic and the 'Spirit' of Capitalism," which was written in 1905, native peoples have been perceived as acting dysfunctionally or irrationally. That is to say that they refuse to act in their own best interests, economically and otherwise, presumably because the "dead hand" of tradition as expressed in their cultural and religious teachings inhibits them from doing so. Weber pointed to the failure of the natives to accumulate capital. In the context of our study of the Lakota, we might point to the failure of the Lakota to take up farming and become completely assimilated, which was perceived as in their best interests by the agents and the government as a whole. As we have seen, the assumption driving the ban was essentially that this refusal could be attributed to traditional religion and the values it enshrined. Given this assumption, banning it was at least a rational attempt to deal with the problem. If people are not acting in their best interests because they are dominated by a dysfunctional religion and culture, as most of the reformers believed, it makes sense to try to destroy it, to save them from their own folly and allow them to participate in activities that truly benefit them.

Alan R. Sandstrom's *Corn Is Our Blood,* a study of a contemporary Nahua village in northern Veracruz, Mexico, casts much light on this situation. The Nahua are the contemporary heirs to the Aztec empire, and their relevance to the Lakota is that they are perceived as Indians by the dominant culture and that they have been heavily missionized by the Spanish Catholic Church. Although there are a number of parallels between the contemporary Nahua and the Lakota, Sandstrom's analysis of the relation of religion to Nahua ethnic identity is particularly relevant to the Lakota.

Sandstrom emphasizes that while ethnicity is to a certain extent ascribed—that is, people are classified as Indian by others on the basis of characteristics such as physical appearance—it is also to a certain extent chosen. One can do little about one's physique and racial heritage, but one can choose or reject other markers of ethnicity such as clothing and religion. As a cultural materialist, Sandstrom proceeds from the premise that people maximize, which is to say that they act rationally to increase their well-being. This means that the reason Nahuas choose to dress, act, and participate in rituals that mark them as Indians is that they perceive certain benefits to being so identified. In other words, Sandstrom rejects the Weberian assumption that native peoples are incapable of rational behavior, and cautions the reader from the outset that certain assumptions must be discarded if traditional communities are to be understood.

> [T]he villagers are quite capable of acting rationally on their own behalf. There is no need to invoke blind obedience to strange customs to account for their behavior. This assertion will become clear in the discussion of Nahua farming practices and the relation of the village to the market system. . . . Indian culture is neither static nor opposed to change, and in fact many changes in village life have been self-generated and achieved through traditional means. (8)

Although we will not examine Sandstrom's argument that economic behavior that is apparently irrational and dysfunctional, such as the native farming practices, is adaptive and rational, his analysis of ethnicity is relevant to the Lakota Sun Dance. In Sandstrom's view, ethnicity can be understood in part as a rational strategy for dealing with the problems raised by political and economic dominance: "Ethnicity, to some extent, can be understood as an effective defense on the part of a subordinated group against social, political, economic, or military domination" (xviii). To show how this can be so, Sandstrom points out that ethnic identity emerges only when at least two groups interact primarily on the basis of their perceived cultural differences (8). The conquest of the native American peoples by people of European origin clearly qualifies as a case in point. One might imagine two broad strategies for dealing with this situation. The first would be to attempt to minimize the objective differences by adopting dress and other customs like that of the conquerors. The second would be to emphasize precisely the features of dress and customs that mark one as different. This second strategy is the ethnic response, and is the one that interests us here.

> When in public . . . a man communicates his identity through his striking white costume, tire-tread sandals, and sheathed steel machete hung at his side. A woman proclaims her Indian identity with her spectacularly embroidered blouse, colorful skirt, and strips of bright cloth braided into her hair. These symbols say, "I am an Indian" to all the world and yet, paradoxically, every one of these items is of Hispanic origin. (9)

Sandstrom points out that the fact that these items are not of traditional origin implies that Indian identity is consciously and actively pursued by the villagers. Along with dress, religion is an obvious ethnic marker. About this, Sandstrom reports that the Nahuas in the village all identify themselves as Catholics to outsiders. That is to say that the village lacks a faction like AIM that totally rejects the religion of the dominant society. Yet traditional religion is the ultimate insider marker to ethnic identity: "In fact the one clear test of whether an individual is an Indian or mestizo is whether or not the person participates in traditional rituals" (9). In this context, the mestizos are not the urban Mexicans, but rural persons whose cultural outlook is Hispanic rather than Indian (63–72). In Sandstrom's village, the practice of traditional religion is thus a marker that distinguishes between Indian and mestizo rather than between Indian and white, for all the villagers identify themselves as Catholic.

In his discussion of Nauha religion, Sandstrom notes that "without exception, religion creates a community of believers and sets them apart from others" (320). Since people subjected to domination develop an ethnic identity "to separate themselves from the ruling group and simultaneously to create an alternate social world" (323), the relevance of religion's creation of community is obvious. The community created by shared religious belief, with its automatic division of the world into insiders and outsiders, is perhaps the ultimate strategy for creating an alternate social world. But for this strategy to succeed there must first be adequate mechanisms for keeping the two worlds apart (338) so that an alternate system of rewards can be established such that "people can be comfortable and feel essentially in control of their lives" (338). This need is met in a special way by the practice of traditional religion, which among the Nahua villagers means participation in what are called in Spanish *costumbres,* or "customs": "The single most important cultural activity in Amatlán that both creates a world view for the villagers and defines the ethnic group to which they belong is participation in the costumbre rituals" (340). The cosmology underlying these rituals is completely foreign to the mestizos, and in fact no mestizos—the group with which difference must be maintained—participate in the *costumbres.* As such, participation in these rituals is the ultimate test of ethnic identity: "Participation in the costumbres is in many ways the ultimate test of Indianness because it is based on a view of the universe and a body of knowledge not shared by most mestizos" (342).

The application of this insight to the Lakota Sun Dance is obvious. In the contemporary situation, which is characterized by competing religious systems as well as by competing economic and cultural strategies for survival, participation in the Sun Dance is the ultimate test of Lakotaness. To pledge to make a blood sacrifice in the dance is the maximum expression of commitment as a Lakota. It was ever thus, since the blood sacrifice in the Sun Dance has always been interpreted by traditionalists as the ultimate test of sincerity. The reader may recall the words of Chased by Bears, one of Densmore's informants, to this effect: "Thus, if a man says he will give a horse to Wakantanka, he is only giving to Wakantanka that which already belongs to him. . . . I must give something that I really value to show that my whole being goes with the lesser gifts; therefore I promise to give my body" (Densmore, 96). To pierce in the Sun Dance is to make the ultimately sincere statement of commitment to the people; it is to be Lakota in preeminent way. Again, as Sword's statement makes clear, this was ever thus: "The scars on my body show that I have danced the Sun Dance, and no Lakota will dispute my word" (Walker 1980, 74). Densmore also attests this in an ironic way: "Yonder man tells too fine a story of his part in the Sun dance—let him show his scars!" (1918, 94).

This function of the Sun Dance cannot be said to be an innovation. The Sun Dance was always a microcosm of the values of the Lakota, and dancing in the Sun Dance was always a test of one's possession of the essential Lakota traits of bravery, generosity, wisdom, and endurance. Dancing the Sun Dance was always a path to leadership. What is different in contemporary times is that traditional identity itself is a choice, and the status to be gained by dancing the Sun Dance is primarily gained in the context of a voluntary community.

In this context, it is important to keep in mind that the traditionalists are one of the two primary political factions on the contemporary reservation. The other faction consists of the more highly assimilated Lakotas who tend to live in the population centers of Pine Ridge and Rosebud and work for the government. Sandstrom's analysis suggests that what matters most in ethnic identity is who is excluded. I believe this insight is the key to understanding certain features of the contemporary dance that have been overlooked or misinterpreted by commentators. For instance, based on his observation of the 1979 dance at Porcupine, Paul B. Steinmetz concludes that the Sun Dance is becoming pan-Indian in orientation, and "the seeking of an individual Indian identity seems more important than a tribal one" (1990, 32). However, Steinmetz notes that the dance he observed was the culmination of four years of dances held by the tribal council at Porcupine, which, as he notes, was an AIM stronghold. The community that AIM seeks to create is indeed a pan-Indian one, and whites are the group that it is most important to exclude in this context. I believe that this accounts for the element of confrontation that Steinmetz says characterizes the contemporary dance (34). Since AIM is oriented primarily to the national political stage rather than to reservation politics, exclusion of other Indians is of secondary importance. Exclusion of whites and "wannabes" is essential, however, for the strategy of AIM is to exploit the advantages inherent in Indianness on a national platform. Based on Sandstrom's model, that is to say that AIM members perceive certain benefits for themselves and their people in choosing to be distinct from whites.

On the other hand, the traditional community on the reservation is primarily oriented to reservation politics. In this context, the exclusion of whites is not the essential issue, as Fools Crow's invitation to Steinmetz to participate in the dance indicates (Steinmetz 1990, 31). At the dance associated with Fools Crow in 1983, the security guards were posted not to exclude whites, but to exclude those who were drinking or those who wished to photograph or tape record the dance. These are precisely the negative (for traditionalists) behaviors associated with the tribal council's Sun Dances. In contrast with the AIM-dominated dances reported by Steinmetz and others, no element of confrontation whatsoever was observed toward whites at this dance. The people this community is most anxious to exclude are those who use alcohol. In this context, the use of alcohol characterizes both the more assimilated Lakotas and the failed and despairing poor of the reservation. For the Fools Crow group, the exclusion of whites is secondary. It could be said they have the tradition on their side in this regard; recall that Walker's informants told him that "anyone may dance the Sun Dance if he will do as the Oglalas do" (Walker 1980, 181). In any case, the reservation traditionalists are fairly secure in their identity with respect to the whites. The point at issue is their identity with respect to their political opponents, the progressive faction symbolized by a former tribal chairman, Dick Wilson. Recall that although I heard no disparaging remarks about whites at the 1983 Fools Crow dance, one spectator referred disparagingly to "the goons" who the traditionalists accuse of enforcing a reign of terror during Wilson's administration.[8]

The above analysis also explains the piercing of women in dances associated with AIM. Since AIM moves in a national political context, the movement for the equality of women has had much more influence on it than on the reservation traditionalists. If piercing in the Sun Dance is to be the ultimate test of commitment to the movement, it is clear that it must be open to women as well as to men. The issue of Christianity is also much more important to the AIM group than it is to the traditionalists. For the AIM group, rejection of Christianity is considered absolutely essential for an Indian identity. On the other hand, the Fools Crow group makes no such demand of its members, many of whom are practicing Christians.

This underscores a point that I made earlier, which is that it matters greatly which Sun Dance one is observing. Given the plurality of dances on the reservation today, it is important not to generalize merely on the basis of the dance(s) that one has happened to observe. The above analysis suggests that there are primarily three classes of contemporary dances described in the literature: (1) those primarily sponsored by the tribal council, (2) those primarily sponsored by AIM, and (3) those primarily sponsored by reservation traditionalists.[9] It might be doubted that the dances sponsored by the tribal council, which are evaluated so negatively in the literature, were primarily religious observances. Their essential motivation seems to have been to make money on tourism and, possibly, to appease the traditionalists (a tactic that ultimately failed). The essential strategy of the AIM dances seems to be to create a pan-Indian iden-

8. Mary Crow Dog describes the activities of the goons graphically in her autobiography (115–16, 192–98).

9. If current trends continue, it may be that a fourth major group may emerge that will consist of dances sponsored by holy men with primarily white or European clients.

tity in an attempt to build a large enough organization of Indians to play effectively on the national political stage. On the other hand, the dominant motivation of the reservation traditionalists, from the point of view of the strategy of ethnicity, is to create a social world that provides an alternative to both the assimilationist tendencies of the more progressive reservation factions and to the rampant alcoholism that both expresses and creates despair. Since this alternative world embodies a political as well as a cultural vision, the traditionalists constitute an alternate political, as well as social, community on the reservation.

Although the Sun Dance was always political, ethnic identity was hardly an issue in the days before the reservation system. In the old days, ethnic identity was not chosen, it was bestowed by birth in the tribe and by language. The dance to a certain extent differentiated the bands from one another, but this is hardly the same thing as ethnic identity in the sense we have been exploring. As a part of the strategy of ethnic identity, the Sun Dance functions to exclude outsiders and reward insiders. In the old days, the dance certainly functioned to provide rewards, but it also functioned to include outsiders, for the Sun Dance was the one function to which even tribes that were hereditary enemies were invited and at which they participated peacefully.

In assessing the development undergone by the Sun Dance in the modern period, it must be remembered that, as the preceding chapters show, there never was a standard Sun Dance. The considerable freedom granted the holy man in the Lakota tradition, the differences in the individual pledges, the traditions of different bands or reservation communities, and changes in the physical and social circumstances of the dance ensure wide variation in this rich and complex ritual. However, the contemporary dance can still be compared fruitfully with the dance before the ban, for the dance has not simply been revived but has also changed and evolved in response to the circumstances and challenges of contemporary life.

In the ritual of the dance itself, perhaps the greatest change introduced in the modern period is the cessation of night dancing. If, as Fools Crow suggests (Mails 1979, 43), night dancing was discontinued during the ban for security reasons, this major change can be traced directly to the ban. The typical shape of the contemporary dance as a four-day, morning-to-afternoon celebration forms a significant contrast to the two-day, all-night dance characteristic of the classic period. The symbolic contrast between night and day is no longer operative, and the dancers sleep after each day's dance, altering the nature of the sacrifice. The symbolic role of the moon as a companion to the sun is no longer emphasized, and the appearance of the sun signals the start of another day's dance, not the end of a long night of dancing. The cessation of night dancing has probably also had a chilling effect on the role of the dance in love.

Another significant change is that the Sun Dance is no longer a major tribal mechanism for the redistribution of wealth, a function that seems to have been taken over to a large extent by the churches (Powers 1987, 114–19). Nearly every account of the classic dance emphasizes this feature, stress being laid on the high cost of the preparations for the pledger and his family and on the giving of valuable gifts, such as horses, to effect the release of relatives or friends. Although, as Mails points out (1978, 78), the costs of giving a Sun Dance continue to be high, the burden to fund the dance tends to fall on the intercessor, who may seek money from outside sources. In some cases, contemporary pledgers have been paid or have received travel expenses. Although the financial involvement of the pledgers and their families is certainly still significant, contemporary Sun Dances do not incorporate the giving away of property to effect the release of the pledger from his bonds. In this sense, the contemporary dance is more egalitarian than the classic dance, in which the less wealthy pledgers faced a much more rigorous ordeal. In the prereservation period, the Sun Dance was essential for the survival of the poor and elderly through the coming winter. Now that this responsibility is taken up to a certain degree by the government and the churches, participation in the Sun Dance is no longer essential for these populations.

Another major change is that the mythological background of the dance as reported by Walker has vanished, the old pantheon being replaced by a generalized traditional cosmos, which retains the four directions, *Wakan Tanka,* and the view of the universe as a web of relationships.[10] Many changes in ritual actions, articles, and sym-

10. Essential documents for understanding the contemporary Lakota religious worldview include Thomas E. Mails (1979), John (Fire) Lame Deer and Richard Erdoes, William K. Powers (1982), and Ed McGaa.

bolism are probably correlated with modernization of the mythological worldview held by Lakotas. Certainly the mythology of war and the buffalo hunt has largely disappeared. The tree is no longer elaborately scouted as an enemy, mock attacks are no longer made on it, the colorful charges no longer take place, the pledgers are no longer "captured," and the tree presents a greener, leafier appearance, in accord with the symbolism of the tree as representative of life. The community is still perceived as threatened from without, but the nature of the threat has changed, and war is no longer the relevant mechanism for the acquisition of wealth and the defense of the people. Although the dance is still a major focus of Lakota pride and militancy, much of the symbolism related to the mythology of war has thus disappeared from the ritual of the dance. As the previous chapter has shown, Black Elk consciously implemented changes in the interpretation of the dance that replaced some of the war symbolism of the dance with modern equivalents.

Although the teaching function of the Sun Dance continues, its influence is attenuated by the relatively short duration of the dance itself. The announcer attempts to fill this void to a certain extent. In the 1983 Fools Crow dance, the microphone was in constant use during rest periods, and the content of all of the remarks could be construed as "instruction." But the announcer's own remarks contained much scolding about breaches of traditional etiquette, indicating that the teaching function of the dance has not been adequately replaced. Although Fools Crow does not require a vision quest, Eagle Feather does, and it can be assumed that some instruction of the pledger is implied in this relationship. However, at least with respect to the Fools Crow dance that I observed in 1983, the "performance standards" were quite high, indicating that considerable care is taken in rehearsal of the dance, which probably includes much broader instruction as well.

The relationship of the Sun Dance to other social rituals and celebrations has also changed. The entire ritual complex once centered on the dance, with essentially every important social and religious observance woven into the fabric of the Sun Dance festival. Today important religious and social rituals take place throughout the year, and the Sun Dance is increasingly celebrated on its own, detached from social dancing and other religious observances. In part, this is a necessary function of the much shorter duration of the festival, the contemporary Sun Dance consuming four days (or five days if one participates in the day of preparation on which the tree is raised) as opposed to several weeks. It also reflects the pluralistic situation on the reservation today. Although the Sun Dance certainly affects the entire reservation, being a major matter of public discussion and controversy,[11] attendance is now limited to persons who voluntarily identify with the portion of the traditional community that is holding the dance. The recent withdrawal of the traditionalists from the dances sponsored by the tribal council (with their subsequent powwow) is part of this trend. Although sole control of the Sun Dance by the holy men is certainly a traditional characteristic, the classic dance was celebrated amid numerous other rituals, secular and religious. The contemporary Sun Dance, as a "stand alone" festival, maintains its distance from these other forms of cultural expression, another indication of its much different position in the community. The need of the traditional community for autonomy and control of the ritual dictated this compromise with traditional practice.

There have also been various changes in the style of dance. Suspending the pledger so that he must dance in place, standing on tiptoe, has not been observed in the contemporary dance. The basic contemporary style of dance, which was also observed in the classic period, is that in which the dancer runs or pulls back from the tree from a greater distance, the feet at all times planted firmly on the ground.[12] The form of the sacrifice in which a dancer is pierced in the chest and back and then attached to four posts, dancing on tip-

11. During the Sun Dance season, the letters published in *Indian Country Today* reflect a variety of points of view on the dance. White participation or observation is a subject of frequent comment and condemnation.

12. It is possible that the form of the dance in which the dancer is suspended on tiptoe is an earlier style of dance than that of pulling back from the tree. It could also be accommodated in a smaller ritual area. In this style of dance, the dancer is "suspended" in a more literal way than is the dancer who pulls back from the tree, and the sacrifice can be considered a more rigorous affair. On the other hand, this style of dance may be indigenous to one or more of the bands, being reported most recently by Frances Densmore, who interviewed at Standing Rock, primarily a Hunkpapa community.

toe, has not been reported in the contemporary period. Full suspension from the tree is a feature of the contemporary dance, as is the form of the sacrifice that involves carrying or dragging buffalo skulls. In general, piercing seems to have been more severe at the start of the reservation period, although the piercing reported immediately before the ban seems comparable to the typical sacrifice reported today. Some contemporary sacrifices, such as those involving full suspension, are clearly more severe than those reported by Fletcher and others who observed these "last" dances. The fasting regulations seem in general to have been relaxed. The total of dancers and pledgers, which seems to have declined in the period immediately before the ban, has returned to a level comparable to that observed in the early reservation period.

Piercing in successive years is strictly a feature of the modern dance. There is no report in the literature of the classic dance of multiple sacrifices in this sense, perhaps in part because the torture was more severe. In some cases, multiple piercing may be interpreted as a "professionalization" of the dance stemming from a shortage of people willing to undergo the sacrifice. This correlates with the need to compensate the pledgers monetarily, which is reported most often in conjunction with dances held by the tribal council. In the case of Eagle Feather's dance, in which a core community reassembles each year to pierce, what is reflected is apparently a yearly recommitment to the values of the community. Especially with alcohol abuse, there seems to be in Eagle Feather's group a subtext of commitment, backsliding, and recommitment that mirrors to some extent the Christian cycle of sin, confession, and forgiveness. But even in the Fools Crow dance of 1983 many of the pledgers exhibited multiple scars. Given the relatively high number of pledgers in this dance, this should probably be interpreted in terms of the increasing role of the dance in personal identity rather than as owing to a shortage of pledgers. Among certain contemporary factions, the number of times one has been pierced probably expresses one's level of commitment to traditional culture.

The nature of the contemporary vow illustrates that the balance between the individual and the community has tipped toward the community. Although pledgers still pledge to obtain shamanic power and to effect healing, the contemporary period has seen the advent of a new type of pledge, emphasized by Black Elk, in which the sacrifice is pledged "for the people," the object of the sacrifice being to obtain power for the community, not for the individual who is pledging. In purely formal terms, this type of pledge is common to both the AIM and Fools Crow dances, although the specific community referenced may not be identical. Although this theme was always latent in the dance, in the classic period Sun Dance vows emphasized the fulfillment of an individual wish. Although the war vow benefited the community indirectly, by stimulating activity necessary to the society, its primary focus was the here-and-now concern of the individual warrior.

Once the broad nature of the cultural changes during the historical period are noted and the basic changes in the interpretation and direction of the dance introduced by Black Elk in response to these changes are understood, the continuity in the dance is remarkable, particularly given the long hiatus in its public performance imposed by the ban. As Thomas H. Lewis points out, the nuclear ceremonial forms are basically intact (48).[13] The Sun Dance is still an annual festival, taking place in the summer, centering on a vow made to *Wakan Tanka* to suffer. The dance still takes place in a circular ritual space defined by a tree cut for the purpose and replanted. The spectators still observe the dance from a shade and the mystery circle is still conceived as brimming with spiritual energy and power. The dancers still wear skirts, blow whistles, and carry sage. Piercing continues, and sacrifice is still the essence of the dance. Flesh offerings are still made in solidarity with the pledgers. There is also considerable continuity in the ritual action itself, despite the many changes detailed above.

As another measure of continuity, the Sun Dance exhibits essential continuity with the "characteristics" reported by Alice Fletcher. The contemporary dance is still well described as issuing from a pledge uttered in time of sickness or trouble, although the "trouble" may now comprise the struggle for survival experienced by the traditional community. Fletcher's mental characteristics, thanksgiving

13. Lewis's observations and analysis are reported in detail in the previous chapter.

and the desire for future benefits, are still prominent, as are her religious characteristics, which are the belief in supernatural powers and a deep sense of religious obligation. The essential belief in the relevance, necessity, and efficacy of blood sacrifice remains prominent in the modern dance, despite its obvious conflict with Christian teaching. The dance continues to serve a teaching function, remaining the focus of a yearly effort to educate the youths in the values of traditional culture.

All concerned in initiating the great experiment in social engineering known as Grant's peace policy were convinced—not only that they were doing good—but that their policies would inevitably prevail. One lesson to be drawn from this policy is clearly that religious oppression is dubiously effective, even when it is carried out on a fairly massive scale. The ultimate failure of the effort to assimilate the Indians by force can perhaps be attributed to naïve assumptions—by both the public and contemporary social scientists—about the nature and function of religion. If men such as Bishop Whipple and the agents from the era of the ban could return to the reservation, they would no doubt be startled and appalled by the vitality of the contemporary Sun Dance. The first question that we can imagine them asking is, Why on earth are they still dancing the Sun Dance?

There is no single, simple answer to this question. For traditionalists, the dance continues to be the central public expression of their religion. Its public revival, after years of repression, is symbolic of the struggle of traditionalism itself to remain a viable part of reservation life. The yearly performance of the Sun Dance both symbolizes and ensures the success of that struggle, being simultaneously an expression of thanks for the survival of the community through the last year and a gathering of strength for the trials of the next. The Sun Dance, the heart of traditional religion, still beats strongly at its center today.

Since the Sun Dance issues from an individual vow, the same question could also be posed in the form, Why do Lakotas continue to pledge to dance the Sun Dance? There are personal reasons for pledging the Sun Dance, which range from a desire to gain status in the traditional community to a desire for personal power or healing.

Because the dance is the focus of traditional identity, it may also be undertaken by the pledger to identify himself or herself more fully as Lakota by a binding of self to the essential expression of traditional cultural identity. On the level of religious belief and ideology, the persistence of the Sun Dance vow indicates that Lakotas continue to believe in the efficacy and necessity of sacrifice, this particular sacrifice being believed necessary to secure not only the survival of the traditional community but also of the entire earth. On this level, participation in the Sun Dance identifies the pledger not only with the daily struggle of the traditional community to ensure its political, material, and spiritual well-being but also with the cosmic struggle and drama.

In addition, it cannot be overemphasized that the Sun Dance is a powerful emotional and spiritual experience. The pledgers and spectators alike participate in the making of a colorful ritual that ripples with astonishing energy. From this point of view, it does not matter whether the energy is perceived as natural or as supernatural in origin. The power generated by the Sun Dance is palpably felt by the community, which in itself provides a sufficient explanation for participation in the dance. To attend the Sun Dance is to stand in the presence of power. The experience itself is its own reward, perhaps more so, since any given traditional community can experience the Sun Dance only once a year. To attend the Sun Dance is to feel the power, to approach religious ecstasy, to experience for oneself the essence of a religion based on power. The Sun Dance sweeps away any possible doubts about the existence of sacred power in a searing emotional catharsis, reinforcing through personal experience the reality and efficacy of traditional religion.

The essential history of the Sun Dance in modern times is its survival of change, repression, and neglect. The ban did not produce its intended result, the complete destruction of traditional belief and ritual. For that matter, the peace policy itself failed to achieve its objective, the solution of the Indian problem through the complete assimilation of the Indian into mainstream American culture. Rather, the efforts to civilize and acculturate the Lakota have resulted in the present pluralistic situation, in which traditional religion coexists with a wide diversity of religious expression. For a significant portion of the reservation community, the result has not been the hoped-for replacement of traditional religion with Christianity but the acceptance of both. As bireligious, many Lakotas profess belief in some form of denominational Christianity while continuing to practice traditional religion. A significant portion of the Sun Dance community thus overlaps with the Christian community.

Note that the result is not syncretism, as the term is usually employed, to designate the blending of two religious traditions. The contemporary Sun Dance does not incorporate Christian symbolism. The observer of the Sun Dance, ignorant of the Christian associations of many participants, would find little that is reminiscent of Christianity. At the dance at Three Mile Camp I observed, the only practice that could possibly be interpreted as incorporating Christian symbolism was the frequent giving of flesh offerings made in the form of a cross. The prominent crossbar, which Feraca interprets as turning the tree into a cross, was not observed, nor was the cross that Black Elk inscribed within the mystery circle. No mention was made of Christianity by the announcer, and no effort was made to verbally associate the ritual with Christianity. Although Catholics have incorporated elements of the Lakota tradition into Christian services,[14] overtly Christian elements are absent from the Sun Dance. There is considerable evidence of change and adaptation in the Lakota tradition, but there is little evidence of blending of Christianity with traditional religion as expressed in the Sun Dance. Rather, Lakotas maintain allegiances in two religious worlds, the Christian and the traditional.

The religious change and adaptation characteristic of native American religion in historical times has often been understood as degeneration, a passive and mechanical response to external pressure. The Lakota Sun Dance reveals a more positive and creative aspect to this rapid religious change. Through the efforts of holy men such as Black Elk, Eagle Feather, and Fools Crow, the Sun Dance is celebrated today, not as a museum piece, but as an authentic and viable expression of Lakota religion in a modern context.

14. Paul B. Steinmetz discusses his use of traditional elements in Catholic worship in (1969), (1970), and (1990).

The Lakota Sun Dance, like traditional Lakota religion itself, has survived considerable repression. It stands as a model case of religious evolution and change, symbolizing the staunch determination of traditionalists to maintain their cultural and religious identity. Through their efforts, traditional religion's uniquely American vision of man, the earth, and the cosmos still presents a philosophical and theological challenge to European thought and culture.

7

Black Elk and Dual Participation

In 1984, Raymond J. DeMallie said that Black Elk's Christianity presents the greatest challenge to our understanding of his life and work: "Today Black Elk's Catholicism presents the biggest gap in our understanding of him as a whole human being. How was it that a nineteenth-century Lakota mystic lived a full half of the twentieth century on the Pine Ridge Reservation in harmony with the encroaching white man's world?" (Deloria 1984, 124). It seems that this is no less the case ten years later, since we are still struggling to produce a whole Black Elk, despite our far greater knowledge of his life and the giant step forward represented by critical work that conceives Black Elk as an active creator of his people's present rather than as a passive victim of acculturation and an informant on the past. But the result of the recent critical inquiry into Black Elk's relationship to Christianity is still to leave us with two essentially incommensurable Black Elks—a traditionalist and a Catholic— where there should be one whole person. The essential issue seems to center on sincerity. Michael F. Steltenkamp's Black Elk is a sincere Catholic who retains some appreciation for the Lakota tradition but whose participation in the Duhamel pageant was insincere. Julian Rice's Black Elk is a traditionalist whose Catholicism was insincere, simply a strategy, a ruse for protecting his people and preserving traditional religion. Paul B. Steinmetz's Black Elk, like Steltenkamp's, has made a sincere and total commitment to Catholicism as the fulfillment of traditional Lakota religion. One of DeMallie's suggestions is that Black Elk was a sincere Catholic convert who relapsed into traditionalism upon meeting Neihardt. This view at least has the ad-

204

vantage of presenting a whole Black Elk, but there is little or no direct evidence to confirm it, and it is not accepted by the other three commentators. It is even questioned by DeMallie's own later remarks, which tend to construe Black Elk's Catholicism along the lines suggested by Rice. It is hardly accidental that these positions tend to mirror the interests and commitments of their proponents. The Catholic commentators understandably claim Black Elk for the church; those more attracted to his traditionalism are inclined to question the sincerity of his commitment as a Catholic. It boils down to an either/or: Black Elk cannot have been a sincere Catholic, for he was a traditionalist; Black Elk cannot have been a traditionalist, for he was a sincere Catholic. Does this mean that we are left with two irreducibly different Black Elks, with the choice between them simply a matter of one's own inclinations and preferences?

William K. Powers, an anthropologist who has specialized in the Lakota, poses the question in the context of the concept of "dual religious participation," a phenomenon that "has perplexed anthropologists, missionaries, and government bureaucrats for decades perhaps because the phenomenon appears to be a contradiction in terms" (1987, 96). Even when one has stripped away assumptions based on one-sided acculturation theories and ethnocentric biases, dual participation remains a puzzle: "[H]ow do we explain the tendency of native peoples to participate in two discrete religious systems? Do they in fact 'adore' two gods, one represented in the ritual paraphernalia of the Grandfathers, the other in the beaded chasuble, maniple, and stole of the priest?" (99).

To make a fresh start, Powers proposes that dual participation cannot be understood if it is assumed that Christianity and native religion "fulfill the same needs rather than disparate ones," since this leads to the expectation that the two belief systems will collide and produce "either tension or conflation" (100). The solution is to discard the assumption that we are dealing with bireligion or "dual religious belief," since participation is different from belief: "I agree that indeed he cannot believe in two religions, but this is not to say that he cannot participate in more than one" (100). If Christianity and traditional religion both functioned as belief systems, the expectation would be that they would be syncretized. Among the Oglala, however, they coexist rather than conflate, which can only be understood on the basis of a structural-functional model: "I will argue that Christianity and Oglala religion coexist because they serve quite disparate functions" (102). In effect, while traditional religion meets religious needs, Christianity meets social and economic needs. The result of the combination of the two is to guarantee the persistence of the values that underlie Oglala cultural and social identity. The answer to the riddle of dual participation is thus the recognition that it is a strategic response to circumstances: "I regard the participation by Oglala in Christian sects as social, political, economic, and religious strategies" (102). The acceptance of Christianity by the Lakota was partly due to the fact that it provided a refuge from the part of the white world that regarded them as savage and hostile. However, the key to understanding Lakota Christianity is the recognition that through structural transformations, Christianity became a vehicle for the preservation of Oglala institutions and values: "Thus the Oglala were not so much to become Christianized as Christianity was to become nativized" (109). In accord with the recent anthropological stress on "ethnicity as strategy," Powers argues that this took place as a conscious strategy, not as a by-product of a supposedly inevitable process called syncretism. Rather, the Oglala "used Christianity consciously and positively in order to survive" (109).

Powers works out the idea of structural replication in concrete terms by suggesting that denominational loyalties in some ways replicate or reflect the former loyalty to the *tiyospaye* (band), including the rule of exogamy, whereby Lakota Christians tend to marry outside the denomination. The structure of the *tiyospaye*, a social organization that is no longer functional, is thus preserved in a Christian context, in effect "nativizing" the Christian institution. In the same way, the Catholic Congresses functioned to replace the Sun Dance as an assemblage of *tiyosapes*.[1] With respect to political strategies, Powers places the most emphasis on church membership as a means to learn to read and write English. Although this does not seem to be an

---

1. As Steltenkamp makes clear, they were designed specifically to fill the void left by the banning of the Sun Dance (1993, 46). Christopher Vecsey describes these congresses in some detail (n.d., 28–32) and points out that one observer indicated that they were dying a natural death in 1962 (32). The decline of the congresses thus coincides with the revival of the Sun Dance.

example of structural replication, it is a skill that is clearly related to survival in the white-dominated world. With respect to economic strategies, Powers notes that the church distributes food and clothing to needy families, so that Lakotas increase their chance of survival through church membership. Previously the band had performed this function, with its own mechanisms for the charitable distribution of wealth to the needy.[2] By way of religious strategies, Powers argues that holy men become Christians to learn about the white man's gods: "Religious strategy in particular explains the participation of medicine men in Christian rituals for the purpose of understanding the supraempirical beings and powers of the white man" (102). He further suggests that the current Catholic involvement in native religion is simply the same process occurring from the other side. With respect to Black Elk, Powers thus seems to be most in accord with Rice, who sees Black Elk's Christianity essentially as a strategy to protect his people. Since Powers insists that we are dealing with a conscious strategy rather than an inevitable process (syncretism), he would presumably also agree with Rice's stress on the active and creative role of holy men such as Black Elk in preserving traditional values and institutions.

In conclusion, Powers quotes Stephen E. Feraca's assessment that Teton religious concepts are essentially unchanged (Feraca 1963, vii) and suggests that the two religions do not interact on the level of belief: "At the level of public ritual, the two religions conjoin; but at the level of private belief, Christianity and native religion, the respective components of dual religious participation at Pine Ridge, are separate and always have been" (123). In other words, the idea that the Lakota have taken to Christianity is simply a myth. Rather than having been doomed to assimilation into Christianity, the Oglala have overcome it by strategically using it to achieve the end of maintaining the structural integrity of their social organization. Whether this is an accurate assessment or not, the current anthropological stress on ethnicity as strategy, with its somewhat belated discovery of the agency of the natives, is a giant step forward

2. Powers's observation that church attendance increases when dinner is served cannot be regarded as decisive, since attendance on many functions increases when dinner is served.

in understanding contemporary native American culture, particularly when it is contrasted with earlier theories of acculturation that simply assumed that native Americans were the passive victims of an inevitable process of change the outcome of which—assimilation—was a foregone conclusion.

Since Powers implies not only that native Christianity is insincere, but also that the missionaries were—and are—simply unwitting dupes of the nativist agenda, his interpretation is hardly congenial to commentators such as Steinmetz and Steltenkamp who regard Black Elk's Christianity as primary. Although Steltenkamp characteristically does not engage Powers directly, Paul B. Steinmetz disputes several key elements in his interpretation. While he does not deny that the kind of structural transformations that Powers notes have occurred and are occurring, he believes that the notion that Lakota Christianity is insincere is simply false. Further, Steinmetz argues that far from being intact, traditional religion has been deeply influenced by Christianity. Moreover, the forms of Christianity found on the reservation have also been influenced by traditional religion. Steinmetz explicitly disputes the correctness of Powers's functional analysis, saying "to claim that Lakota religion satisfies religious needs and Christianity social ones is simply being blind to the facts" (1990, 179). As one example, Steinmetz points out that at the time of death, Lakotas—including the traditional holy men—universally turn to the Christian church.

A more personal issue is also at stake between Powers and Steinmetz, for Powers impugns Steinmetz's motives in adopting the sacred pipe (1987, 99). In response, Steinmetz protests that Powers is incorrectly informed on certain facts and has simply prejudged his motives (1990, xii, 178–79). As for Powers's rejection of the idea that the pipe is a foreshadowing of the Christ, Steinmetz replies: "The truth is that Powers's rejection of this concept is a form of anthropological imperialism in which an anti-Christian bias does not allow him to see the empirical fact that Christianity had a significant influence on Lakota religion" (1990, 178). Perhaps Powers would not dispute the assessment that his estimate of the value of Christianity is extremely low. The influence of Christianity on traditional religion seems quite clear, however, particularly in the light of the basic adjustments that Black Elk made in the ritual and interpretation of the

Sun Dance, which have been largely accepted by contemporary holy men. Powers might argue in reply that these apparent changes are only structural transformations and not essential changes. Without such an argument, it must be said that Powers's claim that Christianity and traditional religion do not interact on the level of belief is demonstrably false—many Lakotas profess both forms of belief, and evidences of mutual influence certainly exist.

In part, Powers's functionalism is simply another way of implying that Black Elk's Christianity is insincere. A few brief philosophical remarks may be in order to help clarify this discussion. To disagree about a man's sincerity is to differ on the extent to which his public actions or utterances or both are in accord with his personal and private beliefs. Such disagreement is intrinsically incapable of final proof, since the ultimate appeal is to something that is subjective, private, and unavailable for public inspection. It seems that beliefs about the sincerity of others are rather strongly held. When we suspect that a person is being insincere, almost no evidence can compel us to change our minds. When we doubt a person's sincerity, we routinely question even their protestations of sincerity, for such protestations are subject to the same doubt that accompanies their other utterances. Since it is possible to doubt even one's own sincerity, it is likely that the matter could not be resolved even if it were possible to access another person's private mental states.

But this does not mean that no public evidence can be adduced as relevant. In general, we have grounds to question a person's sincerity when one or more of the following conditions are met: (1) that person is under duress; (2) that person stands to benefit in some way; (3) that person's statements or actions are contradictory. All three conditions pertain to a certain extent with Black Elk. As for the first condition, an element of duress was clearly present in Black Elk's acceptance of Christianity. According to Lucy Looks Twice, his daughter, Black Elk's conversion was occasioned by physical intimidation and coercion. As I have argued in the first chapter, this story should probably be discounted. It cannot be denied, however, that Black Elk's conversion took place in the context of considerable economic and political duress. In this sense, Lucy Looks Twice's story of Black Elk's conversion tells the essential truth. As the account of the ban shows, considerable pressure was brought to bear to induce the Lakota to accept Christianity. The ban on the Sun Dance and on traditional healing, which hurt the holy men economically, was only one aspect of this pressure.

With respect to the second condition, Black Elk clearly stood to benefit by accepting Christianity, since his income as a catechist was considerable.[3] Since Black Elk subsequently made his living as a catechist, it could be said that the material benefits of his acceptance of Christianity point to the possibility of insincerity. With this in mind, his actions during the recriminations with the Jesuits over *Black Elk Speaks* could be adduced as evidence that he maneuvered to preserve his living in the context of this cause célèbre.[4]

In having economic reasons for accepting Christianity, Black Elk as a holy man was simply a special case, for as Powers has shown, there were economic benefits for all Lakotas in accepting Christianity. Pointing to these advantages is insufficient to prove that Black Elk's acceptance of Christianity was insincere. For one thing, material factors always affect a person's choice of religion and social group. For another, Black Elk's people desperately needed an economic and social strategy, which it was Black Elk's vocation as a holy man to devise. The fact that Black Elk was concerned about his people's political, economic, and social well-being was integral to his religion and role as holy man. Black Elk's vision for his people was necessarily a political and economic strategy. The idea of religion as concerned with the salvation of souls without concern for their economic and social conditions is a feature of certain versions of Christianity, not of traditional Lakota religion, which is oriented decisively

---

3. In his prepublication critique, Paul B. Steinmetz disputes this point, saying that Black Elk made $10 per month, and that "even with the value of money for those days, financial gain could not have been a motive." Steltenkamp reports that estimates of Black Elk's monthly salary vary from $5 to $25 (1993, 70). I am inclined to think that in the reservation economy of the day, any cash income was significant. Steltenkamp also indicates that Black Elk's missionary travels to other tribes were subsidized additionally (71).

4. Christopher Vecsey emphasizes that Black Elk's recantations of *Black Elk Speaks* were signed after his recovery from being run over by a team of horses and a wagon, suggesting that last rites were withheld until Black Elk agreed to recant. "Just how much pressure was applied, we shall never know; however, it is clear that a *quid quo pro* took place" (n.d., 37).

to the survival and well-being of the people on earth. In other words, to say that the acceptance of Christianity by Black Elk was a strategy is only to state the obvious—his people badly needed a strategy for survival.

At the same time, I do not think that it is discourteous to point out that Black Elk may have had his eye on his own interests. Ritual specialists and priests by definition make their living by practicing religion. If Black Elk chose Catholicism in part because he could improve his living, he acted essentially no differently than a Christian minister who chooses a wealthy suburban parish with a large stipend over a poor, inner city ministry. If Black Elk believed that what the Catholic Church taught was to a certain extent true and that it was to a certain extent doing good, he could have served it in good conscience. Although others might assess participation on these minimal grounds as insufficiently sincere, I would point out that raising the bar for sincerity any higher than this might well exclude most of the ritual specialists of any religion.[5] If he felt it was the best course open to his people, he might even have endorsed it despite his personal reservations. But I find it difficult to accept Julian Rice's notion that Black Elk satisfied his conscience by dissembling for a higher good and merely pretending to be a Catholic as a strategic maneuver. Similarly, I find it difficult to accept the implications of Powers's remarks, which is that people such as Black Elk joined the church in a self-conscious effort to subvert it culturally and exploit it materially.

In the first place, this picture seems inconsistent with Black Elk's character as a militant during the Ghost Dance disturbances.[6] In the light of this affair, Black Elk hardly seems to have the character either of a mole or an accommodationist. In the second place, as my analysis has shown, Black Elk accepted some elements of the Chris-

5. In practical terms, a stronger test would be subject to the same dialectic that characterizes the concept of "sincerity" itself. Suppose, for instance, we require a conversion experience. How would we know who is sincere in professing to have had one?

6. Those who are certain that Black Elk would never have endorsed the actions of AIM at Wounded Knee in 1973 seem to have lost sight of Black Elk's actions during the Ghost Dance, during which he advocated armed resistance to the army (DeMallie 1984, 268).

tian critique of traditional religion and modified the Sun Dance in the light of them. Were Black Elk to have occupied the strategic position implied by Rice and Powers, it seems to me that he would more likely have chosen either the path of outright resistance or the path of the nominal Christian, as Fools Crow apparently did. Unlike Fools Crow, Black Elk chose to become deeply identified with the Catholic cause on the reservation, which would seem to indicate that his participation was sincere, given his obvious integrity and pride in himself as a Lakota holy man.

What do we make of the third ground for suspecting insincerity, the presence of contradictory statements or actions? As Powers's discussion makes clear, the fundamental assumption on which suspicion of Black Elk's sincerity rests is that a person cannot believe in two religions at once. This assumption is at bottom the reason that commentators have not produced a whole Black Elk. Given this assumption, at any time, Black Elk has to be either a sincere Catholic or a sincere traditionalist, because he cannot have been both.

Again, a brief philosophical analysis may be helpful in clarifying the discussion. Why is it that a person cannot believe in two religions at once? The answer would seem to be that because they both propose beliefs, their truth claims are contradictory and the person can necessarily credit only one at a time.[7] That is, a person cannot credit two contradictory statements about the same thing. For instance, I cannot believe both that Rapid City is ten miles north and that it is twenty miles south. Similarly, Christianity describes the godhead as a trinity of persons while Lakota religion conceptualized the godhead as the *wakan tanka*. These beliefs seem to be simply incompatible and contradictory. However, the premise on which this argument rests is the perception that religious beliefs are propositions of the scientific type. That is, that they are of the same logical type as scientific propositions, which are themselves assumed to be straightforwardly true or false.

The assumption that religious statements primarily concern mat-

7. In this context, saying that religious beliefs are compartmentalized means that we theorize that a person who professes dual religious belief in fact believes contradictory propositions, but at different times.

ters of fact is far from justified philosophically.[8] Can this assumption even be taken for granted within the everyday Lakota cultural context? In traditional Lakota culture, religion is most consistently equated with supernatural power—the power to overcome enemies, to ensure the bounty of the earth, or to heal the body of sickness. The holy man is the conduit of this power, the intercessor with the spirit world who can bring its power to work for men. There is, in the Lakota cultural context, no concern with salvation in the Christian sense, and no emphasis whatsoever on the Christian notion of salvation through true belief. The very notion of orthodoxy—correct belief—is completely foreign to traditional Lakota culture. Lakota religion exhibited considerable individualism in both belief and ritual expression. There was no credo, no catechism, no prayer book, and no hell to threaten those who failed to believe. The traditional religious obsession, if it could be called that, is with power and not with truth. As Rice points out, the traditional religious concerns most analogous with the Christian concern with salvation through true belief are the Lakota desire for health and for continuity of the tribe on the earth.

Furthermore, the fundamental orientation of an oral culture is to storytelling for the transmission of culture and to ritual for theological and philosophical expression. Each tribe had its own religion, its own origin myth, and its own stories. Each holy man had his own vision, which directed both his storytelling and his ritualizing. Each holy man tells the old stories differently, in accord with his vision. Steinmetz has catalogued eleven basic versions of the myth of the bringing of the sacred pipe to the Lakota by the White Buffalo Calf Woman (1991, 54). It is important to realize that these versions vary not only in detail but also in essential features and meaning. In a Western historical-critical context, such variation would immediately

8. Harold H. Oliver describes the "rational objectivation of myth" that leads to such an assumption: "Despite the judgment of many that the intention of myth is in no way *referential* to those who originated it, it has indeed come to be so to subsequent devotees. With the loss of its original intention, myth is interpreted as establishing a realm of divine objects comparable in reality to the human world, if not indeed more real. Affirming and even defending the reality of these objects becomes the new form of the ancient piety" (1981, 183).

create a demand to know which story was true, and—as critical work on the Gospels testifies—the discovery of discrepancies in such stories leads in this culture to the conclusion that none of them are true. But does anyone seriously propose that the same kind of concern for the literal truth of a text characterizes a traditional oral culture? Are we to assume that each storyteller regards his version alone as true and the others as false? In a traditional culture, it is not that the hearers of different versions of the story do not realize that they are different. It is that they assume that the truth conveyed is symbolic, not literal. Within a traditional context, the hearing of two different stories of the White Buffalo Calf Woman does not create cognitive dissonance, but insight into storytelling and the nature of religious truth. One might say that each story is regarded as true in its own way, or as having some truth of its own. Oliver points out in his critique of the objectivation of myth that myths are not problematical when they are transmitted, but become so only when they are reflected on from the historical-critical point of view.[9] In other words, religious discourse is misconstrued when its contents are objectified. The primary point of the story of the White Buffalo Calf Woman is not that she came on such-and-such a day and said and did such-and-such, but that we are related to her, through this story, in a meaningful way. Even the dullest member of a traditional culture would presumably grasp this point.

This is not to say that contemporary Lakotas do not experience cognitive dissonance when contemplating their dual participation from the point of view of Western science. As we have seen, Ben Black Elk apparently experienced such dissonance. My point is that the concept of religion as conveying essentially factual information is

9. "[M]yths become problematic when they are reflected upon rather than simply transmitted. Prior to the time when the myths are 'broken'—to use Paul Tillich's term—it is unthinkable that questions about the truth of these episodes should be raised. Such questions characterize the critical, not the mythical mind . . . once critical questions arise, they generate an understanding of myth as false objectivation. Subsequent generations influenced by such criticism are unable to re-enter the world of such myths without first becoming convinced that 'objectivizing' misses the intentionality of the mythical worldview. Even the concept of 'mythical worldview' betrays an objectifying mode of thinking which is foreign to the intentionality of myth" (1981, 182–83).

not at all native to the tradition of an oral culture, but arises only within a historical-critical consciousness, with its transformation of myth into objectifying discourse.

In any case, our primary concern is with Black Elk, and not with the common people. Is there any reason to believe that the great holy man took religion—either Catholicism or traditional religion—to be literally true? The essential touchstone of religion for Black Elk was his vision, and as was traditional, he continually modified it throughout his life in response to his unfolding understanding of religious truth and to changing economic and social conditions. The vision is filled with symbols, and there is no reason to assume that Black Elk did not realize that they were symbols. In other words, it is simply ethnocentric to assume without further ado that Black Elk must have experienced Christianity and traditional religion primarily as conflicting belief systems. It seems much more likely that Black Elk was predisposed to see religions statements as symbolic expressions of truths that could not be fully captured outside the context of religious ecstacy. If two holy men could have different visions without threatening the Lakota concept of religion, why could not two cultures have different visions of the sacred?

It may also be that perceiving religions as culture-bound symbol systems might come more easily to those who are forced to live in two cultures than to those who inhabit only one. As a missionized people, the insight that Christianity was the white people's tribal religion must have come fairly naturally. What else could the Lakota have made of the Black Robes and their strange obsession with imposing their beliefs on other people? Whether Christianity was perceived as tribal, however, from the Lakota perspective its efficacy was obvious. As Sword's testimony shows, the question for the Lakota holy man was not necessarily Christianity's "truth" but its power: "When I served the Lakota *Wakan Tanka,* I did so with all my power. When I went on the warpath I always did all the ceremonies to gain the favor of the Lakota *Wakan Tanka.* But when the Lakotas fought with the white soldiers, the white people always won the victory" (Walker 1980, 74). Might this not be the clue to the acceptance of Christianity by the Lakota, that its power was demonstrated in war?

It may be worth digressing a moment to consider whether the view that religions are culturally conditioned symbol systems can be made compelling within a Western philosophical and theological context. As a philosopher of religion, I know well how distressing this view can be to both believers and unbelievers. Believers resist it because it seems to be another way of saying that religion is not true; unbelievers resist it because it seems to be an attempt by religion to place itself beyond scientific criticism. Although it is not a part of the mission of this book to justify this concept philosophically, it might be pointed out that the notion that religious truth claims are of the same logical type as scientific truth claims arose relatively late in the history of Christianity, appearing decisively only as a result of the conflict between science and religion in the Enlightenment. In our own age, this view is expressed most clearly by Freud, who characterized religion essentially as pseudoscientific illusion. That is to say, religion purports to provide scientific information that is not acquired by scientific means or verified by scientific evidence: "Religious ideas are teachings and assertions about facts and conditions of external (or internal) reality which tell one something one has not discovered for oneself and which lay claim to one's belief."[10] In Freud's view, religion is simply science by revelation, which is to say, pseudo-science. It is essentially received belief that has the same aim as science, but is far inferior to it, since it has nothing whatsoever to offer as verification except a lame appeal to ancient authority. It does nothing and provides nothing of value that is not provided by science. To take an obvious example, the Hebrew Bible says that God created the heavens and the earth in a week, where science shows that creation was a process that took millennia. With this absurdly literal reading of the Genesis story, religion becomes knowledge with a very low degree of evidence, which is to say unjustified belief.[11] It could be argued, however, that Freud decisively misunderstood the truth claims of religion, which are not of the same logical type as scientific propositions, but are instead symbolic. It would then be that religion "means" in somewhat the same way as a work of art means— through the medium of culturally conditioned symbolic expression.

10. *The Future of an Illusion.* Trans. W. D. Robinson-Scott and rev. James Strachey (Garden City, N.Y.: Anchor Books, 1964), 37.
11. It is fair to characterize this reading of the creation myth in the Hebrew Bible as absurd, because it is obvious that it was not intended as scientific cosmology.

It is more than a little ironic that after a century of anthropological theorizing about the function of religion and its relation to culture—and almost more than thirty years since Clifford Geertz published "Religion as a Cultural System"—that William K. Powers, an anthropologist, most clearly articulates the assumption that religions are primarily competing systems of propositions.[12] This assumption also underlies the other critical work on Black Elk; the perceived opposition between Black Elk's traditionalism and his Christianity is largely a product of it. In the light of this assumption, Black Elk must be either a sincere Christian or a sincere traditionalist, for he simply cannot have been both. But if Black Elk did not share our culture-bound concept of religion as propositional truth, what reason is there to believe that he even felt the conflict? If they were to him two alternate ways of envisioning the sacred—or two stories about the sacred—not two mutually exclusive and absolute truth claims, it becomes easier to see how he could accept Christianity as a further unfolding of his vision, weaving Christian elements back into his account of his original power vision.

The impression that it was an either/or choice for Black Elk is further dissipated by the recognition that in reality three religions are involved with Black Elk. The assumption has too easily been made that Black Elk repudiated the Ghost Dance and shared the interpretation of Wounded Knee promulgated by the Jesuits and by Neihardt, which was that it was God's judgment on false religion. Just as the ban on the Sun Dance has been underestimated in discussions of Black Elk's religion, the fact is almost universally ignored that the Ghost Dance did not die a natural death, did not wither away, but required vigorous repression even two years after Wounded Knee, as J. George Wright's report from the Rosebud Agency indicates.

> The evidence of the existence of the Ghost Dance and its results has entirely disappeared, although in a few instances, early last spring, it was discovered that ghost shirts were being made and wild talk was indulged in by a few "brave medicine men." Prompt

12. Although my conception of religion is not essentially Geertzian, his essay clearly makes the point, in a social scientific context, that religious discourse is essentially symbolic.

action, however, with solitary confinement and compulsory work for a short time, effectively checked any movement in that direction. (CIA 1892, 460)

The assumption that the Ghost Dance withered away or collapsed under the weight of its own absurdity persists probably because its tenets are completely implausible from a scientific point of view that misconstrues religious discourse as propositional. But in fact nothing in Black Elk's interviews with Neihardt suggests that he repudiated the fundamental thrust of the Ghost Dance.[13] He claims to have been the chief dancer and "the leader in every dance" and also claims to have invented the ghost shirt (DeMallie 1984, 266, 262). These are not the statements of a man who wishes to repudiate the Ghost Dance. Surely if Black Elk had wished to repudiate the dance, he would have repudiated the ghost shirt! What he said, which was interpreted by Neihardt as a repudiation and recognition of error, was that perhaps he should have relied on his original vision during this time because it had more power (DeMallie 1984, 266). Not that the ghost dance vision had no power, or was false or untrue.[14]

Perhaps because Neihardt's interpretation of the Ghost Dance as a tragic mistake has been so pervasive,[15] it has commonly been over-

13. In this context, Steinmetz interprets Black Elk's references to the "son of the Great Spirit" in the Neihardt interviews as referring to Christ, not Wovoka (1990, 179–82). It seems to me that it makes more sense to read them as referring to Wovoka, without disputing the insight that acceptance of Wovoka by Black Elk was a bridge to his acceptance of the Christ. Perhaps in this sense the Ghost Dance served as the template for the Lakota acceptance of Christianity. In his prepublication critique of my manuscript, Steinmetz comments, "Holler misses the point that the wounds in the palms of the Ghost Dance Messiah and his body becoming radiant is an image of the risen Christ. Perhaps the best interpretation is that the Ghost Dance Messiah is Wovoka identified with Christ."

14. Black Elk did express some ambivalence about joining the fighting at Wounded Knee: "I just thought it over and I thought I should not fight. I doubted about this Messiah business and therefore it seemed that I should not fight for it, but anyway I was going because I had already decided to. If [I] turned back the people would think it funny, so I just decided to go anyway" (272). Whatever his doubts at the point of combat, Black Elk continued to accept the Ghost Dance's central religious idea, the revitalization of traditional culture through the practice of traditional religion.

15. I discuss Neihardt's interpretation of the Ghost Dance in more detail in my essay "Lakota Religion and Tragedy" (1984a, 31–37).

looked that there is much Ghost Dance in Black Elk's traditionalism. The Ghost Dance was fundamentally a response to a situation that did not arise in the days of Lakota religion before the whites, the loss of autonomy and the sense that something was radically wrong and needed fixing. There is a striking continuity between the value of the Ghost Dance—to reinvent and restore traditional culture through religious ritual—and the desire of the mature Black Elk to get his people back in the hoop and make the tree of his vision flower. In fact, it is clear from Black Elk's account of his participation in the Ghost Dance to Neihardt that he was attracted to it primarily because of its similarity to his vision: "At first when I heard this I was bothered, because my vision was nearly like it and it looked as though my vision were really coming true and that if I helped, probably with my power that I had I could make the tree bloom and that I would get my people back into that sacred hoop again where they would prosper" (DeMallie 1984, 257). When he attended his first dance, he was overcome by the similarity of the dance to his power vision.

> They had a sacred pole in the center. It was a circle in which they were dancing and I could clearly see that this was my sacred hoop and in the center they had an exact duplicate of my tree that never blooms and it came to my mind that perhaps with this power the tree would bloom and the people would get into the sacred hoop again. It seemed that I could recall all my vision in it. . . . Then happiness overcame me all at once and it got ahold of me right there. (DeMallie 1984, 258)

It also accorded with the fundamental thrust of his vision as he interpreted it in 1931: "Perhaps it was this Messiah that had pointed me out and he might have set this to remind me to get to work again to bring my people back into the hoop and the old religion" (DeMallie 1984, 258). Note that Black Elk judged the validity of the Ghost Dance in terms of his vision, and it is likely that he judged the validity of Christianity in the same way. It is also clear that the fundamental intention of the Ghost Dance as Black Elk interpreted it— to get the people back into the sacred hoop and make the tree of traditional culture bloom—remained valid for Black Elk throughout his life. There is thus as much of the Ghost Dance in his reinterpretation of the Sun Dance as there is of Christianity. A true revision of Black Elk's religion might see him as somewhat equal parts traditionalist, Ghost Dancer, and Lakota Catholic. If this is so, it shows further how wrong it is to conceive Black Elk as either a traditionalist or a Catholic.

In the end, Black Elk's own relation to sacred power, which was expressed as much for the understanding as possible in his account of his vision, was the primary element in his own religion. As a religious genius, there is no reason at all to assume that Black Elk would necessarily have been repelled rather than fascinated by Catholicism and the Jesuits. There is no reason to doubt Fools Crow's testimony that Black Elk spent "many hours talking to the priests about it" (Mails 1979, 45). That is exactly what we would expect a man such as Black Elk to have done. Perhaps in Black Elk's case, susceptibility to religions went hand in hand with susceptibility to visions. In the end, there does not seem much reason to assume either that Black Elk was intellectually intimidated by Christianity or to doubt the essential correctness of Fools Crow's understanding of the position that resulted from these discussions: "Black Elk told me he had decided that the Sioux religious way of life was pretty much the same as that of the Christian churches, and there was no reason to change what the Sioux were doing. We could pick up some of the Christian ways and teachings, and just work them in with our own, so in the end both would be better" (Mails 1979, 45). In other words, where commentators have seen two incompatible beliefs, which has led to disagreements on which one Black Elk held sincerely, Black Elk seems to have seen two basically compatible beliefs, or two modalities of what was primary, the sacred. Just as a man does not stand still, but refines his understanding and vision as he ages, new situations require new adaptations and new religious responses. Nothing in Black Elk's religion suggests that he regarded the sacred as the source of timelessly true propositions or as an ancient tradition to be preserved intact at any cost. Rather, as Steltenkamp points out, for Black Elk, the sacred is the source of the power necessary to face the problems of life with courage and confidence, to innovate with authority.[16] The sacred can be expressed only in symbolic thinking, for

16. Recall that Red Weasel, the intercessor interviewed by Frances Densmore, was taught by his mentor, Dreamer of the Sun, that if he was well prepared, he need

it is beyond the power of the human mind to capture and comprehend. Black Elk's creative and courageous confrontation with Christianity and his engagement with the problems of his people make him so much more than simply a boy who fell sick and dreamed spectacularly of heaven. In fact, his life and work embodies the best that was in his people and justifies his position as the greatest religious thinker yet produced by native North America.

Ultimately, just as nothing can be urged that would necessarily force Rice to retreat from his claim that Black Elk was simply pretending to be a Christian, I do not think that anything can be urged that would force Steltenkamp to retreat from his claim that Black Elk did not intend the revitalization of traditional religion. For one thing, "intend" is a concept like sincerity that refers to private mental states and is hence just as incapable of final proof. Note, however, that given the context of the times, an argument from silence is not convincing. Black Elk doesn't say in *The Sacred Pipe* that he wishes the Sun Dance would be publicly revived. But the most obvious interpretation of what he said in 1931 and 1948 is that traditional religion should be revived. Unlike Neihardt, Black Elk did not believe that the traditional ritual process was dead (Holler 1984a, 38–41). His ritual on Harney Peak, as well as the many rituals surrounding the transmission of his sacred knowledge to Neihardt, clearly indicates that he continued to regard it as living, efficacious, and valid. His fundamental message to the whites in *The Sacred Pipe* was that his tradition had validity and that it was just as worthy of respect as Christianity. His fundamental message to *his* people in the *Black Elk Speaks* interviews seems clear. They should get back in the sacred hoop and make the tree flower. The constant in both books is a commitment to the central idea of the Ghost Dance, religious ritual as the means of reviving traditional culture.

Black Elk's message in *Black Elk Speaks* employs symbolic discourse, a common device when speaking plainly is proscribed by op-

---

not fear the unexpected. In his words, "Dreamer-of-the-Sun told me that if I would obey his instructions I would be a help to the Sioux nation, and that, if properly prepared for the duties of the highest office in the Sun dance, I need have no anxiety when filling the office as the proper thing to do would come to my mind at the time" (1918, 88). The kind of improvisatory attitude toward ritual expressed in this statement is central to traditional Lakota religion.

pression. As DeMallie points out, the hoop and the flowering stick were conventional symbols (1984, 86). Since the hoop clearly represents the Sun Dance circle, and the flowering stick clearly symbolizes the Sun Dance tree, I would argue that Black Elk made himself as clear as he could, given the various constraints on his free speech. In the context of his time and situation, I doubt if he could have made himself any plainer. If he had said flatly, "The Sun Dance should be revived," the furor would have been unimaginable, given the brouhaha created with the relatively tame and veiled symbolic speech he did employ. Note also that the symbols Black Elk used were derived in part from the Ghost Dance. That they are still understood by Lakotas and are still in use by Lakota holy men is indicated by Mary Crow Dog's account of a Ghost Dance held at Wounded Knee in 1973.

> Leonard always thought that the dancers of 1890 had misunderstood Wovoka and his message. They should not have expected to bring the dead back to life, but to bring back their ancient beliefs by practicing Indian religion. For Leonard, dancing in a circle holding hands was bringing back the sacred hoop—to feel, holding on to the hand of your brother and sister, the rebirth of Indian unity, feel it with your flesh, through your skin. . . . In that ravine, at Cankpe Opi, we gathered up the broken pieces of the sacred hoop and put them together again. All who were at Wounded Knee, Buddy Lamont, Clearwater, and our medicine men, we mended the nation's hoop. The sacred tree *is not dead!* (153–55)

Much the same kind of thing might be said about Black Elk's message in *The Sacred Pipe*. The context of the times in 1948 was no more amenable to direct declarations of support for traditional religion than was 1931. The Jesuits were apparently quite concerned about the possibility of a replay of the Neihardt disaster, since Brown remembered Father Zimmerman—one of the principals in the recriminations over *Black Elk Speaks*—as "somewhat of an impediment to fieldwork" (Steltenkamp 1993, 84). All in all, it is unlikely that Black Elk was essentially any more free to express himself frankly in 1948 than he was in 1931. But he places in the mouth of Kablaya numerous exhortations to his people to make a Sun Dance pledge for the good of the people to help them get back in the sacred hoop—essentially the same message and hope Black Elk expressed in the Neihardt interviews. Black Elk must have known this was his final statement; it is difficult to believe, given the level of adaptation, modification, and elaboration in *The Sacred Pipe*—not to mention what Kablaya constantly says—that what Black Elk meant was that his people should respect their former tradition intellectually, for it was great. If he had meant—as Steltenkamp would have it—that the traditional religion was superseded, that his people should forget about attempting to revive it and throw themselves wholeheartedly into Christianity, why didn't he say so? Surely there were no comparable constraints on his speech in this regard.

Ultimately, the question of whether Black Elk intended the contemporary revival of traditional religion and the Sun Dance is one with the question of whether Jesus intended to found the Christian Church. It is too late to ask either Jesus or Black Elk what he intended, which may be a lucky thing for certain factions. The revival of traditional religion is a fact, and the fact that Black Elk is claimed by opposing factions is, in the end, simply another measure of his greatness. For Lakota Catholics, Black Elk's legacy is his pioneering of an authentic Lakota Christianity; for traditionalists, his legacy is the contemporary revival of traditional religion and the contemporary form of the Sun Dance, which is largely in accord with his vision. In fact, the religious situation on the reservation today, in which many Lakotas profess belief in both traditional religion and Christianity, is largely due to Black Elk's own creative and courageous confrontation with Christianity and with the challenges of modernity. His legacy to all contending factions is his lifetime of thoughtful and authentic engagement with the problems of his people, justifying his place in his people's hearts as their greatest *wicasa wakan*.

Glossary

Bibliography

Index

Glossary

Acculturation: Cultural changes ascribed to contact between cultures. Although technically neutral, the term is usually employed to describe the effect on native cultures of contact with white culture. Often viewed as the first step toward assimilation.

AIM: American Indian Movement, a radical political action coalition inspired by the tactics of the Black Panthers in the 1960s. AIM's involvement with the Lakota dates from the occupation of Wounded Knee in 1973, which led to a lengthy siege with much exchange of fire between AIM and government forces.

Assimilation: Acculturation to the point of the disappearance of ethnic identity.

Ban: The official edict forbidding the Sun Dance and other native American religious practices issued on April 10, 1883.

Boas, Franz: The dean of American anthropology (1858–1942). Boas trained or influenced almost all of the anthropologists working on native America in the first half of the twentieth century.

Boasian: Refers to the school of Franz Boas, which is characterized by an inductive approach and an avoidance of theoretical synthesis.

Brulé: One of the subdivisions of the Lakota. Presently occupy the Rosebud Reservation. Also "Burnt Thighs" or "Sicangu."

Candidates: Those who have pledged to make a Sun Dance sacrifice.

Catechist: In the Roman Catholic Church, one who offers instruction in the catechism. Until recently, the highest office a native American could hold in the Catholic Church.

Catku: Lakota term for the place of honor opposite the entrance to a tipi or a Sun Dance circle.

Classic Sun Dance: The Sun Dance during the period from contact until the ban.

Cognitive Dissonance: Term borrowed from social psychology to denote mental discomfort caused by conflicting belief systems.

Compartmentalize: Term borrowed from social psychology to explain how a person operates with apparently contradictory beliefs or behaviors. Use of the term implies that the contradiction is avoided by placing such beliefs and behaviors in separate mental "compartments."

Contact: The point at which a native American group first encounters white culture.

Coup: A warrior struck coup on an enemy by striking him in the context of battle, generally with a stick known as a "coup stick."

Cross-cultural: Used as an adjective, implies a comparative perspective.

Cross-cultural perspective: Critical point of view informed by awareness of the differences among cultures.

Dakota: One of the three dialects of the Sioux. Dakota speakers are also known as the Santee. In the older anthropological literature, the term is used both to designate the Santee (Dakota speakers) and as a technical term to designate the Sioux (Santees, Yanktons, and Lakotas taken together).

Ethnic group: A voluntary community characterized by perceived identity of cultural and religious traits.

Ethnic group markers: Clues to ethnic identity, such as dress, speech patterns, behavior, or beliefs.

Ethnic identity: Personal identity based on identification with an ethnic group.

Ethnocentric: Characterized by the lack of a cross-cultural perspective. Implies the absolutizing of the moral and epistemological values of one's own culture.

Ethnography: The scientific study and description of cultures.

Flesh offerings, scarifications: Small pieces of skin offered as sacrifices.

Functionalism: In the context of religion, the social scientific explanation of religion in terms of its social, political, and economic functions.

Ghost Dance: Pan-Indian messianic movement based on the teachings of Wovoka. The Ghost Dance led to an outbreak among the Sioux and to the subsequent massacre of Big Foot's band at Wounded Knee in 1890.

Holy man: See Wicasa wakan.

Hoop, sacred hoop: The Sun Dance circle.

Hunkpapa: One of the subdivisions of the Lakota. Occupied the Standing Rock Reservation.

Inipi: Ritual of purification by sweat bath. Also known as the sweat lodge.

Intercessor: Denotes the holy man in charge of the Sun Dance.

Lakota: Designates one of the three dialects of the Sioux. Lakota speakers are also known as the Teton (or Teton Dakota in the older anthropological literature).

Leader of the dancers: Ceremonial office in the Sun Dance.

Medicine man: See Pejuta wicasa.

Mellowed earth: Soil that has been pulverized and cleaned of all vegetation and foreign matter.

Mystery circle: The circle defining the ritual space within which the Sun Dance takes place. Also "hoop" and "sacred hoop."

Nakota: One of the three dialects of the Sioux. Nakota speakers are also known as the Yankton.

Oglala: One of the subdivisions of the Lakota. Presently occupy the Pine Ridge Reservation.

Peace policy: Denotes the Indian policy promoted by the reformers, which was based on civilizing and Christianizing the Indians.

Pejuta wicasa: Lakota for "medicine man." A healer as opposed to a wicasa wakan, or holy man.

Piercing: Cutting of the flesh to allow the insertion of a skewer to be torn loose as a sacrifice during the Sun Dance.

Precontact: Denotes the period before contact with white culture.

Preparations tipi: Tipi reserved for the use of the intercessor during the Sun Dance. Employed for rehearsals and ancillary rituals.

Prescriptive present: Designates the issuance of ritual prescriptions in present tense.

Reformers: The churchmen and philanthropists who prevailed on President Grant to initiate the Peace Policy.

Religious studies: Scholarly discipline that investigates religion from a dispassionate point of view.

Romanticism: In the context of native American studies, the projection of contemporary values on historical events. Implies the tendency to equate aboriginal culture with utopia.

Sacrifice: In context of the Sun Dance, a wound that causes the blood to flow.

Sage: Herb used in ritual purification.

Salvage anthropology: Ethnography characterized by the collection of physical or mental artifacts without regard to their contemporary context. Often employed as a pejorative characterization of Boasian anthropology.

Santee: One of the three social/political divisions of the Sioux. Santees speak the Dakota dialect. Occupied the easternmost position geographically.

Scarification: See Flesh offerings.

Shade: The spectator area for the Sun Dance. An "awning" made of evergreen boughs.

Singers: Those who accompany the Sun Dance with songs.

Sioux: Designates Lakotas, Dakotas, and Nakotas taken as a totality. In the older anthropological literature, "Dakota" is used as a technical term for Sioux.

Smudging: Ritual purification though use of the smoke of burning sweetgrass.

Sunwise: All Lakota ritual takes place in a circle oriented to the cardinal points and all movement within that circle is properly sunwise or clockwise.

Syncretism: Technical term for religious change brought about by cultural contact. Often implies the blending or combining of religious traditions that were separate before contact.

Taku Skanskan: The spirit of motion or release. Associated with the sky and symbolized by blue.

Teton: One of the three social/political divisions of the Sioux. Tetons speak the Lakota dialect. Occupied the westernmost position geographically.

Teton Dakota: See Lakota.

Tiyospaye: Lakota for "band," or tribal subgroup.

Vision: A holy man's call to vocation, obtained through religious ecstasy. Also, the product of a vision quest undertaken by an adolescent seeking personal identity or a holy man seeking an answer to a specific question or pressing problem.

Vision quest: Ritual whereby a vision is sought. In former times, was required of all males as a rite of passage into adulthood. May be required of male Sun Dance pledgers.

Wakan: Designates anything that is strange, powerful, mysterious, or unknowable. Translated into English in religious contexts as "sacred" or "holy."

Wakan Tanka: Lakota term for the godhead. Appropriated by the missionaries as a translation of "God."

Wicasa wakan: Wakan man or holy man. As opposed to the pejuta wicasa, the holy man was primarily an intercessor with the spirit powers. He might also function as a healer.

Yankton: One of the three social/political divisions of the Sioux. Yanktons speak the Nakota dialect. Occupied a geographic point midway between the Santee and the Teton.

Yuwipi: Lakota ritual in which the holy man is bound in a darkened room and obtains release through the mysterious intercession of helping spirits. Employed in contemporary times for spiritual direction and to find lost objects.

Bibliography

Amiotte, Arthur. 1987. "The Lakota Sun Dance: Historical and Contemporary Perspectives." In *Sioux Indian Religion: Tradition and Innovation,* edited by Raymond J. DeMallie and Douglas R. Parks, 75–89. Norman: Univ. of Oklahoma Press.

Anderson, John Alvin. 1971. *The Sioux of the Rosebud: A History in Pictures.* Norman: Univ. of Oklahoma Press.

Beckwith, Paul. 1889. "Notes on Customs of the Dakotas." *Annual Report of the Smithsonian Institution 1866.* I: 245–57.

Bennett, John W. 1944. "The Development of Ethnological Theory as Illustrated by Studies of the Plains Sun Dance." *American Anthropologist* 46: 162–81.

Black Elk. 1971. *The Sacred Pipe: Black Elk's Account of the Seven Rites of the Oglala Sioux.* Recorded and edited by Joseph Epes Brown. 1953. Reprint, Harmondsworth, Eng.: Penguin.

Black Elk, Wallace H. and William S. Lyon. 1990. *Black Elk: The Sacred Ways of a Lakota.* San Francisco: Harper and Row.

Bray, Edmund C., and Martha Coleman Bray, eds. and trans. 1976. *Joseph N. Nicollet on the Plains and Prairies: The Expeditions of 1838–39 with Journals, Letters and Notes on the Dakota Indians.* St. Paul: Minnesota Historical Society.

Brown, Joseph Epes. 1982. *The Spiritual Legacy of the American Indian.* New York: Crossroad.

Brumble, H. David III. 1981. *An Annotated Bibliography of American Indian and Eskimo Autobiographies.* Lincoln: Univ. of Nebraska Press.

Bruner, Edward M. 1986. "Ethnography as Narrative." In *The Anthropology of Experience,* edited by Victor W. Turner and Edward M. Bruner. Urbana: Univ. of Illinois Press.

Buechel, Eugene, S.J. 1970. *A Dictionary of the Teton Dakota Sioux Language:*

Lakota-English, English-Lakota with Considerations Given to Yankton and Santee. Edited by Paul Manhart, S.J. Pine Ridge, S.Dak.: Red Cloud Indian School.

Castro, Michael. 1983. *Interpreting the Indian: Twentieth Century Poets and the Native American.* Albuquerque: Univ. of New Mexico Press.

Commissioner of Indian Affairs. 1872–92. Annual Report of the Commissioner of Indian Affairs to the Secretary of the Interior. Washington: Government Printing Office.

Crow Dog, Mary, and Richard Erdoes. 1991. *Lakota Woman.* New York: Harper Perennial.

Curtis, Edward S. 1970. *The North American Indian.* Vol. 3. 1908. Reprint, New York: Johnson Reprint Corporation.

Curtis, Natalie, ed. 1907. *The Indians' Book.* New York: Harper and Brothers.

Deloria, Ella C. 1929. "The Sun Dance of the Oglala Sioux." *Journal of American Folklore* 42: 354–413.

———. 1978. *Dakota Texts.* Vermillion, S.Dak.: Dakota Press.

———. 1979. *Speaking of Indians.* Vermillion, S.Dak.: Dakota Press.

———. 1988. *Waterlily.* Lincoln: Univ. of Nebraska Press.

Deloria, Vine, Jr., ed. 1984. *A Sender of Words: Essays in Memory of John G. Neihardt.* Salt Lake City: Howe Brothers.

DeMallie, Raymond J. 1978. "George Bushotter: The First Lakota Ethnographer." In *American Indian Intellectuals,* edited by Margo Liberty, 91–102. St. Paul: West Publishing.

———. 1982. "The Lakota Ghost Dance: An Ethnohistorical Account." *Pacific Historical Review* 51: 385–405.

———, ed. 1984. *The Sixth Grandfather: Black Elk's Teachings Given to John G. Neihardt.* Lincoln: Univ. of Nebraska Press.

DeMallie, Raymond J., and Douglas R. Parks. 1987. *Sioux Indian Religion: Tradition and Innovation.* Norman: Univ. of Oklahoma Press.

Densmore, Frances. 1918. *Teton Sioux Music.* Smithsonian Institution, Bureau of American Ethnology, Bulletin 61. Washington: U.S. Government Printing Office.

———. 1920. "The Sun Dance of the Teton Sioux." *Nature* 104, no. 2618: 437–40.

———. 1941. "The Study of Indian Music." *Annual Report Smithsonian Institution,* 527–57.

Doll, Don, S.J., and Jim Alinder, eds. 1976. *Crying for a Vision: A Rosebud Sioux Trilogy 1886–1976.* Photographs by John A. Anderson, Eugene Buechel, S.J., and Don Doll, S.J. New York: Morgan and Morgan.

Dorsey, James Owen. 1894. "A Study of Siouan Cults." *Annual Report Smithsonian Institution, Bureau of American Ethnology* 14: 361–544.

Eastman, Charles A. 1971. *Indian Boyhood.* 1902. Reprint, New York: Dover Publications.

———. 1977. *From Deep Woods to Civilization: Chapters in the Autobiography of an Indian.* 1936. Reprint, Lincoln: Univ. of Nebraska Press.

———. 1980. *The Soul of the Indian: An Interpretation.* 1911. Reprint, Lincoln: Univ. of Nebraska Press.

Eastman, Mary. 1975. *Dahcotah: Or Life and Legends of the Sioux Around Fort Snelling.* 1849. Reprint, New York: Arno Press.

Feraca, Stephen E. 1963. *Wakinyan: Contemporary Teton Dakota Religion.* Studies in Plains Anthropology and History, 2. Browning, Mont.: Museum of the Plains Indian.

Fletcher, Alice C. 1883. "The Sun Dance of the Ogalalla Sioux." *Proceedings of the American Association for the Advancement of Science* 31: 580–84.

———. 1884. "Indian Ceremonies." *Report of the Peabody Museum of American Archaeology and Ethnography* 16: 260–333.

Fools Crow, Frank. 1977. *To My People.* Tatanka Records.

Forbes, Bruce David. 1985. Review of *Pipe, Bible and Peyote among the Oglala Lakota* by Paul B. Steinmetz. *American Indian Quarterly* 9, no. 1: 84–87.

Fritz, Henry E. 1963. *The Movement for Indian Assimilation, 1860–1890.* Westport, Conn.: Greenwood Press.

Geertz, Clifford. 1966. "Religion as a Cultural System." In *Anthropological Approaches to the Study of Religion,* edited by Michael Banton, 1–46. London: Tavistock Publications.

Giago, Tim A., Jr. 1978. *The Aboriginal Sin: Reflections on the Holy Rosary Mission School (Red Cloud Indian School).* San Francisco: The Indian Historian Press.

Grobsmith, Elizabeth S. 1981. *Lakota of the Rosebud: A Contemporary Ethnography.* New York: Holt, Rinehart and Winston.

Haas, Marilyn L. 1983. *Indians of North America: Methods and Sources for Library Research.* Hamden, Conn.: Library Professional Publications.

Hagan, William T. 1966. *Indian Police and Judges: Experiments in Acculturation and Control.* New Haven: Yale Univ. Press.

Harris, Marvin. 1968. *The Rise of Anthropological Theory: A History of Theories of Culture.* New York: Thomas Y. Crowell.

———. 1980. *Cultural Materialism: The Struggle for a Science of Culture.* New York: Vintage Books.

Hassrick, Royal B. 1964. *The Sioux: Life and Customs of a Warrior Society.* Norman: Univ. of Oklahoma Press.

Hodge, William. 1976. *A Bibliography of Contemporary North American Indians: Selected and Partially Annotated with Study Guide.* New York: Interland Publishing.

Holler, Clyde. 1984a. "Lakota Religion and Tragedy: The Theology of *Black Elk Speaks.*" *Journal of the American Academy of Religion* 52, no. 1: 19–45.

———. 1984b. "Black Elk's Relationship to Christianity." *American Indian Quarterly* 8, no.1: 37–49.

Hoover, Herbert T. 1979. *The Sioux: A Critical Bibliography.* Bloomington: Indiana Univ. Press.

Howard, Oliver O. 1972. *My Life and Experiences among Our Hostile Indians.* 1907. Reprint, New York: Da Capo Press.

Howe, M. A. DeWolfe. 1912. *The Life and Labors of Bishop Hare: Apostle to the Sioux.* New York: Sturgis and Walton.

Hultkrantz, Åke. 1980. "The Development of the Plains Indian Sun Dance." In *Perennitas: Studi In Onore di Angelo Brelich.* Rome: Edizioni dell'Ateneo.

Hyde, George E. 1937. *Red Cloud's Folk: A History of the Oglala Sioux Indians.* Norman: Univ. of Oklahoma Press.

———. 1956. *A Sioux Chronicle.* Norman: Univ. of Oklahoma Press.

———. 1961. *Spotted Tail's Folk: A History of the Brulé Sioux.* Norman: Univ. of Oklahoma Press.

Kneale, Albert H. 1950. *Indian Agent.* Caldwell, Idaho: Caxton Printers.

Lame Deer, John (Fire), and Richard Erdoes. 1972. *Lame Deer: Seeker of Visions.* New York: Simon and Schuster.

Lewis, Thomas H. 1972. "The Oglala (Teton Dakota) Sun Dance: Vicissitudes of Its Structures and Functions." *Plains Anthropologist* 17: 44–49.

Linden, George W. 1977. "Dakota Philosophy." *American Studies* 18, no. 2: 17–43.

———. 1984. "*Black Elk Speaks* as a Failure Narrative." *Heritage of the Great Plains* 17, no. 2: 35–45.

———. 1985. "Warrior and Mystic: Nicholas Black Elk and John G. Neihardt." *Proceedings, 16th Dakota History Conference.* Jan. 1985, 482–96.

Lynd, James William. 1864. "The Religion of the Dakotas." *Collections of the Minnesota Historical Society* 2: 150–74.

McCluskey, Sally. 1972. "Black Elk Speaks: And So Does John Neihardt." *Western American Literature* 6: 231–42.

McGaa, Ed. 1990. *Mother Earth Spirituality: Native American Paths to Healing Ourselves and Our World.* San Francisco: Harper San Francisco.

McGillycuddy, Julia B. 1941. *McGillycuddy Agent: A Biography of Dr. Valentine T. McGillycuddy.* Palo Alto: Stanford Univ. Press.

Macgregor, Gordon. 1946. *Warriors Without Weapons: A Study of the Society and Personality Development of the Pine Ridge Sioux.* Chicago: Univ. of Chicago Press.

McLaughlin, James. 1910. *My Friend the Indian*. Boston: Houghton Mifflin Co.

Mails, Thomas E. 1978. *Sundancing at Rosebud and Pine Ridge*. Sioux Falls, S.Dak.: The Center for Western Studies, Augustana College.

———. 1979. *Fools Crow*. New York: Doubleday and Co.; New York: Avon Books, 1980.

———. 1991. *Fools Crow: Wisdom and Power*. Tulsa: Council Oaks Books.

Marken, Jack W., and Herbert T. Hoover. 1980. *Biography of the Sioux*. Metuchen, N.J.: Scarecrow Press.

Mattheissen, Peter. 1983. *In the Spirit of Crazy Horse*. New York: Viking Press.

Melody, Michael E. 1976. "The Lakota Sun Dance: A Composite View and Analysis." *South Dakota History* 6: 433–55.

Miller, David Humphreys. 1959. *Ghost Dance*. Lincoln: Univ. of Nebraska Press.

Mooney, James. 1965. *The Ghost Dance Religion and the Sioux Outbreak of 1890*. Abridged, with an introduction by Anthony F. C. Wallace. Chicago: Univ. of Chicago Press.

Murdock, George Peter. 1960. *Ethnographic Bibliography of North America*. New Haven, Conn.: Human Relations Area Files.

Neihardt, Hilda. 1995. *Black Elk and Flaming Rainbow: Personal Memories of the Lakota Holy Man and John Neihardt*. Lincoln: Univ. of Nebraska Press.

Neihardt, John G. 1931. Transcript of Black Elk interview. Joint Collection: Univ. of Missouri Western Historical Manuscript Collection–Columbia and State Historical Society of Missouri Manuscripts.

———. 1951. *When the Tree Flowered: An Authentic Tale of the Old Sioux World*. New York: Macmillan.

———. 1979. *Black Elk Speaks: Being the Life Story of a Holy Man of the Oglala Sioux*. 1932. Reprint, Lincoln: Univ. of Nebraska Press.

———. 1980. New Transcript of Black Elk interview (with drafts of Neihardt's correspondence relating to *Black Elk Speaks* and Enid Volnia Neihardt Fink's diary of the Black Elk interview). Joint Collection: Univ. of Missouri Western Historical Manuscript Collection–Columbia and State Historical Society of Missouri Manuscripts.

Nurge, Ethel. 1966. "The Sioux Sun Dance in 1962." *Proceedings of the XXVI Congreso Internacional de Americanistas* (Seville, Spain) 36, no. 3: 105–14.

———, ed. 1970. *The Modern Sioux: Social Systems and Reservation Culture*. Lincoln: Univ. of Nebraska Press, Bison Books.

Olden, Sarah Emilia. 1918. *The People of Tipi Sapa*. Milwaukee: Morehouse Publishing.

Oliver, Harold H. 1980. "Relational Ontology and Hermeneutics." In *Myth,*

Symbol and Reality, edited by Alan M. Olson, 69–85. Notre Dame: Univ. of Notre Dame Press.

———. 1981. *A Relational Metaphysic.* The Hague: Martinus Nijhoff Publishers.

Olson, James C. 1965. *Red Cloud and the Sioux Problem.* Lincoln: Univ. of Nebraska Press, Bison Books.

Overholt, Thomas. 1974. "The Ghost Dance of 1890 and the Nature of the Prophetic Process." *Ethnohistory* 21, no. 1 (Winter 1974): 37–63.

———. 1978. "Short Bull, Black Elk, Sword and the 'Meaning' of the Ghost Dance." *Religion* 8 (Autumn): 171–95.

Paige, Darcy. 1979. "George W. Hill's Account of the Sioux Indian Sun Dance of 1866." *Plains Anthropologist* 25: 99–112.

Pomerance, Bernard. 1987. *We Need to Dream All This Again.* New York: Viking Penguin.

Pond, Gideon H. 1854. "Power and Influence of Dakota Medicine-Men." In *Information Respecting the History, Conditions and Prospects of the Indian Tribes of the United States,* edited by Henry R. Schoolcraft, vol. 4, 641–51. Philadelphia.

———. 1867. "Dakota Superstitions." *Collections of the Minnesota Historical Society* 2: 215–55.

Pond, Samuel W. 1986. *The Dakota or Sioux in Minnesota as They Were in 1834.* 1908. Reprint, St. Paul: Minnesota Historical Society Press.

Poole, D. C. 1988. *Among the Sioux of Dakota: Eighteen Months' Experience as an Indian Agent, 1869–70.* St. Paul: Minnesota Historical Society Press.

Porter, Joseph C. 1986. *Paper Medicine Man: John Gregory Bourke and His American West.* Norman: Univ. of Oklahoma Press.

Powers, Marla N. 1986. *Oglala Women: Myth, Ritual, and Reality.* Chicago: Univ. of Chicago Press.

Powers, William K. 1977. *Oglala Religion.* Lincoln: Univ. of Nebraska Press.

———. 1982. *Yuwipi: Vision and Experience in Oglala Ritual.* Lincoln: Univ. of Nebraska Press.

———. 1986. *Sacred Language: The Nature of Supernatural Discourse in Lakota.* Norman: Univ. of Oklahoma Press.

———. 1987. *Beyond the Vision: Essays on American Indian Culture.* Norman: Univ. of Oklahoma Press.

Prescott, Philander. 1854. "Manners, Customs, and Opinions of the Dacotahs." In *Information Respecting the History, Conditions and Prospects of the Indian Tribes of the United States,* edited by Henry R. Schoolcraft, vol. 4, 59–72. Philadelphia.

Priest, Loring Benson. 1942. *Uncle Sam's Stepchildren: The Reformation of United States Indian Policy, 1865–1887.* New Brunswick, N.J.: Rutgers Univ. Press.

Prucha, Francis Paul. 1976. *American Indian Policy in Crisis: Christian Reformers and the Indian, 1865–1900*. Norman: Univ. of Oklahoma Press.

———. 1984. *The Great Father: The United States Government and the American Indians*. 2 vols. Lincoln: Univ. of Nebraska Press.

Prucha, Francis Paul, ed. 1973. *Americanizing the American Indians: Writing by the "Friends of the Indian" 1880–1900*. Cambridge: Harvard Univ. Press.

———. 1975. *Documents of United States Indian Policy*. Lincoln: Univ. of Nebraska Press.

Reat, N. Ross. 1983. "Insiders and Outsiders in the Study of Religious Traditions." *Journal of the American Academy of Religion* 51, no. 3: 459–76.

Rice, Julian. 1991. *Black Elk's Story: Distinguishing Its Lakota Purpose*. Albuquerque: Univ. of New Mexico Press.

———. 1992. *Deer Woman and Elk Men: The Lakota Narratives of Ella Deloria*. Albuquerque: Univ. of New Mexico Press.

Riggs, Stephen Return. 1893. *Dakota Grammar, Texts, and Ethnography*. Department of the Interior, Contributions to North American Ethnology, IX. Washington: Government Printing Office.

———. 1971. *Mary and I: Forty Years with the Sioux*. 1880. Reprint, Williamstown, Mass. Corner House Publishers.

———. 1972. *Tah-koo Wah-kan: Or, The Gospel among the Dakotas*. 1869. Reprint, New York: Arno Press.

Robinson, Doane. 1967. *A History of the Dakota or Sioux Indians*. 1904. Reprint, Minneapolis: Ross and Haynes.

Ruby, Robert H. 1955. *The Oglala Sioux: Warriors in Transition*. New York: Vantage Press.

Sandstrom, Alan R. 1991. *Corn Is Our Blood: Culture and Ethnic Identity in a Contemporary Aztec Indian Village*. Norman: Univ. of Oklahoma Press.

Schwarz, O. Douglas. 1981. *Plains Indian Theology: As Expressed in Myth and Ritual, and in the Ethics of the Culture*. Ann Arbor: Univ. Microfilms International.

Schwatka, Frederick. 1890. "The Sun-Dance of the Sioux." *Century Magazine* 17: 753–59.

Skinner, Alanson. 1919. "Notes on the Sun Dance of the Sisseton Dakota." *Anthropological Papers of the American Museum of Natural History* 16: 381–85.

Smith, J. L. 1964. "A Ceremony for the Preparation of the Offering Cloths for Presentation to the Sacred Calf Pipe of the Teton Sioux." *Plains Anthropologist* 9, no. 25: 190–96.

———. 1967. "A Short History of the Sacred Calf Pipe of the Teton Dakota." *Univ. of South Dakota Museum News* 28: 1–37.

———. 1970. "The Sacred Calf Pipe Bundle: Its Effect on the Present Teton Dakota." *Plains Anthropologist* 15: 87–93.

Sneve, Virginia Driving Hawk. 1977. *That They May Have Life: The Episcopal Church in South Dakota 1859–1976.* New York: Seabury Press.

Spier, Leslie. 1921. "The Sun Dance of the Plains Indians: Its Development and Diffusion." *Anthropological Papers of the American Museum of Natural History* 16: 450–527.

Standing Bear, Luther. 1933. *Land of the Spotted Eagle.* Lincoln: Univ. of Nebraska Press.

Steinmetz, Paul B., S.J. 1969. "Explanation of the Sacred Pipe as a Prayer Instrument." *Pine Ridge Research Bulletin* 10: 20–25.

———. 1970. "The Relationship Between Plains Indian Religion and Christianity: A Priest's Viewpoint." *Plains Anthropologist* 15: 83–86.

———. 1980. *Pipe, Bible, and Peyote among the Oglala Lakota: A Study in Religious Identity.* Stockholm Studies in Comparative Religion, 19. Stockholm: Almqvist and Wiksell International.

———. 1984. *Meditations with Native Americans—Lakota Spirituality.* Sante Fe: Bear and Co.

———. 1990. *Pipe, Bible, and Peyote among the Oglala Lakota: A Study in Religious Identity.* Rev. ed. Knoxville: Univ. of Tennessee Press.

Steltenkamp, Michael F. 1982. *The Sacred Vision: Native American Religion and Its Practice Today.* New York: Paulist Press.

———. 1993. *Black Elk: Holy Man of the Oglala.* Norman: Univ. of Oklahoma Press.

Teller, Henry M. 1883. *Report of the Secretary of the Interior.* Serial 2190. Washington: Government Printing Office.

Terrell, John Upton. 1979. *The Arrow and the Cross: A History of the American Indian and the Missionaries.* Santa Barbara: Capra Press.

Thomas, Owen C. 1973. *Introduction to Theology.* Cambridge, Mass.: Greeno, Hadden, and Company.

Twiss, Gayla. 1969. "The Role of the Pipe in Dakota Religion." *Pine Ridge Research Bulletin* 10: 7–19.

Utley, Robert M. 1963. *The Last Days of the Sioux Nation.* New Haven: Yale Univ. Press.

Vecsey, Christopher. 1987. "Sun Dances, Corn Pollen, and the Cross: Native American Catholics Today." *Commonweal.* June 5, 1987, 345–51.

———. n.d. "A Century of Catholicism at Pine Ridge." Unpublished manuscript.

Vestal, Stanley. 1934. *New Sources of Indian History 1850–1891.* Norman: Univ. of Oklahoma Press.

———. 1957. *Sitting Bull: Champion of the Sioux—A Biography.* Norman: Univ. of Oklahoma Press.

———. 1984. *Warpath: The True Story of the Fighting Sioux Told in a Biography of Chief White Bull.* 1934. Reprint, Lincoln: Univ. of Nebraska Press, Bison Books.

Voices from Wounded Knee: The People Are Standing Up. 1974. Mohawk Nation at Akwesane: Akwesane Notes.

Walker, James R. 1906. "Tuberculosis among the Oglala Sioux Indians." *American Journal of Medical Science,* n.s. 132: 600–605.

———. 1979. *The Sun Dance and Other Ceremonies of the Oglala Division of the Teton Dakota.* Anthropological Papers of the American Museum of Natural History, vol. 16, part 2. 1917. Reprint, New York: AMS.

———. 1980. *Lakota Belief and Ritual.* Edited by Raymond J. DeMallie and Elaine A. Jahner. Lincoln: Univ. of Nebraska Press.

———. 1982. *Lakota Society.* Edited by Raymond J. DeMallie. Lincoln: Univ. of Nebraska Press.

———. 1983. *Lakota Myth.* Edited by Elaine A. Jahner. Lincoln: Univ. of Nebraska Press.

Wallis, Wilson D. 1921. "The Sun Dance of the Canadian Dakota." *Anthropological Papers of the American Museum of Natural History* 16: 317–80.

Webb, H. G. 1894. "The Dakota Sun Dance of 1883." MS. no. 1394a, National Anthropological Archives, Smithsonian Institution, Washington, D.C.

Whipple, Henry Benjamin. 1899. *Lights and Shadows of a Long Episcopate.* New York: Macmillan.

Wissler, Clark. 1912. "Societies and Ceremonial Associations in the Oglala Division of the Teton-Dakota." *Anthropological Papers of the American Museum of Natural History* 11, no. 1: 1–99.

Zimmerly, David. 1969. "On Being an Ascetic: Personal Document of a Sioux Medicine Man." *Pine Ridge Research Bulletin* 10: 46–71.

Index